South Africa's Transkei

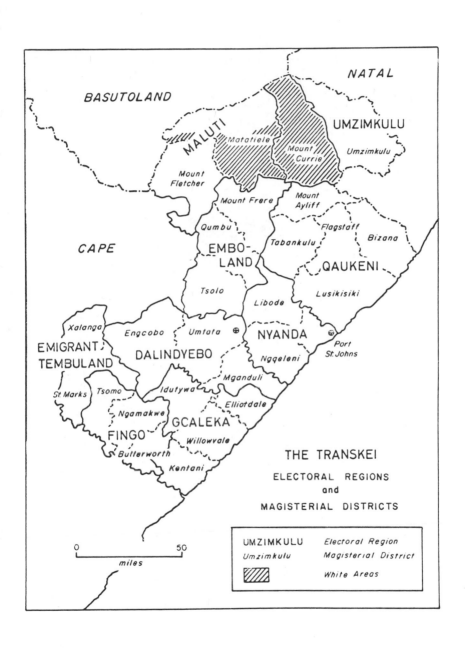

BASUTOLAND

NATAL

MALUTI

UMZIMKULU

Matatiele

Mount Currie

Umzimkulu

Mount Fletcher

CAPE

Mount Frere

Mount Ayliff

Qumbu

EMBO-LAND

Tabankulu

Flagstaff

Bizana

QAUKENI

Tsolo

Libode

Lusikisiki

Xalanga

Engcobo

Umtata

NYANDA

EMIGRANT TEMBULAND

DALINDYEBO

Ngqeleni

Port St.Johns

Mganduli

St.Marks

Tsomo

Idutywa

Elliotdale

Ngamakwe

GCALEKA

FINGO

Willowvale

Butterworth

Kentani

THE TRANSKEI

ELECTORAL REGIONS
and
MAGISTERIAL DISTRICTS

UMZIMKULU — *Electoral Region*
Umzimkulu — *Magisterial District*
— *White Areas*

0   50
miles

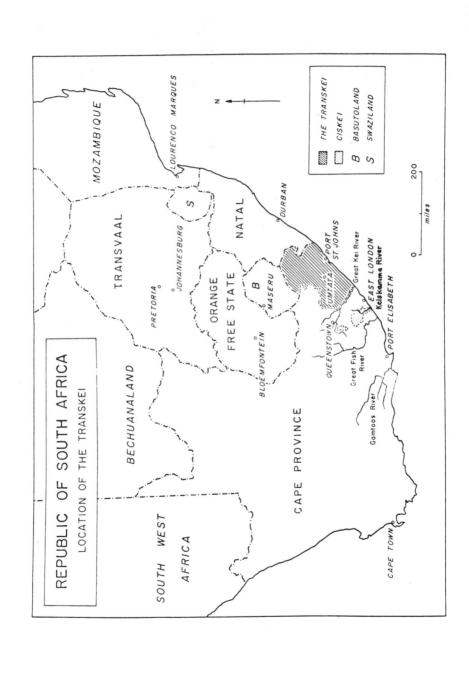

REPUBLIC OF SOUTH AFRICA
LOCATION OF THE TRANSKEI

THE TRANSKEI
CISKEI
B BASUTOLAND
S SWAZILAND

0   200
miles

N

MOZAMBIQUE

LOURENCO MARQUES

SOUTH WEST AFRICA

BECHUANALAND

TRANSVAAL

PRETORIA

JOHANNESBURG

S

NATAL

ORANGE FREE STATE

MASERU
B

BLOEMFONTEIN

DURBAN

CAPE PROVINCE

PORT ST JOHNS
UMTATA
Great Kei River
EAST LONDON
Keiskanna River

QUEENSTOWN
Great Fish River
PORT ELISABETH

Gamtoos River

CAPE TOWN

South Africa's

The Politics of

NORTHWESTERN UNIVERSITY   African Studies

Number Nineteen

Transskei

Domestic Colonialism

Gwendolen M. Carter
Thomas Karis
Newell M. Stultz

Northwestern University Press

Evanston 1967

Gwendolen M. Carter is Melville J. Herskovits Professor and Director, the Program of African Studies, Northwestern University.

Thomas Karis is Professor of Political Science at the City College of the City University of New York.

Newell M. Stultz is Assistant Professor of Political Science at Brown University.

Contents

Preface

THIS STUDY was undertaken in a spirit of open-minded inquiry. The authors had closely followed developments in South Africa since the National government came into power in 1948. They had seen one avenue of potential influence after another closed to the African majority of that country. After June, 1960, Africans no longer had representatives in the South African House of Assembly and Senate, thereby losing their last small share of national representation. (There had never been any illusion, however, that the three Whites that Cape Province Africans could elect to the House of Assembly and the four selected more indirectly, though by a wider group, for the Senate could exercise any genuine political influence on their behalf.) Both African nationalist organizations—the African National Congress, established in 1912, and its breakaway rival, the Pan-Africanist Congress—had been banned after the Sharpeville demonstration and shootings in March, 1960, and it seemed likely that this ban would continue indefinitely. In this perspective, the projected development of local semi-autonomy for the Transkei, largest of the African reserves, which is situated in the eastern Cape Province, seemed the only open-ended situation in South Africa for African political opportunities. Moreover, whatever the government's intentions, it seemed there might be unforeseen implications from the Transkeian situation for all groups in South Africa. The plans for this study were drawn up with these possibilities in mind.

During two intensive research trips (June–August, 1963, and January–April, 1964) the members of our small team—Gwendolen M. Carter, Thomas Karis, Newell Stultz, and Sheridan Johns, III—ably supported on the first trip by Molly Wise, Linda Christiansen, and Peter Bascoin, and on the second by Catherine Eglin, Molly Wise, and Margaret Anderson, worked in the field to gather material from individuals as well as from official sources. The individuals included many Africans in diverse fields of activity and from different parts of the country, as well as Whites and, where relevant, Coloureds and Asians. The objective was to test opinion regarding policies of "separate development" of the African in South Africa in addition to securing factual material. Periods of research in the Transkei, Ciskei, Zululand, the Northern Transvaal, and other African areas were interspersed with those in major cities: Cape Town during the 1964 parliamentary session; Pretoria for detailed consideration of Transkeian electoral procedures and returns; Johannesburg for its rich contacts with all sections of the economy and of the people; Port Elizabeth and East London with their substantial Transkeian populations and potential border industries; Durban and Pinetown as major industrial areas drawing heavily on African labor. Work was also undertaken in the then British-controlled territories of Basutoland, Swaziland, and Bechuanaland for purposes of comparison, and in Southwest Africa, for which the South African government was also considering plans for separate territorial developments.

In addition to this intensive group research, which drew on library facilities as well as those provided by official and unofficial channels, one member of the team, Newell Stultz, was in South Africa continuously from September, 1962, to April, 1964. Initially in that country as a Ford Foundation fellow preparing his doctoral dissertation on the National party prior to the election of 1948, Mr. Stultz concentrated between our two periods of group research on following the handling of the election in the Transkei. He provided the basic research for Section VII.

We also wish to acknowledge the contribution of material on Transkeian land, people, and administration by Professor David Hammond-Tooke of Rhodes University, at one time a government ethnographer in the Transkei and author of several detailed anthropological studies. We wish to point out, however, that responsibility for the final formulations and judgments in this work rests with the authors.

All four members of the full research team had had field research experience in South Africa before undertaking this particular assignment. Miss Carter went first to South Africa from November, 1948, to

February, 1949; returned for thirteen months of field research from August, 1952, to September, 1953; and spent briefer periods of time in 1957, 1959, and 1961 before undertaking the field research of which this book is the outcome. Her major previous publications on South Africa are *The Politics of Inequality: South Africa since 1948* (Praeger, New York, and Thames and Hudson, London, 1958, rev. 1959), and "African Nationalist Movements" in *Southern Africa in Transition,* edited by John A. Davis and James K. Baker (Praeger, 1966; pp. 3–19). Two lectures, published as pamphlets, are *African Concepts of Nationalism in South Africa* (Melville J. Herskovits Memorial Lecture, University of Edinburgh, March 1965) and *Separate Development: The Challenge of the Transkei* (the Nineteenth Alfred and Winifred Hoernlé Lecture, South African Institute of Race Relations, 1966).

Dr. Karis' first visit to South Africa was in 1955 as a member of the research staff of the United States Department of State, and during 1957–59 he was a Foreign Service Officer in the United States Embassy in Pretoria. His primary publications on South Africa are "South Africa" in *Five African States: Responses to Diversity,* edited by Gwendolen M. Carter (Cornell University Press, Ithaca, N.Y., 1963); *The South African Treason Trial: A Guide to the Microfilm Record of the Trial* (Hoover Institution, 1965); and *South Africa: The End Is Not Yet* (Foreign Policy Association booklet, April, 1966). During 1964–65 he was the research secretary for a discussion group on South Africa at the Council on Foreign Relations.

Dr. Stultz's first trip to South Africa, 1955–56, was for a year of study on a Fulbright fellowship at Pretoria University. He has published articles on the Transkei in *Africa Report* and in a series of Syracuse University papers.

Dr. Johns, who joined the group for the second field trip, had undertaken field research during 1962 for his doctoral thesis on early left-wing movements in South Africa. All four were able to build, therefore, on extensive contacts in every sphere of life.

Research in South Africa on African affairs is never easy. Restrictions on entering African areas, whether rural or urban, inhibit contacts. There are few places in the country where it is possible to meet even prominent Africans without surveillance. In 1964 the only place in Stanger where a White person could talk with Chief Albert Luthuli was in a car parked on a busy street; since May, 1964, he has not even been allowed to go to Stanger. In a small Ciskei town a conversation by the research group with the widow of a distinguished, widely known African was interrupted by police inexplicably (to her) demanding official permits to be in that area. In Alice, seat of Fort Hare College, once the independent university college for non-Whites and now the Xhosa college under the Department of Bantu Education, there was constant surveillance by the Special Branch of the police, and a mysterious disappearance and reappearance in a police station of a briefcase from a locked hotel room. In Umtata, the capital of the Transkei, an opposition member of the Transkeian legislature (to whom we were explaining our questionnaire for legislators that, as it happened, had been filled out that morning by Chief Minister Kaiser Matanzima and his brother George, Minister of Justice) was roughly and loudly turned out of one of our hotel rooms by the innkeeper on the ground that "this hotel is only for Whites" and was questioned by the Special Branch immediately thereafter. Two members of our team were searched by the Special Branch on leaving the country.

Apart from these and certain other smaller incidents, no specific impediments were placed in our way. Moreover, whenever we were under formal government guidance, we received generous aid, which we greatly appreciated. Nonetheless the cumulative effect of experiences such as those just described could not help but be disturbing. It is also greatly regretted that Miss Carter's request to the Minister of Bantu Administration and Development and to a senior official in the Department of Information for an opportunity to check the material in this book with relevant South Africans went unanswered. In addition, the long delay in issuing a visa toward the end of 1965 made it necessary for her to cancel her arrangements to present the Hoernlé Memorial Lecture in person and to participate in the discussions of separate development held in Cape Town in January, 1966.

While this study draws heavily on published documents, it also gained much from the cooperation of many people inside and outside of South Africa who have shared their information, data, and views most generously. Our very warm thanks go to all those who recognized the value of presenting a frank and objective study of the subject with which the authors were concerned. Great appreciation is expressed to the Ford Foundation for the financial aid that made the field trips possible and to Smith College for administering the funds.

Introduction

The Challenge of the Transkei

$\mathcal{S}$EPARATE DEVELOPMENT is no longer merely a theory; since the Transkei became a semiautonomous territory in December, 1963, racially separate territorial development has begun to take form in practice. In its broadest meaning, separate development is the South African government's policy of providing separate institutions and, where feasible, separate areas for each of the country's major racial groups. Popularly, the policy is epitomized by the so-called Bantustan program of developing the rural tribal reserves as "homelands" for the major African tribal groups.

The Transkei reserve has become the first Bantustan and the most prominent feature of the government's broad policy of separate development. It is important, therefore, to examine its status within South Africa in relation to the genesis and theoretical characteristics of separate development. Is the Transkeian type of development only an imposed measure of decentralization, or does it represent the first step in what may ultimately be a far-reaching partition of South African territory? Is it a new kind of cover for control and repression of the African, or has it possibilities of establishing "areas of liberty," to use a phrase of a noted South African liberal, Dr. Alfred Hoernlé?

To the South African government, the Transkei's new status—under which an all-African assembly, composed of a majority of ex officio chiefs and a minority of popularly elected members, directed by a Chief Minister and Cabinet, exercises limited but broader powers than previously possessed—is decisive evidence that what it calls the "separate development" of the African in South Africa is on the way to becoming a reality. And the government maintains that "separate development" will ultimately provide a positive feature within the complex South African racial situation, which will counterbalance the pervasive restrictions and onerous discrimination against Africans[1] and other non-Whites in the so-called White areas.

"Separate development," in the government's vocabulary, has two aspects: the introduction of new institutions and revival of fading ones considered appropriate to the Africans' heritage and nature, and their establishment in areas traditionally reserved exclusively for African occupancy. These areas are generally known as "native reserves." Of these reserves the Transkei in the eastern Cape Province is by far the largest in extent and population. Moreover, the Transkei has a relatively homogeneous population, speaking or at least understanding the Xhosa language. Thus it was natural that it should be the first African area within South Africa selected for the government's experiment in providing local semiautonomy, a status, said Prime Minister Verwoerd in 1962, that might be the first step toward ultimate independence.

But what the South African government called its "answer to the racial problem" of that country seemed to most persons who had fol-

1. The terminology used for the indigenous people of South Africa varies by speakers and attitudes. They themselves prefer to be called Africans, and the authors do so as far as possible throughout the book. The ruling Afrikaner Nationalists call them Bantu, which more correctly describes a particular language group found widely south of a line drawn from Gabon in the west to Kenya in the east. Among this group the word Bantu means people. Members of the opposition United party, and Nationalists, too, often use the term Natives, as will be seen in many quotations, and Africans themselves formerly used this term which they now consider derogates from their dignity. In using the word African in descriptions of debates, and other comparable situations, the authors are indicating their own sense of respect for the majority group in South Africa, whereas the wording used by White South Africans, other than progressives or liberals, is likely to have been one or the other of the two terms mentioned above.

The word Coloured refers to persons of mixed blood although the racial amalgam usually occurred many generations ago soon after the original contact with Whites. Asians are commonly Indians, including both Hindus and Moslems, mainly descendants of the indentured labor brought to the sugar plantations in Natal from 1860 on or of traders who followed them, although a few Chinese remain from the period when they were brought as indentured labor for the mines. The Whites (in South Africa commonly called Europeans) include Afrikaans- and English-speaking who are in roughly a 60–40 per cent ratio (bilingualism is high, however, in South Africa).

Population figures for South Africa in the 1960 census were 15,841,128, of whom there were 3,067,638 Whites; 1,488,267 Coloureds; 477,414 Asians; and 10,807,809 Africans. The population of the six largest urban areas with more than 100,000 people was: Johannesburg—413,153 Whites and 739,372 non-Whites (Coloured, Asians, Africans); Cape Town—305,155 Whites and 502,056 non-Whites; Durban—196,398 Whites and 485,094 non-Whites; Pretoria—207,202 Whites and 215,388 non-Whites; Port Elizabeth—94,931 Whites and 195,762 non-Whites; Germiston—86,314 Whites and 128,079 non-Whites.

lowed the evolution of colonialism in the past decade to be little more than an early stage of colonial organization within limited enclaves in South Africa. Further, the lack of exploitable resources of the African reserve areas—including the Transkei—their overcrowding, and the dependence, even for subsistence, of a high proportion of their inhabitants on the earnings of migratory labor make them still more dependent on the sources of capital and the organization of commerce and industry outside their boundaries than even the least developed of the African colonies had been in their pre-independence period. Without vast and systematic capital inflow and industrial development is there thus a chance that these African areas, including the Transkei, can be other than rural slums?

Highly relevant to the potentialities of separate development is the national setting within which the Transkei experiment is taking place. The 10,900,000 Africans at the time of the 1960 national census accounted for approximately 66 per cent of the total South African population. Only 37 per cent of these Africans were living inside reserve areas, i.e., only a little over a third of the total African population. Looked at the other way, the census disclosed that the 6,874,000 Africans in the so-called White areas totaled approximately twice the number of Whites in the whole country. Equally significant is the fact that those Africans living in urban areas in 1960 numbered 3,400,000, nearly a million more than the Whites in these cities.

Moreover these figures did not reflect any startlingly new configurations. Even at the 1951 census 58 per cent of all Africans were in the so-called White areas, and 26.7 per cent in urban areas. It is true that some of the Africans outside the reserves are migrant workers who periodically return to families in the "homelands": about 525,000 Africans at the time of the 1951 census. At that time there were also nearly 650,000 "extra-Union Natives"—Africans from outside South Africa—in that country.[2] But this meant that about three-quarters of the 4,900,000 Africans *outside* the reserves in 1951—that is, 3,700,000—were domiciled there, while about 1,500,000 of them were in the urban areas of the country.[3] Moreover, throughout the 1950's, the urban African population grew at a markedly faster rate than the African population as a whole.

It is these urban Africans, most outside observers agree, who form the crux of the racial problem in South Africa, for they are an integral and essential part of the most highly articulated and developed economic structure in Africa. Moreover, for more than a century some Africans in South Africa had taken advantage of political opportuni-

2. *Union of South Africa, Summary of the Report of the Commission for the Socio-Economic Development of the Bantu Areas Within the Union of South Africa* (Union Government [hereafter cited as U.G.] 61/1955), p. 40.
3. *Ibid.,* p. 28.

ties, though these opportunities had been steadily and inexorably diminished during that period by White-run governments and administrations. Africans had voted in the Cape for the same parliamentary candidates as Whites until they were removed from the common roll in 1936. Subsequently they voted on a separate roll for three Whites for the House of Assembly and, nationally, by an indirect process for four White senators, until both opportunities were removed in 1959. Also, Africans had operated one or more national organizations from 1912 until the African National Congress (ANC) and the Pan-Africanist Congress (PAC) were banned in 1960, and thus they had a longer continuous experience of nationalist associations than any other Africans on the continent. The objectives of the major African nationalist organizations—ANC, the All African Convention, and, from 1959, the PAC—had focused both on removing non-White restrictions within South Africa as a whole and on securing those civil and political rights that are extended, at least in principle, to the adult members of every other developed country in the world. Today, African nationalists continue to oppose separate development on principle as the fragmentation of what they believe should be a united country in which they share political rights and power appropriate to their numbers.

Separate development is obviously based upon racial differentiation. To approve separate development for Africans in the Transkei and other comparable territories might well seem to justify White control in so-called White areas. Within the Transkei itself, the opposition Democratic party upholds the principle of multiracialism and advocates rights for Africans in the White areas as well. Its policy is based partly on long ties of friendship between Africans and Whites residing in the Transkei and on the view that the contributions of Transkeian Whites should be reflected in a sharing of responsibilities and opportunities. Equally in the national sphere, the constructive economic results from the working together of Whites, Africans, Asians, and Coloureds affirms the equity of their full sharing of political, economic, and social rights, as well as in the returns of a prosperous, expanding economy.

Yet, however harsh the criticism and widespread the doubts, both inside and outside the country, the South African government was determined to establish the new institutions in the Transkei and to claim far-reaching implications for them. In Parliament it brushed aside United party and Progressive party objections. In the Transkei itself, substantial though somewhat inept opposition, particularly from the Thembu, an important tribal group, was ineffective in stopping or even slowing down the process. In late 1963, new institutions for separate territorial development came into being in the Transkei.

In choosing the Transkei, the government could take advantage of that area's long experience of representation in local advisory bodies and of the acceptance in 1955 of the Bantu Authorities system, designed to bolster the position of the chiefs. Moreover, in Chief Kaiser Matanzima the South African government had an intelligent and effective ally who accepted the notion of territorial separation with the shrewd awareness that it offered scope for political maneuvering not otherwise available within the South African context.

There were other reasons why the Transkei was the obvious place for the government to attempt its experiment. Whereas most African reserve areas are composed of scattered pockets of land—there were 264 in all in 1959 making up just under 13 per cent of South Africa's land area—the Transkei is a consolidated area, though only its rural sections fall under the new institutions. In addition, as compared to other African reserve areas in South Africa, the Transkei has a substantial proportion of its people living within its borders: approximately 60 per cent, or 1,400,000 of the 2,400,000 thought in 1963 to be of Transkeian origin and thus eligible for Transkeian citizenship. Thus while Transkeians number between a fifth and a quarter of all Africans in South Africa, those resident within the Transkei include well over one-third of all those Africans—4,026,000 in 1960—whose *de facto* homes are in reserves.

Turning these figures the other way, the 40 per cent of Transkeians who live outside the Transkei include only about one-seventh of the total number of Africans in White areas. At the same time, the small number of local employment possibilities forces most African males in that territory, as in other reserve areas, to seek work for varying lengths of time in or near urban areas outside. Thus there is, and has long been, a constant movement of African labor that must be taken into account in interpreting these and other figures on African residence.

Why did the South African government begin to implement its policies of separate territorial development in the Transkei at the point it did? What were the stakes at issue? The internal and external pressures that form the setting in which the government's decision was made are spelled out in detail in the first chapters of this book. In that perspective it is sharply apparent that to establish new institutions under the rubric of potential ultimate independence was playing with high stakes—no less than risking the possible fragmentation of South Africa in an attempt to persuade Africans inside and outside its boundaries and the world at large that separate territorial development offers an acceptable alternative to the extension of national political and other rights in an undivided country.

The challenge of the Transkei has been to demonstrate that the South African government has provided its people with sufficient opportunities to counterbalance the disabilities suffered by Africans in the so-called White areas. How the government went about implementing its policies and toward what ends forms much of the body of this book. The judgments on its success or failure can be left to the conclusion.

Section I
South Africa under Pressure

1

The Setting of Domestic Colonialism

THE RISE of an Afrikaner-dominated republic, the intensification of world hostility to White racial dominance, and the acceleration of domestic colonialism in the Transkei reflect historic timetables, moving at different speeds toward contradictory ends. Afrikanerdom seeks to maintain undisputed White dominance in South Africa; the world outside is pledged to procure equality of individual rights for all the inhabitants of this area, of whom the Africans total over three-quarters. The domestic colonialism reflected in the so-called Bantustan program opens possibilities for aiding either one or the other of these objectives. The government hopes that this program will damp down the fervor of African nationalism by providing an alternative to African nationalist efforts to gain their share of national power, and that this alternative will become acceptable both to Africans and to international opinion. In sharp contrast, those Africans and others who are willing to exploit the possibilities they feel inherent in the government's policy of separate development hope that they can use it as a Trojan horse from which to challenge the national policies and ultimately the power of the White-controlled government of South Africa. However illusory this latter possibility may seem now, there is a dynamic in the implementation of separate territorial development that may produce unexpected results in the long run.

These developments have interacted and continue to interact with others in South Africa that are hardly less important: the growth of industrialization and of the economic interdependence of all racial groups; the frustration of African protest and its turn to violence; and the steady tightening of repressive controls on the expression of opposition to government policies, leaving the rural Transkei virtually the only ground where Africans can voice nonviolent opposition to the actions of a regime in which they have no representation. It is clear that South Africa's future will be shaped in the urban areas, not in the rural Bantustans of which the Transkei is the first and, despite all its liabilities, the most promising. Yet no territorial segment of South Africa nor any sphere of its life can be insulated from the impact of a dynamic economy or from the influences of radical change abroad. Not only will the Transkei itself be affected but, as we have suggested, what happens there may in turn affect the timetables operating both inside and outside South Africa. Thus, developments in the Transkei and implications drawn from them may have an effect on the power of the White regime, the stance of interested parties outside, and future relations between White and Black.

Prime Minister Hendrik Verwoerd's announcement in Parliament on January 23, 1962, that "the Government will . . . grant the Transkei self-government" was "dramatic," as he described it, only insofar as it indicated that the government had decided on a radical acceleration of the Bantustan timetable. Dr. Verwoerd himself said it was "dramatic" only "inasmuch as people did not believe that we were honest . . . that we were in earnest . . . "[1] What needs explanation, in fact, is not the announcement's substance but its timing. The announcement itself can be seen as the logical outgrowth of ripened policy. But pressures inevitably affected the timing, for the policy had not only been the product of Afrikaner nationalist values and goals but was also a response to the challenge of African nationalism, to White disquiet at home, and to the threat to South Africa that Ethiopia and Liberia had launched in November, 1960, by asking the International Court of Justice to judge whether South Africa had violated its obligations as Mandatory over the Territory of Southwest Africa.

The relationship and interaction between the Transkei project and South Africa's public relations posture regarding Southwest Africa were of particular significance from 1960 to July, 1966, when the Court decided on technical grounds to make no judgment on the issues presented to it. In that period, Ovamboland and the Transkei became the two far-separated horns of the apartheid bull. Some acute South Afri-

---

1. *House of Assembly Debates,* cols. 74–75. Two weeks earlier, Victor Leibbrandt, Chief Magistrate of the Transkei, was reported to have told a journalist that self-government could not possibly come to the Transkei as early as 1963. "Our hand is being forced, there is no doubt about that, but the Transkei is just not ready for self-government." (*Forum,* March, 1962, p. 11.)

can observers believed that Dr. Verwoerd was speeding up and extending the political development of the Transkei largely to provide a prototype for separate development in Southwest Africa and to add credence to official claims that apartheid, in the form of racial territorial segregation, was fair to all groups and even idealistic in its ultimate aims rather than an ugly manifestation of prejudice and self-interest.

There is much evidence for this interpretation. In 1958, Dr. Verwoerd changed the draft bill for removal of the three Native Representatives from the House of Assembly, after protests from within his own party that so negative a bill, without some positive compensation, would alienate some domestic opinion as well as provide foreign critics with much ammunition against South Africa. It became the glorified "Promotion of Bantu Self-Government Act" of 1959. Not until after Liberia and Ethiopia pressed charges of the incompatibility of apartheid with the Mandatory's responsibilities did Dr. Verwoerd drag his party all the way to phrases indicating the possibility of eventual independence. At the same time, the South African government was hurrying plans for applying the Bantustan principle to Southwest Africa. The northern reserves in Ovamboland offered a prospect similar to the Transkei: a solid block of African territory largely homogeneous in language. Less advanced in education and in experience with Western institutions, however, Ovamboland could not provide the dramatic demonstration of the Bantustan principle that the Transkei, with its heritage of experience with representative advisory councils and of territorial individuality, might provide.

The interaction of the two concepts of the Transkei State and an Ovambostan was prematurely revealed to the press by the Deputy Minister for Southwest African Affairs on January 31, 1962.[2] Although the Odendaal Commission on Southwest African development programs was not appointed until September, 1962, the South African government plainly was far advanced at the end of 1961 in its plans for the application of "groot" (great) apartheid to Southwest Africa. Since the Prime Minister acted both as the Minister in charge of Southwest African affairs and as the master architect of the overall Bantustan program, the utility of the Transkei project to the credibility of the program for Southwest Africa could hardly be a chance development. Certainly the Prime Minister and the mass media controlled by him, together with the government's information service, made the most of the new institutions established in the Transkei, bringing Ovambo chiefs and headmen there to see their operations and presenting elaborate testimony before the International Court by lawyers and witnesses about the significance of the Transkeian development for Southwest Africa.

2. *Cape Times,* February 1, 1962, and S.A.B.C. broadcast of same date.

13

In the parliamentary no-confidence debate of January, 1962, in which Dr. Verwoerd spoke, Sir de Villiers Graaff, leader of the opposition, had accused the government of having failed for nearly fourteen years to convince South African and world opinion that apartheid had a moral basis. Pressures were becoming "so menacing and so dangerous," internally and externally, he pointed out, that the government should act immediately, if ever, in implementing the "positive aspects" of apartheid. What was the timetable, he asked contemptuously, for the enlargement and conversion of existing Bantu reserves into "independent homelands" for the Bantu? These and other Nationalist plans (for example, cutting back the supply of Black labor from the reserves and giving up land) would be so expensive and so disruptive of White convenience, declared Sir de Villiers, that the government did not have "the guts" to implement them.[3]

Dr. Verwoerd replied at length, maintaining that "the building up of the Bantu homelands, the development of border industries . . . the institution of influx control . . . are all processes which of necessity take time."[4] Not until 1978, he declared, as he had on earlier occasions, would a turning point be reached at which the rising influx of Africans into cities would level off and begin to decline. Meanwhile, in what he called leading "the Bantu nations in our midst" to adulthood, the government refused to be rushed. But now the time was opportune, he believed, to make his announcement even though he could not prophesy how long it would take before all functions of government could be transferred. Yet distinctive changes could be produced in a short time under certain circumstances. A few years earlier, he recalled, Sir de Villiers had taunted M. D. C. de Wet Nel, the Minister of Bantu Administration and Development, for saying, "Give me two years . . . and then you will see what peace, what order, and what co-operation [with the Bantu] we will be able to obtain." But De Wet Nel had also said: "Give me two years without continual attacks and obstruction by the Press and the parties and without the incitement and without the interference from outside and without the coddling of rebels and agitators!" His implication was clear that it was the activities not only of "rebels and agitators," English-language newspapers, and the United, Progressive, and Liberal parties but also of tribal chiefs and other moderate Africans, and of Afrikaner politicians and intellectuals in the National party that had held back and hampered the government's Bantustan policy.

Many factors, in effect, had acted to influence the implementation of the government's racial policies, some to slow it down and others to accelerate certain aspects, particularly separate territorial development. The Transkeian program appears to have been affected by threat-

3. *House of Assembly Debates,* cols. 39–41, 47.
4. *Ibid.,* cols. 63, 73, 75, 77.

ening changes in the nature of the African nationalist challenge, by increasing expectations of Transkeian Africans, and by the dangers of mounting hostility abroad, on the one hand, and by the diverse moral and political pressures of South African Whites and by the government's growing political strength and resulting freedom of action on the other. The years 1960–61, marked by national emergency and disturbances in the Transkei, comprise a distinct period and, to an undetermined but important extent, precipitated the acceleration marked by Dr. Verwoerd's announcement of January, 1962. But the stage was set for this crucial time during the dozen preceding years of Afrikaner Nationalist rule.

Within these years three periods may be distinguished: the five years of the Nationalists' first term in office, from May, 1948, to April, 1953; the nearly four years that culminated with the large-scale arrests in December, 1956, of leaders, mainly non-White, from the extra-parliamentary opposition; and the three turbulent years of 1957–59. When the pressures culminated during the two years of 1960–61, the regime felt sufficiently threatened to declare a national emergency.

1948–53

The African National Congress (ANC), since 1912 the historic organ of the African's national aspirations, reached its high point of organized challenge to apartheid during the Nationalists' first term. Traditionally led by liberal professional men and church leaders, the ANC became more militant in 1949, when leaders of its Youth League rose to dominance. A new "Program of Action" was adopted, calling for a 1 end to cooperation with governmental institutions and for boycotts, strikes, and civil disobedience.

Boycott was not a new tactic. It had long been urged by the All African Convention (AAC), a federation of organizations that the ANC had helped to form during the all-African protest against the 1936 legislation which had removed qualified Cape Africans from the common voting roll and had placed them on a separate roll to elect three Whites to the House of Assembly. Especially after 1943, when it took the lead in organizing the Non-European Unity Movement (which included Coloureds as well as Africans), the AAC became particularly active among teachers and voters in the Transkei. It called for a boycott of such "dummy institutions" as the Natives' Representative Council—a national elective African advisory body set up as part of the 1936 "settlement"—and the Bunga—the partly elected African advisory council of the Transkei.

Unlike the AAC, however, the Youth League's members were nondoctrinaire, at least regarding tactics, and were inspired by militant African nationalism. Although initially anti-Communist and opposed

15

to joint action with non-Africans, many leaders of the Youth League moved during the early fifties toward closer interracial cooperation and acceptance of Indian and Communist support in their opposition to governmental legislation and action that appeared to threaten the entire extraconstitutional antigovernment front.

The high point of African protest was reached in the "defiance" or passive resistance campaign of 1952. The demonstrators deliberately violated minor apartheid regulations, for example, by entering public premises reserved for Whites. In this way, they sought to publicize their opposition to a number of laws, in particular, the long-existing pass laws (laws requiring Africans to carry identification passes). As a protest against lack of land, they opposed measures aimed at culling cattle to reduce overgrazing. They protested, also, against the Bantu Authorities Act of 1951, which strengthened the position of tribal chiefs, and against other legislation designed to confine each racial group to its own "group area," to remove Coloureds from the common voting roll in Cape Province, and to suppress "Communism," which was defined so broadly in the legislation that it could be made to apply to African nationalists. The ANC's membership of around 15,000 to 20,000 grew to 100,000, and about 8,500 volunteers, including some Indians and Coloureds, went to jail. But by the end of the year the campaign petered out amidst some rioting and violence, and early in 1953 severe legislation was enacted against civil disobedience undertaken as a means of protest.

The defiance campaign was conducted mainly in urban areas, but many of its aims were supported by politically minded Africans in the reserves. Although the Transkei remained relatively quiet, and conservative members of the Bunga occasionally expressed suspicions of the ANC, the Bunga had aligned itself with urban protests regarding political rights since the 1920's. It expressed continuing concern over the years for the maintenance and extension and, after 1936, the restoration of African eligibility to vote on the common roll. The Bunga also voted unanimously on a number of occasions that Africans should become eligible to stand as members of Parliament. Thus it acted consistently when it adopted a resolution at the beginning of the defiance campaign rejecting the principles of the Bantu Authorities Act.

During the Nationalists' first term in office, the Bunga repeated its requests for greater authority over local government in the Transkei and for the appointment of qualified Africans to higher administrative positions. These proposals were coupled with a rejection by the Bunga of the national policy of political inequality; early in April, 1949, for example, the Bunga resolved that "This council deplores the Government's policy of apartheid as a serious injustice . . . "[5] On the other

5. South African Press Association Report (April 28, 1949).

hand, as is spelled out in more detail later, one proposal had been made in the Bunga in 1944 that the Transkei should become fully self-governing. This proposal reflected not only personal opportunism but also the frustration and despair that underlay a minor strand of African thought that had been expressed since the 1920's.[6] If equal rights were not to be extended in a multiracial or nonracial society, the argument ran, then Africans themselves should demand territorial independence.

1953-56

During the second period, from April, 1953, through 1956, there was a growing polarization of Afrikaner and African pronouncements regarding apartheid and separate development, and the stage was set in the Transkei for development on the government's own terms. The period began with the Nationalist government's return to office with an enlarged parliamentary majority and an enlarged popular vote among the White electors, although it still gained less than a popular majority.

The Bantu Education Act of 1953, enacted shortly afterward, was an integral part of the government's policy of separate development and therefore, although the Act itself dealt with administrative matters, came under heavy attack from both White and African opponents of the government. Africans were particularly suspicious of the consequences of transferring African education from mission and provincial control to the Union Department of Native Affairs rather than the Union Department of Education. They feared that "Bantu education" meant inferior education, that the Nationalist emphasis on teaching through the vernacular or mother tongue and on relating education to tribal culture was designed to confine the African to a position of subordination. Nevertheless, whatever was to be the future content of education, urban Africans were generally anxious to have their children in school. The ANC sought to protest the transfer of the schools to the Department of Native Affairs in April, 1955, by urging boycott, but the campaign was confused and proved abortive.

In the face of new punitive legislation that seriously increased the personal risk, including whipping, to be run in any campaign of protest, non-White tactics shifted from disobedience to demonstration. Efforts to form a multiracial popular front culminated on June 25-26, 1955, when the ANC and allied Indian, White, and Coloured organizations, which included some members of the banned Communist party, held a Congress of the People. Nearly 3,000 delegates adopted a Freedom Charter, which demanded the vote for every individual and also equal rights of development for "all national groups and races." During this

6. Gwendolen M. Carter, *African Concepts of Nationalism in South Africa* (Melville J. Herskovits Memorial Lecture [Edinburgh: University of Edinburgh, 1965]), pp. 16–17.

period the opportunities of the ANC and its allies to engage in legal protest were steadily constricted, however, by bans on individual activity and by official harassment and intimidation. Finally, in December, 1956, major officials of the Congress alliance were arrested on a charge of high treason that was based essentially on such documents as the Freedom Charter. (The accused in that trial were found not guilty in March, 1961, the court saying it could not conclude from the evidence that the ANC had pursued a policy of attempting to overthrow the State by violence.)

Earlier in 1956, widely representative and, of course, separate conventions of Afrikaners and Africans had accepted and rejected, respectively, the "ultimate separate development" proposed by the Tomlinson Commission, a government-established body to determine the population capacity of the African reserves. An Afrikaner *volkskongres,* called to discuss the Report and attended by some 800 delegates representing 540 organizations, resolved in June, 1956, to support territorial separation on the ground that "there is no possibility of the peaceful evolutionary development of White and Black in South Africa into an integrated society."[7] Four months later, the Tomlinson Report was considered by some 400 Africans at the most widely representative conference (sponsored by the Interdenominational African Ministers' Federation) to be held since the conferences of 1935–37 that had opposed the removal of Africans in Cape Province from the common voting roll to a separate roll. The 1956 African conference denied that "cooperation and interdependence between the various races" would threaten the survival of the White man and recorded its "total rejection" of the Tomlinson Report. With reference to what the Commission called "the political aspect," the conference maintained, however, that "an arrangement on their own [the Afrikaners'] premises could logically only mean sovereign independence for the so-called Bantu Areas." But the statement from the conference did not speculate on the possibility of such a development. It rejected the notion of "separate national homes" since that policy was coupled with the deprivation of African rights in the rest of the country. The conference further asserted that the government's rejection of some of the economic recommendations of the Tomlinson Commission demonstrated that the government's claim to be acting in the interests of the Africans was "a hollow political bluff."[8]

Nevertheless, among the members of the Bunga—most of them chiefs or headmen—the government's powers of persuasion, mixed with the promise of enhanced authority and hard evidence that opposition was

7. Quoted in L. E. Neame, *The History of Apartheid* (London: Pall Mall Press, 1962), p. 126
8. *The Statement by the All-In African Conference held at Bloemfontein on the 4th–6th October 1956* (mimeographed).

fruitless, produced what appeared to be a successful breakthrough for official policy: the unanimous vote of the Bunga members in April, 1955, to accept the Bantu Authorities system in principle. Just what this decision meant to the Bunga cannot easily be determined. The night before the vote, most of them attended a meeting addressed by two of the parliamentary Native Representatives, who were advocating the restoration of Africans to the common voting roll, and gave them a unanimous vote of confidence.[9] During the Bunga's discussions on the following day one prominent member coupled his support for Bantu Authorities with his hope for eventual "direct representation in Parliament." But the prevailing hope for the present was for wider authority within the Transkei.

"There seems to be a tendency among the Natives," said Walter Stanford, the Transkei's White representative in Parliament, "to take whatever they can get . . . "[10] Stanford believed that Africans, by collaborating, were prejudicing their chances for wider political rights. A different conclusion was reached by Nelson Mandela, one of the founders of the ANC Youth League, who was destined to become the commanding figure in the ANC underground after that organization was banned following Sharpeville. The Bunga decision, he wrote in mid-1955, indicated how little impact ANC propaganda had made in the Transkei and threw doubt on the tactic of boycotting government-sponsored bodies. "Will participation in these bodies," he asked, "not serve as a means of maintaining connection and contact with the great masses of the people in the Reserves? Should these bodies not be used as platforms to expose the policies of the Nationalist Government, and to win the people over to the liberation movement?"[11]

1957–59

During the third period, from 1957 to 1959, some elements of the African opposition became more racially assertive, more identified with Pan-Africanism, more impatient, and more disposed to take direct and often undisciplined action. Ghana's independence in March, 1957, was an inspiration for Africans everywhere. The ANC's leadership, however, was partly immobilized by the treason trial (which attempted to blur the distinction between long-standing aspirations and Communist aims) and was thus diverted from effective or large-scale campaigns of protest and activity against its African nationalist rivals. Meanwhile, the readiness of Africans who shared an economic grievance to cooperate effectively and almost spontaneously in local protests was evident

9. *The Star* (Johannesburg), April 22, 1955.
10. *Ibid.*
11. *Fighting Talk,* a left-wing magazine, July, 1955, p. 7.

in the successful boycott of Johannesburg buses by more than 50,000 Africans during a period of three months early in 1957. In the following year, while the treason trial continued, the Congress alliance sponsored a three-day stay-at-home demonstration immediately prior to the general election of April, 1958. Because of confused leadership, African dissension, and effective countermeasures by the government, however, the demonstration was a fiasco.

Much of the discord within the organization was caused by "Africanist" challengers of the ANC's leadership, that is, nationalists opposed to the Congress alliance and imbued with zeal for African self-reliance and assertion. In April, 1959, the Africanists formally established the Pan-Africanist Congress (PAC). During the same month the ANC celebrated its own Africanism at an "Africa Week" rally. ANC leaders as Westernized and sophisticated as Oliver Tambo, Duma Nokwe, and Dr. Arthur Letele appeared uncharacteristically in tribal dress. By wearing the dress of tribes other than their own they demonstrated their respect for the tribal heritage of all Africans.

In December, the ANC Annual Conference endorsed March 31 as Antipass Day to commemorate the antipass demonstrations of 1919 and to be celebrated for the first time in 1960. Later, the PAC decided to launch its antipass campaign—in which Africans would refuse to carry passes as a protest—on March 21, 1960, which was destined to become the day of the Sharpeville shootings.

While African political organizations continued to limit themselves to traditional forms of nonviolent demonstration during this period, violence flared up in the usually quiet rural areas. Popular opposition to various measures of agricultural reform had erupted in the reserves in earlier years, especially after the Smuts government's introduction in 1945 of its Rehabilitation Scheme. In August, 1947, for example, before the Nationalists came to power, police reinforcements were necessary in the Mount Ayliff district of the Transkei, where the local Paramount Chief's cooperation with the government in stock culling and soil conservation met substantial opposition led by a rival chief. In response, government officials warned that chiefs who stirred up trouble would be deported from the territory.[12] After 1948, the Nationalist government banished some troublesome chiefs and enlarged the authority of those who remained in office. (In 1957, for example, a significant regulation, Proclamation 110, shifted important powers, such as the allocation of land, from headmen to chiefs.) Some government-appointed chiefs were disliked because they were often autocratic and occasionally (like some headmen) corrupt. But the explanation of hostility that erupted into riots and led to hut burning and murder varied from area

12. *The Star* (Johannesburg), August 9 and 27, 1947.

to area, depending on circumstances of local rivalries and grievances as well as opposition to official policies.

Other incidents of serious disorder and bloody clashes with the police occurred at Witzieshoek, near Basutoland, in 1950 and in Eastern Pondoland in the Transkei in 1953. Meanwhile, government officials became increasingly industrious in seeking popular support. Officials toured the reserves with propaganda units equipped with loudspeakers, and at important junctures the government raised the salaries of chiefs and headmen. At the same time, tribal representatives were warned that their groups would lose financial and social services if they did not accept the Bantu Authorities system, which not only strengthened the position of tribal chiefs but also, Africans felt with justification, brought still more government control into the system of indirect rule.

Despite these warnings, resistance and violence reached the stage of open revolt in 1957 in the Sekhukhuneland and Zeerust areas of the northern Transvaal, and disorder and rioting occurred in Eastern Pondoland. In 1958, tensions became higher in some reserves when official teams arrived to begin to issue passes to African women, who had not previously had to carry these much-hated documents of control.

In Tembuland in the Transkei, unrest and resentment arose in part from hostility between its Paramount Chief, Sabata Dalindyebo, and the chief of a historically separate segment of the Thembu, Kaiser Matanzima. The weakness of Sabata's intervention on behalf of factions opposed to Matanzima, who was a leading government collaborator, was illustrated, however, in October, 1957. In response to a letter from Sabata complaining that followers of a headman deposed by Matanzima had been severely assaulted in the presence not only of Matanzima himself, but also of the Bantu Affairs Commissioner and the police, the Chief Bantu Affairs Commissioner warned Sabata that further "impertinent letters composed and written by your secretary" would lead to cancellation of his appointment.[13] In June, 1958, Sabata's secretary and four other advisers were deported to distant areas.[14]

Partly as a result of these local and national evidences of serious African discontent and opposition to government policies, vigorous debate continued during 1957–59 on the future direction of public policy. This was true also in the Transkeian Territorial Authority (TTA), the body of chiefs and councillors that replaced the partly elected Bunga in 1957. The TTA seemed occasionally to be as ambivalent in its attitudes to government policies as was its predecessor. Acting within the framework of official policy, it asked in 1957 that qualified Africans be appointed to all posts occupied by Whites in the Transkei.[15] In 1959, on

13. Quoted in unpublished, typewritten manuscript by W. M. Tsotsi.
14. *New Age* (Johannesburg), June 12, 1958.
15. *Fighting Talk* referred to these demands in its issue of March, 1962, and commented (page 4): "The new constitution is going to speed up this process."

the other hand, there was still support in the Territorial Authority for retention in Parliament of the Native Representatives.[16]

Within the White political arena, more vigorous opposition to the government's policies was promised in November, 1959, when the Progressive party was formed. Among its leaders were eleven members of Parliament who had become increasingly impatient with the United party's lack of a positive racial policy and had finally resigned from the party over an issue, apparently relatively minor, but one of principle, regarding the purchase of additional land for the Native Reserves. The Progressives adopted essentially the same position that had been occupied by the Liberal party when it was formed after the 1953 election, that is, support of high but nonracial qualifications to determine the right to vote and rigid constitutional safeguards. Like the White Liberals, who had been moving toward a closer identification with the Africans, the Progressives insisted on the need for more communication with African leaders and began privately to engage in consultations. In this respect, they were in accord, interestingly enough, with some progovernment Afrikaner intellectuals. Following the 1958 election, Afrikaner members of the unofficial South African Bureau of Racial Affairs, despite Dr. Verwoerd's disapproval, began holding a series of private meetings with Africans, including ANC leaders on trial for treason, and PAC leaders.

To such internal criticism of the government's policy were also joined external pressures. Apartheid continued to receive its chief opposition from the United Nations where perennial and impassioned attacks on South Africa's racial policy had taken place since 1946. In October, 1958, however, a new development occurred: the United States ended its practice of abstaining on resolutions critical of apartheid and joined 69 other countries (with five, including the United Kingdom, against, and four abstaining) in expressing "regret and concern" that South Africa had not modified its racial policy. This action disturbed Afrikaner nationalist leaders more than had all preceding actions of the United Nations and intensified existing anxiety about the course of American policy.

Trouble in the reserves attracted some international attention, but trouble of international significance occurred on the night of December 10–11, 1959, in Windhoek, Southwest Africa, the mandated territory that the United Nations insists—and South Africa agrees—has an international character. About a thousand Africans rioted after nearly a

---

16. During debate on the Promotion of the Bantu Self-Government Bill, Stanford described "a sorry story of intrigue and pressures being brought to bear upon the Africans" and charged that a pending motion supporting retention of the Native Representatives had been avoided by postponing the meeting of the Authority, on technical grounds, until a time when the motion could be ruled out of order. (*House of Assembly Debates* [May 19, 1959], cols. 6145–46.)

week's boycott of African facilities that had been conducted to protest the intended removal of residents from an old residential quarter to a new site some distance from town. In response to attacks by stone throwers and to the fear of being overwhelmed, the police fired, killing 11 Africans and wounding 44 others.[17] Reactions in the United Nations foreshadowed those that were to follow the Sharpeville shootings some three months later.

1960-61

The political relations of White and Black were radically transformed during 1960–61, and White confidence in the continuation of White domination in South Africa was temporarily shaken. The crucial event was precipitated on March 21, 1960, a historical watershed for the country. On that day in Sharpeville, south of Johannesburg, the police killed 72 Africans and wounded about 186 in a crowd that was demonstrating its support for a new defiance campaign against the carrying of passes and, according to the police, was threatening to overrun them. The program that occasioned these and later disturbances was initiated by the PAC and had originally been opposed by the ANC on the grounds that it was "sensational" and might not succeed. After the shooting, however, Chief Albert Luthuli, leader of the ANC, called for a "stay-at-home" Day of Mourning and made the defiant gesture of burning his pass.

The government, seeking a showdown, exercised for the first time the power granted to it by legislation enacted after the passive resistance campaign of 1952 and proclaimed an emergency, thus freeing itself from the restrictions of habeas corpus. By enacting legislation that resulted in the outlawing of both the ANC and the PAC, the government took a major action that it had obviously expected to take if the prosecution were successful in the treason trial. By arresting and indefinitely detaining 1,900 persons seized in early-morning raids, the police cracked down on political suspects whose names were apparently on a standing list. (More than 17,000 African "idlers" were also detained.) By jailing leaders of the anti-Communist Liberal party without explanation and for the first time, the government fulfilled the predictions of critics who had seen danger to all opponents of official policy in the breadth of the prosecution's treason trial argument. By convicting the PAC leaders during the first six weeks after Sharpeville for incitement and by imposing penalties ranging from whipping to three years in jail,

17. *Report of the Commission of Enquiry into the Occurrences in the Location on the Night of the 10th to the 11th December, 1959, and into the Direct Causes Which Led to Those Occurrences* (U.G. 23/1960).

the government demonstrated again its readiness to act speedily and forcefully in cutting down African leadership.

Following the end of the emergency on August 31, 1960, the surface of South Africa's life resumed the appearance of normality. The ANC and the PAC, still under ban (a ban that has been renewed annually), attempted to maintain their structures underground. Meanwhile organizations allied to the ANC and many persons who had been detained, including members of the Liberal party and ANC and PAC members who were not under individual bans, again became publicly active. At the same time, leading Whites, including supporters of the government and representatives of commerce and industry, made the most urgent appeals for consultation with Africans that had ever been heard in South Africa.

During the period between the end of the emergency and South Africa's becoming a republic outside the Commonwealth on May 31, 1961, African opponents of apartheid made a final effort to construct the widest possible, or "all-in," front for public protest. Again the call for a national convention came to the fore. Although there was no expectation that such a convention would take place, there was some hope that at least a multiracial conference might be held. Such hope was encouraged by the series of private discussions that had been taking place between Whites (including Afrikaans-speaking intellectuals) and non-Whites. An African "Consultative Conference" met in Johannesburg in December, 1960; its participants included members of the ANC and the PAC who were not individually banned and others whose orientation ranged from Communist to Progressive. Plans were made for an African conference, but later the united front was broken as a result of the suspicions of persons sympathetic to the PAC that former ANC members were distorting the mandate for unity and imparting to the future conference an ideological slant that covered Communist ends.

When what was called the All-In Conference was held, it was in fact dominated by former ANC members. Meeting in Pietermaritzburg, Natal, in March, 1961, it attracted more than a thousand Africans from all parts of the country. The Conference demanded the calling of a national convention and urged Africans to participate in a three-day stay-at-home prior to the proclamation of the Republic on May 31. From the earliest stages of the planning, however, the organizers encountered the usual harassment of raids and arrests.

The stay-at-home failed to mobilize mass support, partly because of PAC opposition, but it also revealed the extent of White insecurity and dampened the republican festivities. The demonstration triggered the largest mobilization of White forces and systematic intimidation (including that of private employers) yet seen. In early-morning raids, the police arrested from 8,000 to 10,000 Africans who were suspected of intimidating other Africans who wanted to go to work. Virtually all meetings were banned, including those the Liberal party wished to sponsor. Military forces were closely coordinated with the police. Police loudspeakers broadcast attacks on African leaders, maintaining that they had absconded. Military planes flew low over African urban areas, and Saracen tanks were stationed at their gates.

The attempted stay-at-home was surely the last of its kind. Circumstances are no longer likely to recur in which any segment of the African opposition will be able or will wish to organize a mass public rally for the announcement of widespread demonstrations to be held many weeks later. The proclamation of the Republic inaugurated a period in which both ANC and PAC leaders began publicly to accept that violence was unavoidable. Much later (in the Rivonia sabotage trial of 1964) Nelson Mandela testified that he and others had concluded at the beginning of 1961 that "all channels of peaceful protest had been barred to us" and that violence was inevitable.

Disturbances in the Transkei

Although an urban stay-at-home represented a potentially grave threat to the regime, the most prolonged and troublesome disturbance that the regime faced during this period was in Eastern Pondoland in the Transkei. Opposition to unpopular chiefs and headmen, and to unpopular soil conservation schemes, increased taxation, and other official policies, resulted in sporadic and violent protests, beginning in February, 1960, and occurring throughout the year. These protests took the form of the occasional stoning of White motorists, mass meetings of tribesmen, refusals to pay taxes, rioting, the burning of huts and kraals, and the murder of fellow-Africans considered to be government collaborators. There was some violence also in Tembuland, after September, and danger that unrest would spread beyond these districts.

The government instituted drastic measures in return. On November 30 and December 14, 1960, Regulations 400 and 413 provided for detention without right to habeas corpus, and a ban on all meetings, without official permits, of ten persons or more. These regulations still continue in effect, because of the support of government-appointed and salaried chiefs in the Transkei Legislative Assembly. By the end of 1960, large areas had been sealed off from newsmen and other observers, and thousands of specially trained riot police and heavily armed troops, with helicopter support, had moved into the Transkei.

Some of the opponents of progovernment chiefs hid in the mountains and appear to have organized a cell-based movement known as the "Congo" (or Congress), with a hierarchy of leadership called "the Hill." There is evidence, also, that they maintained contact with and sought financial aid from Pondos living in urban areas. The left-wing newspaper, *New Age,* and, to a lesser extent, the pro-Liberal periodical, *Contact,* gave prominent coverage to Pondoland developments, and

Roley Arenstein, a White Durban Communist, gave valuable legal assistance to individual Pondos. Though the role of Whites seems, in fact, to have been only personal and of negligible importance, government officials charged that Whites had instigated the disturbances by exploiting intratribal feuds. Accordingly, toward the end of 1960, senior chiefs in the Transkei were granted power to apprehend and hand over to the police persons described by the Minister of Bantu Administration and Development as "White Communist agitators."[18]

Mass arrests of Africans were made for tax and pass violations, for possession of dangerous weapons, and for more serious offenses. Mass trials were held. In January, 1961, the Minister of Justice disclosed that 4,769 Africans had been taken into custody in Pondoland and that 2,067 had already been brought to trial.[19] At the end of January, the Minister of Bantu Administration and Development admitted that 25 Africans had been murdered in Pondoland, including two chiefs; 26 Africans had been injured by other Africans; and 15 Africans had died as a result of what was called "self-defense action by the South African Police."[20] On April 20, the Minister of Justice added that 524 Africans were still in detention in Pondoland: 114 were to be charged with murder, 121 with arson, and 289 "for multifarious breaches of the law."[21] By this time, government control had been restored in Pondoland, and by the end of May, 1961, most of the troops had been withdrawn.

Other Effects of Turmoil

This period of turmoil had its effect on South Africa's relations with outside countries. The Sharpeville shootings and subsequent emergency greatly aggravated the apprehensions of foreign investors. During 1960, a large volume of capital left the country, and the outsurge was renewed in March, 1961, when Dr. Verwoerd, in the face of harsh criticism of his country's racial policies at the Prime Ministers' Conference, withdrew his request that South Africa, when it became a republic, be allowed to continue its membership in the Commonwealth. Moreover, early in April, 1961, the United Kingdom, which had previously abstained or voted against UN resolutions critical of South Africa, voted alongside the United States for a resolution calling on all states to consider taking such action as was open to them to bring about the abandonment of apartheid.

A few days later, Dr. Verwoerd stated frankly that "in the light of the pressure being exerted on South Africa," the government would gradually have to introduce the elective system into the Bantu Authori-

18. Quoted in Muriel Horrell, *A Survey of Race Relations in South Africa: 1961* (Johannesburg: S. A. Institute of Race Relations, 1962), p. 43.
19. *House of Assembly Debates* (Jan. 27, 1961), col. 226.
20. *Ibid.* (Jan. 31, 1961), col. 438.
21. *Ibid.* (April 20, 1961), col. 4999.

ties system and allow the development of separate Bantu states, possibly even to the point of full independence.[22] Before the month was over, a member of the Transkeian Territorial Authority had presented the Authority with a motion—similar to one presented in 1960 by Chief Kaiser Matanzima—requesting the South African government "to declare the Transkeian Territories as a whole a self-governing state under the control of the Bantu people." (See Chapter 6.)

The internal and external challenges to South Africa were chronic; pressures for acceleration of the Transkeian timetable promised to persist. Yet by May 31, 1961, when South Africa became a republic outside the Commonwealth, there seemed no likelihood that any such move would be allowed to jeopardize White control of the whole country. By that date, the economy was on the way to strong recovery from the scare of the 1960 emergency. As the leaders of the ANC and the PAC abandoned their traditional tactics of nonviolence, police controls became tighter and more efficient; and in the face of growing hostility abroad, South African defensive strength and self-sufficiency were rapidly being enlarged.

By the end of 1961 the deep entrenchment of Afrikaner Nationalist political power was so evident that the party's leadership had a remarkably wide discretion as to how to interpret and implement the Bantustan policy. The party's strength lay in its role as the political organ and protector of the Afrikaans community, but the greater priority given to racial issues after Dr. Verwoerd became Prime Minister and the growing urgency of appeals to English-speaking Whites for unity in "the White nation" muffled the traditionally militant and exclusive spirit of Afrikanerdom. As events in Africa, especially in the Congo, aroused White fears, and as the maintenance of internal security and economic prosperity contributed to White satisfactions, the National party slowly encroached upon the traditionally English-speaking support of the United party. The National party's popular vote and parliamentary representation had increased steadily since 1938, but not until the October, 1960, referendum on the question of becoming a republic did it, in effect, win a clear majority of the vote—52.04 per cent—a majority that probably included a small number of English-speaking persons.

On October 18, 1961, for the first time the National party won a clear majority of the estimated popular vote (estimated because some seats were uncontested) in a general election—53.5 per cent. With this vote, it

22. Horrell, *op. cit.*, p. 97.

won more than two-thirds of the seats in the House of Assembly.[23] This winning trend occurred despite the charges of some United party spokesmen that the Nationalists were doing too much for the Africans and the fears of some English-speaking farmers and businessmen, especially in Natal, that their interests would be sacrificed by the expansion of Bantustan areas. Among Afrikaners, Nationalist defectors of various persuasions failed to attract support, and rumors of insurgency by the party's right-wing members proved to be little more than wishful thinking. On the other hand, a substantial number, nearly 70,000, of Whites voted for Progressive candidates in 1961, though only one, Mrs. Helen Suzman, of the eleven United party members of Parliament who had become Progressives (about one-fifth of the United party's parliamentary strength) retained a seat.

Problems Continue

While the domestic challenge to White supremacy appeared crushed, or dormant, toward the end of 1961, external pressures were undiminished. Among the latter were two new developments, both of which served to emphasize the significance of the Transkei. In the first place, the British High Commission Territories of Basutoland, Bechuanaland, and Swaziland were obviously moving toward self-government and independence. Beginning in 1961, Dr. Verwoerd described as politically unrealistic South Africa's fifty-year-old hopes of incorporating the territories and began to express his desire for the development of a southern African common market and the eventual abatement of African hostility toward South Africa.

Secondly, in June, 1960, Liberia and Ethiopia, as former members of the League of Nations, but on behalf of all the independent African states, agreed to ask the International Court of Justice to decide whether South Africa had violated its League mandate in Southwest Africa since it had "failed to promote to the utmost the material and moral well-being and social progress of the inhabitants of the Territory." In the case that followed, South Africa, while continuing to challenge the Court's jurisdiction, argued that its policies of racial separation were not only best for Southwest Africa but also had a worldwide validity, thereby putting its apartheid and separate development policies on trial.

23. In the provincial council elections of March, 1965, the National party made significant gains among English-speaking voters in all provinces, winning seats in traditional United party strongholds in Natal. On March 30, 1966, the Nationalists won their fifth general election in a row, increasing their popular majority to an estimated 60 per cent of the total vote, including uncontested districts, and winning about three-fourths of all the seats in the House of Assembly. Both the progovernment and opposition press saw the results as a mandate for separate development leading to independent Bantustans. (*South African Scope*, May, 1966, p. 3; Denis Worrall, "South Africa's 'Partition Election,' " *Africa Report*, May, 1966, pp. 25–26.)

The year 1961 came to a close with a renewal of demands for self-government in the Transkei and—an unrelated development—sporadic sabotage and violence to public property. On November 10, 1961, Chief Tutor Ndamase, son of Paramount Chief Victor Poto of Western Pondoland, said publicly to the Minister of Bantu Administration and Development, "We want self-government for the Transkei by the end of 1963, and complete independence as soon as possible after that."[24] He did not make this statement, he said, because of letters from White agitators urging independence, as the Minister had suggested; the only letters he had seen were from Pondos threatening him with death if he continued to collaborate.

In urban areas, meanwhile, isolated acts of sabotage proved to be amateurish, but the promise of more advanced forms of sabotage lay in leaflets distributed on December 16, announcing the formation of a new organization (later to be identified as an arm of the Congress alliance), "Umkonto We Sizwe" in Zulu, or "Spear of the Nation." December 16, it may be noted, is Dingaan's Day, when Afrikaners commemorate the defeat of the Zulus at Blood River in 1838.

The events described in this chapter form the background for the announcement by Prime Minister Verwoerd on January 23, 1962, of impending self-government for the Transkei. Obviously this announcement was a response to internal and external pressures. Nonetheless the policy of territorial separate development had long been deep-rooted in Nationalist thought and plans, as the next chapter makes clear.

24. Quoted in *Fighting Talk,* March, 1962, p. 3. See also Randolph Vigne, "Birth of Bantustan," *Forum,* March, 1962, p. 10.

Section II
Bantustans: The White Position

2

Theory and Programs of Separate Development

ALTHOUGH the policy governing the tempo and scope of the Bantustan program has been responsive to hostile domestic and external pressures, it has also responded to sympathetic pressures from within Afrikanerdom and to some degree has been self-generating and even inexorable. Over the years the government has moved with pragmatic flexibility toward its own doctrinaire goals; these are widely labeled as negative and repressive, though if one accepts the Nationalists' frame of reference they can be interpreted at times as positive and potentially liberating. It has moved sometimes with deliberate slowness and sometimes—especially after the events of 1960-61—with great speed. Throughout, it has been affected by White attitudes regarding racially separate territorial development as expressed both before and after 1948.

BEFORE 1948

No concept in South Africa has been turned to more varied purposes in the past than that of separate development. Intellectuals and church leaders, particularly among Afrikaner nationalists, have seen in separate development a means to provide Africans with their own area within which to develop freely according to their own will, thereby salving White consciences troubled by the overt discrimination against Africans in the so-called White areas of the country. Others have looked to separate development as a means of distracting nationalistic Africans from their country-wide objectives. Some support separate development as the most promising way of diverting the criticisms of racial discrimination made by outside countries and of justifying South African control of Southwest Africa. There have been and are a few Africans, notably those who can expect to benefit personally from newly provided local opportunities, who are prepared to accept a partial territorial separation as an alternative to the White-controlled, legally enforced national system of colour and racial discrimination.

Much of the rhetoric in support of so-called positive apartheid resembles that used in defense of the old Transkeian system of local government. This system, begun in 1894, bypassed tribal institutions, which were considered barriers not only to the spread of civilization but also to the movement of African workers into a wage-earning economy. Through this system, African councils were established with a majority of elected members. In the Transkei, the councils sent representatives to a General Council, known colloquially as the Bunga, or "place for discussion," where they sat under White magistrates. The councils, it must be emphasized, were little more than advisory bodies. But the quality of the Bunga debate was often high. Much expert opinion agreed with the judgment made in 1931 by Jan H. Hofmeyr (who was to become Prime Minister Jan Smuts's deputy during the 1940's and leader of the liberal-minded members of the United party) that the administration of the Transkeian Territories was the "most effective and successful expression" of the policy of "constructive segregation." This "constructive segregation," said Hofmeyr, gave "the black man . . . the facilities and the encouragement to develop along his own lines. . . . The end which it envisages is a white nation and a black nation dwelling side by side in the same land." But "it is inconceivable," he added, "that the white man should be able completely to dispense with the black man's labour on his farms, in his mines, in his factories; it is just as inconceivable that there should be set aside for the black man's occupation land sufficient to provide for all his needs independently of the white man's wages."[1]

One of the earliest Afrikaner statements on separate territorial development was included in the 1942 draft republican constitution that declared in Article IX, Section 2:

To each of such segregated race groups of Coloured subjects of the Republic, self-government will be granted within their own territory under the central management of the general government of the country, in accordance with the

---

1. *South Africa* (London: Ernest Benn, Ltd., 1931), pp. 313–14.

fitness of the group for the carrying out of such self-government for which they will have to be systematically trained.[2]

A further encouragement to the concept of autonomous African development came from the 1944 People's Congress of nearly 200 Afrikaner organizations on the race question called by the Federation of Afrikaans Cultural Associations. One of the key speakers, Dr. E. G. Jansen, who became the first Minister of Native Affairs in Dr. Malan's Cabinet in 1948, declared:

It is time the Afrikaner policy of separate development be given a chance to be put into practice. . . . it will have to be a system based on the principle that whites and non-whites should develop separately and be treated separately.[3]

The Reverend J. G. Strydom carried this proposal a step further by advocating that African tribes should be developed into Christian-National units in their own areas. Moreover, this proposal was not limited to him. Significantly the congress conceded a measure of African autonomy in its resolution "that it is the Christian duty of the whites to act as guardians of the non-white races until such time as they reach the stage of being able to manage their own affairs."[4] But the central issue considered was not what kind of dispensation the Africans should receive, nor how gradually to end White trusteeship, but the immediate methods for differentiating Africans by statute.

Typical of the dualism of Afrikaner thinking at this time was a resolution of the 1944 Transvaal Synod of the Dutch Reformed Church that only through racial apartheid could "the coloured and black races . . . achieve the highest possible level of racial independence." But "independence" was to be qualified by White trusteeship. "The policy of the Church," they stated, "is founded on the principles of Christianity which support the policy of racial separation and guardianship of whites over the native."[5]

Others foresaw, however, that it would not always be possible to limit African self-expression in separate areas by White control. By far the most articulate of the group that looked so far was Professor G. Cronje. In 1948, he predicted the inevitable demise of guardianship and its replacement by Black autonomy. "While the execution of guardianship means that the Bantu must develop under the guidance of the white man," he wrote, "it must be considered that the logical development of this will eventually end in emancipation, maturity and self-determination."

Toward the end of the 1940's, the thinking of Afrikaner intellectuals

2. The full text of the draft constitution is Appendix B of the report of the International Commission of Jurists, *South Africa and the Rule of Law* (Geneva, 1960).

3. *Inspan,* October, 1944.

4. *Ibid.*

5. This quotation and the subsequent ones are from the Dutch Reformed Church newsletters immediately following the Synods.

and theologians about the Africans' political future converged. In 1947, the Dutch Reformed Church in a national congress on the theme of "Our Church and the Colour Question," urged more territory for the Africans where they "could achieve the right to govern themselves and advance to the highest positions."

According to two pro-apartheid sociologists, "the Apartheid idea" —that is, the idea of developing Bantu national units into homelands and eventually into sovereign states—"crystallized" by 1945–48. After 1948, they maintain, there was merely progressive elaboration but no change in "the fundamental core," although there was "accelerated tempo" after 1959.[6]

AFTER 1948

The distinction between crystallization before 1948 and elaboration afterward may be overly sharp. Yet it is clear that with reference to separate territorial development, tempo and scope—rather than direction and substance—were primarily the matters on which Nationalist leaders differed after 1948. Unlike Hofmeyr, Prime Minister D. F. Malan, who became the head of the Union's first all-Afrikaner cabinet in 1948, was able to conceive of "total apartheid" as an ideal, "the ultimate goal of a natural process of separate development."[7] Like Hofmeyr, however, he rejected as economically impractical proposals for total territorial separation and "full nationhood" for the African in the foreseeable future. Such proposals were made, however, by Afrikaner intellectuals in the South African Bureau of Racial Affairs and endorsed at a special congress of the Dutch Reformed churches in 1950. In contrast, Malan's successor as prime minister, Johannes Strijdom (1954–58), while also accepting "total apartheid" as an ideal, was in practice a blunt exponent of White *baasskap* or boss-ship.

Dr. Hendrik Verwoerd, who was prime minister from September, 1958, until his assassination in September, 1966, was the foremost ideologist of so-called positive apartheid or separate development, as well as the leading policy-maker of so-called petty or negatively restrictive apartheid. His government's "great vision," which he set forth in 1959 in introducing the Promotion of Bantu Self-Government Bill (described in Chapter 3), was new only in the degree of his emphasis on African homelands and on their future constitutional relationships with

6. N. J. Rhoodie and H. J. Venter, *Apartheid: A Socio-historical Exposition of the Origin and Development of the Apartheid Idea* (Cape Town: H.A.U.M., 1960), pp. 16, 21, 28.

7. "Race Relations Policy of the National Party" (a pamphlet issued in late 1947 and reprinted in D. W. Krüger, ed., *South African Parties and Policies, 1910–1960: A Select Source Book* [Cape Town: Human and Rousseau, 1960], p. 403).

the so-called White areas. The culmination, it was suggested, would be a South African Commonwealth of Nations.

He was publicly more optimistic than his predecessors about the tempo at which South Africa could move toward total separation, or—as even he qualified it—"separation in the political sphere at any rate,"[8] though whether he believed African tribal groups could govern themselves effectively in the foreseeable future without the "White Republic's" guidance and control was widely doubted by South Africans, including his own followers and intimates. Like him, apartheid idealists agree that the aims of the old system were not necessarily different from the aims of the government's Bantu Authorities system; but, also like Dr. Verwoerd, they argue that these aims are to be attained on a more realistic (therefore slower) timetable. The period would depend upon the natural and guided evolution of tribal institutions toward Western forms.

The belief that national groups are organisms and attain maturity through slow, evolutionary growth is put forward by Afrikaner Nationalist theorists as valid both for the Afrikaner nation and the several African "nations" within South Africa. The Afrikaner's historic sense was evident in certain formulations of the Tomlinson Report which commented that the development of "the European [sic] population of the Union . . . into an autonomous and complete national organism" had occurred "over the past 300 years."[9] An explicit premise of the 1959 bill, which provided for the development of the Bantustan concept, is that unlike the Europeans "the Bantu peoples . . . do not constitute a homogeneous people, but form separate national units on the basis of language and culture."[10] While educated Africans and tribal chiefs had founded the African National Congress in 1912 in order to promote a sense of national identity among all Africans within South Africa, apartheid theorists consider that this aim is a liberal and cosmopolitan aberration. Afrikaner nationalists believe that they gain insight into the aspirations of the Africans and the preconditions for healthy African nationalism by reflecting upon their own long (though not so long) progress toward nationhood. According to Dr. Verwoerd in 1962, each member of an African or, as he called it, Bantu nation will move "step by step" from the tribal to a Western or parliamentary system "as and when he becomes ripe for it as a result of the experience we allow him to gain."[11]

8. *House of Assembly Debates* (Jan. 27, 1959), col. 62.
9. *Summary of the Report of the Commission for the Socio-Economic Development of the Bantu Areas within the Union of South Africa* (U.G. 61/1955), p. 103.
10. First clause of the Bantu Self-Government Bill of 1959.
11. See p. 12, n. 1.

BANTUSTANS: THE WHITE POSITION

The Transkei's Readiness for Political Advance

Was the Transkei "ripe" for the announcement of January 23, 1962? Was it "ripe" for the direct election (held in November, 1963) in which Transkeian Africans, men and women, throughout the Republic as well as in the Transkei, elected a substantial minority of a new legislative body organized on parliamentary lines? In 1959 the prospect that the Transkei would progress to this level of Western electoral practice in three or four years had seemed slight. For Dr. Verwoerd, in fact, the Transkei's previous electoral experience had seemed dangerously misleading to Africans and needed to be redressed since it left open the possibility of national political integration through representation in Parliament.

In the judgment of liberal-minded Whites, on the other hand, the Transkei was more than ready for further political advancement. Transkeian Africans had had long experience, as we noted earlier, in directly electing a majority of the members of district councils and indirectly electing nearly a two-thirds majority of the Bunga. Furthermore, from 1853, when representative government was granted to Cape Colony, until 1910, when the Union was formed, Transkeians who met certain qualifications—not based on race—voted (along with other similarly qualified Africans in Cape Province) on the same electoral roll with Whites. The common electoral roll was to elect White or (in theory) non-White members of the Cape Colony Parliament. In the eastern Cape, during some dozen years before Union, Africans had held the balance of power in seven constituencies. Though excluded from Parliament by the South African Constitution, qualified Transkeians and other Africans in Cape Province had been eligible from 1910 to 1936 to vote on the common roll and from 1937 to 1960 to vote on a separate or communal roll. In the latter period one function of the African members of the Bunga had been to serve as an electoral college to select one of the four White senators who were expected to represent African interests in Parliament. They had also elected three members of the national Natives' Representative Council, which existed from 1936 to 1951 and whose very existence implied that Africans had national interests.

Before the United party's defeat by the Nationalists in 1948, Prime Minister Smuts had proposed giving the Natives' Representative Council some authority over both local government and the development of the Native reserves, and allowing local councils to become wholly elective. Furthermore, it had been widely expected that future racial policy would be influenced by the 1948 report of the Commission headed by Judge Henry Fagan, which recognized that the urban areas not only included migrant laborers, as was the common belief, but also "a settled, permanent Native population." The Fagan Commission recommended, as a result, that representative boards of Africans should be in close liaison with the White-controlled municipal councils.[12]

But after 1948, Africans could expect that Afrikaner Nationalist guidance would provide them with a different kind of experience. Their transition to Western forms of government was to be made separately within each Bantu "nation," according to Nationalist ideology, and was to be based upon what was called "sound foundations of the Bantu's own essentially democratic system of self-government."[13] In 1951, the essentials of the Bantustan policy, designed to bolster and invigorate or, where necessary, re-create separate tribal institutions and loyalties, were embodied in the Bantu Authorities Act. This Act abolished the Natives' Representative Council, already disillusioned with its own impotence, and provided for replacing other advisory and partly elected councils by tribally based authorities. The tribal authorities were to be composed of a chief and advisers, who were appointed by the government. Above and derived from this base was a hierarchy of authorities at the district (in the Transkei only), regional, and territorial levels.

By agreeing in 1955, though for mixed reasons and under strong pressure from the government, to reconstitute itself in accordance with the principles of the Bantu Authorities Act, the Bunga consented to the elimination of popular election. (One exception in the Transkei's application of the government's system was the election of a minority of the members of the tribal authorities.) The new Transkeian Territorial Authority was thus composed of chiefs and councillors who had been members of the Bunga and some others who had been appointed as chiefs in newly subdivided areas or in areas which formerly had no chiefs. In one respect, in addition to some new administrative powers, there was superficial advancement toward self-government: the chairman was African rather than White and membership was exclusively African, with African members now sitting on the front benches in place of White magistrates, who now sat as observers.

At the ceremonial opening of the first Transkeian Territorial Authority on May 7, 1957, Dr. Verwoerd, then Minister of Native Affairs, spoke of "this tree of separate development. . . . Let it grow slowly. Do not be impatient."[14] In less than two years, however, that is, within a few months after becoming Prime Minister, he announced at the beginning of the 1959 parliamentary session that the time was ripe to take the next step "towards placing the Natives on the road to self-government in their own areas."[15] Parliament proceeded in that session

12. *Report of the Native Laws Commission, 1946–48* (U.G.28/1948), pp. 19, 49.
13. Union of South Africa, *Memorandum Explaining the Background and Objects of the Promotion of Bantu Self-government Bill, 1959,* White Paper 3, 1959, p. 5.
14. *Separate Development (The positive side):* Speech by Dr. H. F. Verwoerd, Minister of Native Affairs, on the occasion of the opening of the Transkeian Territorial Authority, Umtata, May 7, 1957 (Pretoria: Department of Native Affairs, 1958).
15. *House of Assembly Debates* (Jan. 27, 1959), cols. 63–64.

to enact the Promotion of Bantu Self-Government Bill, 1959, abolishing the provision of the 1936 "settlement" that, in partial compensation for removing them from the common roll on which they voted with Whites, had given to the Africans in Cape Province a vote for three Whites to represent them in the House of Assembly, and to the Africans in the four provinces an indirect vote for four Whites in the Senate. The 1959 Act also recognized eight Bantu "national units" and provided for White commissioners-general to serve as liaisons between the government and these units. In addition, tribal representatives (commonly described as ambassadors) would serve as links between a national unit and members of it who were working in the urban areas.

By 1961, reacting to strong criticism, domestic and foreign, of their policy as an attempt to revive outworn tribalism, government spokesmen were talking about the gradual reintroduction of the elective principle and Western forms as part of the process of development.[16] And on January 23, 1962, as we have seen, Dr. Verwoerd announced that "the full franchise . . . although separated from that of the Whites" was to be given to Transkeian Africans. He declared that "Bantu agitators" and their organizations, the African National Congress and the Pan-Africanist Congress, "who ask for one man, one vote and for Black domination" would not be satisfied; but he felt that the government's policy would enable the Western nations to reply to the Afro-Asians: "No. Here we have a method which does not violate international morality and international demands."[17]

The Tempo of Changing Policy

The acceleration of the Bantustan policy was undoubtedly a part of the government's strategy for counteracting domestic and external pressures and improving South Africa's case for retention of the international territory of Southwest Africa. Yet during most of the years after 1948 the statutory elaboration of what was called positive apartheid (educational, social, and ultimately, political institutions given to Africans, as contrasted to restrictions imposed on them) proceeded not only with doctrinaire certainty but also with remarkable caution and sometimes even apprehension. Some of the factors that helped to slow the government's pace were its preoccupation with the preliminary task of defining and implementing negative apartheid (by enacting an extraordinary amount of detailed legislation to provide a mandatory statutory base for customary segregation, to reduce interracial contacts to a minimum, and to remove long-standing rights such as freehold title to land owned by Africans outside the reserves); the Nationalists' legalistic use of parliamentary formalities; their occasional willingness to provide for

16. *Ibid.* (April 11, 1961), col. 4315.
17. *Ibid.* (Jan. 23, 1962), col. 98.

investigations and to make minor concessions in proposed legislation; their pragmatic readiness to delay implementation of policy in the face of difficulties or opposition; and their anxious desire to entrench Nationalist political control more deeply before making departures in policy that might offend their own or potential White support.

A more fundamental explanation of the government's deliberate pace toward separate territorial development before 1962 lies in the view that legislative provisions for positive apartheid represent the unfolding of an ideological scheme rather than a pragmatic response to changing circumstances. This interpretation suggests that once certain principles were embodied in the 1951 Bantu Authorities Act and the direction of policy toward Africans was clearly enunciated, the theorists among Nationalist politicians could be satisfied that rapid implementation or statutory extension were not matters of particular urgency. In 1952, for example, the government introduced its Bantu Urban Authorities Bill providing for replacement of the advisory boards that had been created by municipalities to represent all Africans living in certain areas rather than separate ethnic groups of Africans. But the time did not appear ripe for the creation of tribally related bodies, and passage of the legislation was delayed for years. Following the Sharpeville shootings in 1960, Dr. Verwoerd reasoned that the disturbances, "seen in the right perspective," had helped to prepare public opinion for a further movement toward separate development, including the institution of Bantu authorities in urban areas.[18] In 1961 the Urban Bantu Councils Act was finally passed, and in November, 1963, the first councils were established.

Although undoubtedly the motives governing the tempo of policy formulation were complex and responsive to the uncertainties of a fluid situation, the government's preparation for legislation had the appearance of systematic thoroughness. Legislation was preceded sometimes by a theoretical exposition of the underlying ideological rationale. These characteristics were displayed by the Native Education Commission and the Commission for the Socio-Economic Development of the Bantu Areas, known as the Tomlinson Commission, both appointed in 1949.

The report of the former was completed in 1951. One of its basic conclusions was that the existing system of African education was not "an integral part of a plan of socio-economic development" of the Bantu people and failed to propagate the "culture" of separate Bantu groups.[19] Two years later, the Bantu Education Act of 1953 provided for the transfer of African education from mission and provincial control to the Department of Native Affairs. An important feature of the

18. *Ibid.* (May 20, 1960), col. 8338.
19. Quoted in Gwendolen M. Carter, *The Politics of Inequality: South Africa since 1948* (New York: Praeger, 1958), p. 102.

Act's implementation, the appointment of African school committees and school boards, subject to ministerial approval, was related to the developing structure of tribal authorities. Furthermore, emphasis on instruction through the medium of the vernacular or mother tongue was intended to bolster tribal self-consciousness.

Expansion of the new policy awaited further studies and legislation. Only in 1959, in the Extension of University Education Act, was provision made for closing the doors of the "open" universities of Cape Town and of the Witwatersrand to non-Whites, unless the non-Whites were already enrolled or had special ministerial permission. (In June, 1958, 73 Africans and 180 Coloured and Indians were enrolled at the University of the Witwatersrand and 37 Africans and 515 Coloureds and Indians at the University of Cape Town. Non-Whites also attended the University of Natal but in separate classrooms.) In keeping with the legislation's title, the government proceeded with the building of separate, tribal-related colleges for Africans and separate colleges for Coloureds and Indians. But in the process, under other legislation, the academic reputation and freedom of the highly respected University College of Fort Hare were severely damaged (in the judgment of many observers, destroyed). On January 1, 1960, its independence ended when it came under the control of the Minister of Bantu Education. The student body had previously been composed of non-Whites from all parts of the country, but the college was now restricted to being an institution of higher education for the Xhosa, whose homeland was the Transkei.

The Tomlinson Commission

The government's most important commission, established to investigate possibilities for the socio-economic development of the reserves and named after its chairman, Professor F. R. Tomlinson, collected 7,687 folio sheets of evidence and produced a report of 3,755 mimeographed pages (later summarized in over 200 printed pages), with 598 tables and 66 large-scale maps. This contrasts with the far more limited, though no less significant, report of the Fagan Commission on Native Laws, prepared for the Smuts United party government in 1948: 84 printed pages, including annexures. Despite the obvious relevance of the Tomlinson investigation to Nationalist thinking on separate development, the Tomlinson Report was not submitted to the Cabinet until October, 1954, and the government's White Paper on the Report, which rejected some of its basic recommendations, was not issued until May, 1956.

The foremost reason why Africans leave the reserve areas is and always has been the poverty of their land, which in any case, as we have seen, includes less than 13 per cent of the area of South Africa. The

Tomlinson Commission found that 30 per cent of the reserve land was badly eroded and that another 44 per cent was moderately so.[20] Moreover, since 1936 the "real" income produced in the reserves had remained almost unchanged; while per capita income had actually declined over the preceding twenty years.[21] Thus it documented the belief that a considerable proportion of what was necessary to keep those in the reserves even at subsistence level was earned by Africans in the White areas of the country.[22]

The Commission thus proposed a sweeping reorganization of the economic and social life of the reserves. One-half their present population should be removed from the agricultural land, it maintained, so that those remaining might have sufficient space to grow enough food to feed themselves. Even so, there would be little or no food surplus available for the nonfarming population, unless agricultural methods were greatly improved.[23] Thus the Africans leaving the land perforce, and those who might return from the White areas of the country, would have to find their livelihood in commerce and manufacturing in the reserves. The Commission estimated that 50,000 new jobs a year, apart from agriculture, would have to be created in the reserves during the ensuing 25 years. Of these jobs it proposed that 20,000 be in secondary or manufacturing industry and the remainder in tertiary or service activities.[24] The magnitude of this task was underlined by the Commission's own statement that "as far as industries are concerned, the Bantu Areas are in fact a desert."[25]

To begin to meet the obvious needs that it had pointed out, the Commission proposed an extensive development program, including the establishment "without delay" of more than 100 urban townships.[26] For industrial development, the Commission recommended that the government expend £25 million ($70 million) during the first five years.[27] Altogether the estimated cost of the whole program during its first ten years amounted to £104 million ($291,200,000).[28] With this sort of beginning, the Commission anticipated that the reserve areas could be made to support a population of about seven million persons in 25 to 30 years' time. It also foresaw that an additional one and one-half million persons could be housed in the reserves and supported by the earnings of migrant laborers. Still, even if its recommended rate of development was achieved, the Commission concluded that by 1981 the reserves

20. U.G. 61/1955, p. 51.
21. *Ibid.*, p. 99.
22. *Ibid.*, p. 94.
23. *Ibid.*, p. 114.
24. *Ibid.*, p. 184.
25. *Ibid.*, p. 49.
26. *Ibid.*, p. 150.
27. *Ibid.*, p. 138.
28. *Ibid.*, p. 206.

would be able to accommodate *de facto* only about 60 per cent of what it estimated would then be the African population of South Africa.[29] Thus there would still remain more Africans than Whites in the so-called White areas of the country.

The Tomlinson Commission and the government differed basically in their view of how economic development in the reserves should be financed. Aware that African resources for the required capital formation were "meager," the Commission proposed that the "necessary stimulus to development" be provided by White private enterprise. Otherwise it considered that "the desired tempo of development will probably not be attained."[30] Significantly, however, while seven of the nine members of the Commission, including M. D. C. de Wet Nel, the future Minister of Bantu Administration and Development, signed this recommendation, two members of particular importance to the future of the program opposed the suggestion that White entrepreneurs should be allowed to establish industries in the reserves. C. B. Young, who was soon to become Secretary of the newly named Department of Bantu Administration and Development, and C. W. Prinsloo, who subsequently became Undersecretary of the Department of Information, wrote in a minority report that to grant concessions in the reserves to Whites would create "White spots" in the "Bantu areas" and would be contrary to the policy of separate development.

The government accepted this minority view.[31] Moreover, it concluded that the Commission's recommendation for the government to spend £25 million over five years to stimulate industrial development in the reserves was based on the assumption that there would be large White-owned industries in those areas and, since this would not be the case, the recommendation no longer applied.[32] In fact, however, the Commission had declared that "this amount should be provided by the Government, irrespective of whether other sources of capital can be found or not."[33] The government's alternative was to propose a Bantu Areas Investment Organization (later established as the Bantu Investment Corporation) to be capitalized initially at £500,000 ($1,400,000) from funds at the disposal of the Native Trust. But the financing of industrial development in the reserves would be "based chiefly on the principle of self-aid," the government declared, which meant in effect that it would be substantially left to the Africans themselves.[34]

Although the government subsequently mentioned a sum of £36.6

29. *Ibid.,* p. 184.
30. *Ibid.,* p. 132, 142.
31. *Memorandum: Government Decisions on the Recommendations of the Commission for the Socio-Economic Development of the Bantu Areas Within the Union of South Africa,* White Paper F-1956, Decision 9 (i).
32. *Ibid.,* Decision 10.
33. U.G. 61/1955, p. 138.
34. White Paper F-1956, Decision 9 (iii).

million ($102,480,000) for investment in the reserves, only £7.9 million ($22,120,000) was actually expended on their development in the five years from 1956 to 1961. In 1961 a five-year development program for the reserves was inaugurated, which projected an expenditure of an additional £57 million ($159 million). But two-thirds of this latter amount was allocated for town planning, while the next largest item—£7.3 million ($20,440,000)—was for soil conservation.

The government proposed two programs to increase employment opportunities for Africans in the reserves. The one was the Bantu Investment Corporation and the other the so-called border-industries scheme, which was first announced in 1956. This latter program involves encouraging White-owned industry to relocate on the White side of the borders of the reserves by offering various financial inducements including the lowering of minimum standards of wages. This scheme assumes that Africans employed in these industries will be able to return nightly, or at least weekly, to their homes inside the reserves, an assumption not realized to any considerable extent.

Basic to the government's approach was the assumption that an economically underdeveloped area was still capable of political advance. The aim of political independence was thought to be a greater driving force than economic independence in the national development of the various Bantu "nations," as it had been for the Afrikaner nation. A more cynical or practical explanation of the great emphasis on the forms of political structures and constitutions was that these were both inexpensive and valuable in impressing opinion at home and abroad with the idealism motivating apartheid as a means of progress. It is to the legislative provision for such changes, and the parliamentary attitudes accompanying it, that we now turn.

3

Legislative Provision for Separate Development, 1951, 1959, and 1963

SEPARATE DEVELOPMENT, carried out politically by the Bantu Authorities system, is the Nationalist government's distinctive approach to South Africa's racial situation. It is designed to provide a system of local government for Africans by Africans under White control. It is the corollary of the Nationalists' primary purpose of excluding Africans from any direct participation in, or even influence on, the White structure of government.

Due to opposition from N. C. Havenga, whose Afrikaner party was at first essential to Nationalist control of Parliament, the National party leaders did not immediately exclude the Native Representatives as they had wished, but waited until the Promotion of Bantu Self-Government Act of 1959 to do so. An integral part of the first legislative step toward territorial separate development, the Bantu Authorities Act of 1951, was, however, the abolition of the Natives' Representative Council in favor of the Bantu Authorities system.

THE BANTU AUTHORITIES ACT, 1951

The Nationalists could and did argue that the Natives' Representative Council, set up under the 1936 legislation as a national advisory body, was no longer a functioning body and that the Africans themselves found it quite unsatisfactory. Never influential, the Council had gone into voluntary recess in 1946 in protest over the government's failure to consult it in connection with the African mine strike that year on the Witwatersrand. It is also true that the Council saw no future for itself when Dr. Verwoerd called it into session in December, 1950, to explain the apartheid policy to its members. After this explanation, it appears that he refused to let them discuss the character and implications of apartheid. In the debate on the Bantu Authorities Bill in 1951, one of the Native Representatives, W. H. Stuart, taunted the Minister with not having wanted to "face the criticism needlessly, which obviously, necessarily and rather spontaneously arose from the nature of his speech."[1] Other opposition members in that same debate accused the Minister of wishing to abolish the Natives' Representative Council in order to cut short the case that Council members were pushing through the courts to force the government to listen to the advice—which under the 1936 Hertzog legislation it had the constitutional right to give—on policies affecting Africans. Whether or not there was some validity to this charge (and the Minister declared that, on the contrary, the National party's action was because of an election promise to abolish the Natives' Representative Council), it is clear that this action was an essential part of the new approach to the relations between Africans and Whites that was implicit in Nationalist philosophy.

The opposition fought hotly against the abolition of the Natives' Representative Council although its members agreed that the body had never been successful. Since the United party had established the Council and had been in office throughout most of its life, the criticism leveled at the Nationalists had not much substance. In general, United party speakers agreed that there were inherent weaknesses in this kind of institution, whose functions were purely advisory, and found themselves criticizing the lack of responsibilities for this national body of representative Africans. Thus Major Pieter van der Byl, former Minister of Native Affairs, declared that the trouble with the NRC was that it

. . . had no responsibility, financial or otherwise. They had no bone to chew on . . .; and another important factor which the Minister did not bring out— they were much too small a body to represent the vast population, consisting of seven or eight million Natives.

Mrs. Margaret Ballinger who, as a Native Representative since 1939, had no responsibility for the establishment of the system, pointed out still more sharply the basic difficulty in the functioning of the NRC:

1. The source of all statements about the 1951 debate and of quotations from it is in one or more of the following columns of the *House of Assembly Debates:* June 18—cols. 9808 (Verwoerd), 9811-12 (Verwoerd), 9824-25 (Van der Byl), 9829 (Steenkamp), 9838 (J. A. S. Nel), 9843-45 (J. A. S. Nel), 9847 (Stuart), 9861 (Hughes), 9869 (Van Coller), 9876 (Maree), 9879-80 (Ballinger), 9884-85 (Ballinger), 9902 (Verwoerd); June 19—col. 10054 (Stuart); June 21—cols. 10258 (Smit), 10261 (Ballinger).

. . . it was that in fact nobody paid the slightest attention to its essential recommendations at a time when society was changing and the pressure of old outmoded policies was becoming extremely harsh. . . . There is a very close connection between the fact that, throughout the war years, the Native People lost rights, they did not gain them, and the fact that an intransigent spirit grew up in the Natives' Representative Council. . . . The Natives' Representative Council did represent their people but they represented their people with a sense of frustration because they could not get their views home to this Parliament.

Unable to justify their own handling of the Natives' Representative Council, the opposition members took refuge in supporting the abortive proposal by General Smuts for its reconstitution into a body of fifty elected Africans under an elected African chairman with responsibilities for coordinating all African councils and with the possibility of moving from its advisory position to one in which it would have power to make laws for Africans, with the approval of the Governor-General, to impose taxes, and to take on administrative functions. This proposal had fallen by the way, as we have seen, when the Nationalists came into office, and there is no way of knowing whether the United party would have implemented it had that party been successful in 1948.

It was not difficult, in any case, for Dr. Verwoerd to go to the heart of the issue raised by Smuts's proposal and, at the same time, to make clear the basic context within which Nationalist action was taking place.

Those proposals were not very warmly welcomed by the Bantu leaders, for they had but one desire—they repeatedly said so—and that was equality and representation in the Union Parliament together with the Europeans. They very expressly said that this was their sole aim in their constitutional development. . . .

Subsequently Verwoerd said of the NRC ". . . that the body wants other rights, absolute equality of rights for the Natives, and they are not satisfied with the Natives' Representative Council."

The opposition could not and did not deny this basic desire of the Africans for equality. Stuart summed up the African position:

They said that the Natives' Representative Council was no satisfaction to them; but they want to stand on their vote; that they want to stand on the proposition of equal rights for civilised men in the main channel together with everyone else; that they did not want the stigma of being separate; that they do not want the stamp of the ghetto placed upon them in their political representation.

The abolition of the Natives' Representative Council was only one side of the coin: provision of the Bantu Authorities system was the other. The Nationalist argument in support of the substitution consisted of two parts: that constitutional development should build from the bottom up, not from the top down as with the NRC; and that this structure should be built on the basis of tribal authorities which, said the Minister, "is the basic form of government, the primary form of authority." The objective, he maintained, was the "restoration of the prestige, the authority of Native law and custom," which would be achieved by providing the Bantu Authorities with administrative, executive, and judicial powers. The structure was to be pyramidal in form, with tribal authorities headed by the chief at the lowest level; then a regional authority, created by two or more tribes, communities, or combinations of tribes and communities; and at the apex, when these regional authorities had achieved sufficient maturity to satisfy the national government, there would be territorial authorities under African control. Detailed provision for these territorial authorities was made in the 1959 legislation, the Promotion of Bantu Self-Government Act.

This relatively simple structure, in which White control was assured at each level, evoked a disproportionate degree of enthusiasm from Nationalist ranks. J. A. S. Nel maintained that by implementing the Native tribal system, it would become "known as a Magna Charta of the Bantu people in South Africa." More realistically, he noted that "It is an approach and a policy that does not rest on the tottering pillars of fine-sounding theories but that is based on the bitter experience of the established section of the European population. . . ." Again reiterating the Nationalists' fear of Whites sharing control with Africans in South Africa, Nel said later:

The idea of making the Natives an integral part of our whole national life, as advocated by those honorable members on the other side, the idea of giving them their own Council in our national life is definitely one of the most dangerous things we can do. If we do that, we shall not be eliminating the points of friction; we shall be creating points of friction. We shall be creating volcanoes and clashes.

On the positive side, Nel maintained that:

Here we have a basis on which the Native will henceforth be able to give expression to his own inner self, to develop his family life and his national life. Henceforth, according to this Bill, he will have the opportunity also to be a recipient of those human rights and privileges for which we are all yearning in this life.

The point was echoed by W. A. Maree, who declared that:

To my mind this is a Bill by which we are doing our utmost to save what can still be saved of the tribal life of the Bantu which embodies the whole basis of his social, political and economic structure.

Opposition criticism, voiced in the bare three days during which the bill was considered, denied the basic Nationalist assumption that the tribal structure was still intact and a viable basis for a constitutional structure. They pointed to the high percentage of Africans living outside the reserves and maintained that "the tribal head exists only in theory."

Turning to the reserves themselves, Mrs. Ballinger remarked wryly:

Given an adequate amount of land where the people could live their own lives, it is remotely possible that a tribal society might be resuscitated, and might in the course of centuries evolve into something different—provided the people are left alone to do it; but I doubt if even in those circumstances that can happen.

She endorsed the Minister's view that there must be a modern system of land holding, scientific methods of agriculture, and industries for the Africans to provide them with economic opportunities in the reserves, but she questioned skeptically "the assumption that you can build up this pattern on the basis of and control it by tribal organization."

The opposition also pointed out the fact that some tribes, or groups derived from various shattered tribes, such as the Fingos, have no acknowledged chiefs—a problem that made it necessary for a government anthropologist, Professor David Hammond-Tooke, to "find" the appropriate people to fill such offices. Moreover, as Gray Hughes, member of Parliament from the Transkei whose law offices were in Umtata, pointed out, the growing middle class in the reserves "had nothing to do with the chiefs," and, in effect, these commoners were being disenfranchised by placing all emphasis on a tribal structure.

Most of these difficulties could be avoided, it seemed to some members of the opposition, by making the tribal councils elective rather than having them appointed by the chief and the government. An elective council system could provide a voice for each of many splinter groups within a given area, such as the Transkei. In the judgment of C. M. Van Coller:

We have tried to experiment with the small Bunga in the Transkei and it has proved an unqualified success.

In the Bunga you have Pondos, you have Tembus, you have Fingos, and you have Xhosas, all represented, working together for the benefit of the people in that territory.

And this point was followed up by Dr. D. L. Smit, who said that the advantage of the Bunga system used in both the Transkei and Ciskei

. . . over the purely tribal authorities, created under this Bill, is that it enables not only the chiefs, but the educated and detribalized Natives, by a system of election, to take part in local government. In order to meet the rapid changes in Native life, we need, not this retrograde Bill, but institutions, to meet new needs rather than to look solely to traditional institutions, whose bonds among their people have broken down.

During the following decade, the government sought to promote the acceptance of the Bantu Authorities system. But nationalist African leaders, from their side, attacked the 1951 Act as a reactionary effort to resuscitate a divisive tribalism, and specifically protested against it in the African defiance campaign of 1952. In 1955, however, the government scored a success when the Transkeian Bunga voted to accept the Bantu Authorities system in principle. Meanwhile, the Tomlinson Commission had completed its report proposing "ultimate separate development," to which, as we have seen, major conferences of Afrikaners and Africans in 1956 responded in fundamentally divergent ways. In September, 1958, Dr. Verwoerd became Prime Minister. His readiness to restore and extend popular elections in the Transkei and thus to move away from tribal institutions toward Western forms was still more than three years in the future. The 1959 Parliament, however, set the newer tone of full political and partial territorial separation that was to mark the Verwoerd period.

PROMOTION OF BANTU SELF-GOVERNMENT ACT, 1959

The debate on the Promotion of Bantu Self-Government Bill of 1959 provided a wide-ranging expression of parliamentary attitudes at a crucial point in the development of the government's Bantustan policy. As in all legislative debates, much of the rhetoric was stale, and much of it appeared again in the 1963 debate on the Transkei Constitution Bill. Nevertheless, the 1959 debate occurred within a wider frame of reference than any other legislation bearing on Bantustans and is particularly revealing of the assumptions, values, and expectations that had characterized White political thought since the early 1950's. The extravagance of some of the rhetoric may have been no greater than in, say, the *Congressional Record;* yet the debate had a more elusive quality since it was preoccupied with speculation about long-run consequences.

Both the National party and the United party were essentially in agreement on the necessity of maintaining White supremacy for the foreseeable future. There was also much truth, however, in the agreement of Dr. Verwoerd and Sir de Villiers Graaff, leader of the United party, that the directions of their policies in other respects were "diametrically opposed." The parties expressed basically divergent attitudes regarding the trends toward economic integration in South Africa and the growth of an urban class of Africans. Accepting these trends and the permanence of African residence in so-called White urban areas, United party leaders talked of the unity of all the people as "South Africans" and of gradual movement under "White leadership" toward a federation in which all races would be represented in the central Parliament. The Nationalists, conceiving of the people of South Africa as divided into many racial or ethnic nations, of which the White nation was one, rejected the political implications that followed from accepting urban Africans as a growing and permanent class.

The Governor-General's speech, at the opening of Parliament on January 23, 1959, emphasized the "positive elements" of separate development and announced the forthcoming elimination of all the Native

Representatives from Parliament. Their removal was the culmination of the long process of deterioration in African political rights, marked earlier by the exclusion in 1910 of Africans from eligibility for membership in Parliament, by their removal from the Cape Province common voting roll in 1936, and by the abolition of the national Natives' Representative Council in 1951.

Government spokesmen claimed during the debate that the elimination of the Native Representatives should have occasioned no surprise and required no protracted debate. The National party had called for elimination of the three Native Representatives from the House of Assembly (but not from the Senate) in its pre-1948 election manifesto. And other provisions of the Bill, said M. D. C. de Wet Nel, Minister of Bantu Administration and Development, were "the logical outcome" of the Bantu Authorities policy enacted in 1951. For this reason, there had been no need, he said, to consult the Bantu since their support for the Bill was implicit in their support for the system of Bantu authorities.[2]

Sir de Villiers, however, during the no-confidence debate, expressed surprise regarding the proposal to eliminate the Native Representatives in the Senate since it had never been clearly proposed to the electorate. His contention that there was no mandate for this aspect of the Bill was supported by J. D. du P. Basson, a young Nationalist from Southwest Africa, who had once been a member of the United party and was to switch back again later. Furthermore, the timing of the Bill had "shocked" him, Basson said, because it was unfair to deprive the Africans of their small share of political power before compensatory developments had occurred in the Bantu areas. Much later, after expulsion from the National party caucus, Basson stated that the Prime Minister had not consulted any of the senior bodies of the party or even the parliamentary caucus before introducing the Bill into the House.

The main United party attack on the Bill was far-reaching. The Bill was the most important, or one of the most important, measures in the history of South Africa not only because it repealed the Representation of Natives Act of 1936—part of the so-called settlement of the Native problem—but also because it accepted in principle the eventual partition of the country. Sir de Villiers, therefore, took the unusual step of opposing the introduction of the Bill on March 24 and refused in mid-

2. Quotations from and other references to the 1959 parliamentary debate are in the *House of Assembly Debates* for the period January 23–June 29 as follows: Abraham, 6071; Ballinger, 6124–26, 6137, 7113; Basson, 6166–74, 9498; Bekker, 7095; Coertze, 6751; Cronje, 6272–73; De Wet Nel, 247, 3084–86, 3363, 6002–9, 6013–14, 6019–24, 6292–98, 6698, 6704, 6729, 6731–34, 6780–84, 6798, 6829, 7185–95; Dönges, 6148–50, 6155; Governor-General, 5; Graaff, 28–35, 3072–73, 6024, 6027–41, 6857–59, 7095–98; Lawrence, 6158, 6288, 6290–92, 6797; Lee-Warden, 6696; Louw, 6053, 6082; Malan, 6065; Marais, 6774; Mentz, 3363, 6812; Mitchell, 6209, 6807–8; Potgieter, 6693, 7156; Sauer, 6695; Smit, 6048, 6835; Stanford, 6144–48, 6755, 6864–67; Steenkamp, 6158–59, 6164; Steyn, 3075; C. R. Swart, 6189; R. A. F. Swart, 6777, 7126; Tucker, 6080; Van der Byl, 7159, 7162; Verwoerd, 50, 60–64, 4126, 6215–36; Wentzel, 7129.

April to agree to a limitation on debate. The government, having just been forced through a long debate and an all-night sitting on a bill to exclude non-Whites from the open universities (see Chapter 2), imposed a guillotine on the Bantu Self-Government Bill. The total time spent on this Bill in the House of Assembly from the second reading, beginning on May 18, to final passage on June 3, was only 37 hours. Even less time was allocated in the Senate.

The opposition accused Dr. Verwoerd of violating the spirit of parliamentary democracy. He responded to challenges regarding the urgency of the Bill by accusing the opposition of trying to use the discussion of pending bills "to besmirch the good name of South Africa, not only in this country but also abroad." The Bill should be enacted after "business-like discussion," he said, and the world could then judge South Africa by its practice and not by the words of the opposition.

What did the Bill itself provide? One of its sixteen clauses provided for the removal of the three Whites in the House of Assembly and the two in the Cape Provincial Council who were elected by African voters in Cape Province, and the removal of the four Whites in the Senate who were elected by Africans by an indirect process in all four provinces.[3] This was the original purpose of the Bill. Precisely what other changes the Bill would immediately effect in African policy were not clearly evident. The significance of the remaining provisions of the Bill was mainly symbolic of the direction of the government's policy.

As a summary of the government's rationale for its Bantustan policy, the preamble of the Bill is worth quoting almost in full. (A government White Paper, published about the same time as the Bill, in March, presented a more elaborate explanation.)

Whereas the Bantu peoples of the Union of South Africa do not constitute a homogeneous people, but form separate national units on the basis of language and culture:

And whereas it is desirable for the welfare and progress of the said peoples to afford recognition to the various national units and to provide for their gradual development within their own areas to self-governing units on the basis of Bantu systems of government:

And whereas it is therefore expedient to develop and extend the Bantu system of government for which provision has been made in the Bantu Authorities Act, 1951, with due regard to prevailing requirements, and to assign further powers, functions and duties to regional and territorial authorities:

And whereas the development of self-government is stimulated by the grant to territorial authorities of control over the land in their areas, and it is

---

3. In Cape Province, the number of African men registered to vote had declined as a result of the raising of qualifications (see Chapter 5, p. 93) to 6,633 in 1909; reached a high point of 16,480 in 1927; declined as a result of stringent enforcement of qualifications to 10,628 in 1935; and after removal to a separate roll rose to some 18,000 in 1959.

therefore expedient to provide for the ultimate assignment to territorial authorities of certain rights and powers . . . .

And whereas it is expedient to provide for direct consultation between the
various Bantu national units and the Government of the Union: . . .

Accordingly, the Bill recognized eight "national units," that is ethnic
entities rather than geographical areas: North-Sotho, South-Sotho,
Swazi, Tsonga, Tswana, Venda, Xhosa, and Zulu. Five commissioners-
general, appointed by the Governor-General, were to represent the government with either one or two of the units. De Wet Nel explained
during the debate that since the new official would be "on the same
footing as a foreign representative," thought had been given to using
the title High Commissioner. He was a "link" or "liaison" between the
government and the Bantu. Or, as described by Harry Lawrence, a former Minister of Justice on the United party's front bench, he was like a
Russian commissar since his mission was indoctrination. Key words in
the Bill describing the functions of the commissioner-general in relation
to his Bantu unit were: "furnish guidance and advice . . . promote the
development of . . . consult with . . . enlighten the population . . . "

Another new official was to represent a territorial authority in desig-
nated urban areas. The group to which he would be assigned was defined in the Bill as: "that portion of the Bantu community in the said
areas, which belongs to the national unit concerned." Thus, as Douglas
Mitchell, the conservative leader of the United party in Natal, pointed
out, each of the eight ethnic units might send a representative to Durban. But "for the first time in the history of South Africa," said F. E.
Mentz, Deputy-Minister of Bantu Administration and Development,
". . . the Natives in the urban areas will enjoy the privilege of having
a direct link with their national units from which they stem and to
which they belong."

No title was provided for the representative, whom the Bill referred
to simply as "a Bantu person" but whom De Wet Nel during the debate
occasionally referred to as an "ambassador." He was to hold his office
subject to the government's approval. Meanwhile, De Wet Nel explained, African advisory boards composed of members elected in the
urban townships would continue to function. In time, however, he
presumed they would be supplanted by boards formed by the new
ambassadors.

"But the most important consideration," said De Wet Nel, "is that
this Bill makes it possible for the Governor-General to transfer his
legislative powers systematically" to territorial authorities. Envisaging
this eventuality, the Bill empowered such authorities to "make enactments" regarding any matters that the Governor-General might assign
to them, in accordance with existing law, or "matters which Parliament
may from time to time assign." The Bill also amended the Native Trust
and Land Act of 1936 to empower the Governor-General to transfer to

African representatives land held in trust. "In due course," said the Minister, such lands would be transferred.

The longest clause of the Bill listed "powers, functions and duties." The 1951 Act had provided only sketchily for territorial authorities, which were to be the apex of the pyramidal system of Bantu Authorities. Not until the Governor-General's Proclamation 180 of 1956, and then only with reference to the Transkei, were detailed provisions made for the constitution and functions of a territorial authority.[4] Proclamation 180 retained the elective principle: certain African taxpayers were to elect just under one-third of the membership of tribal authorities and indirectly some members of the district authorities. The great majority of Bantu authority members, however, were appointed (or recognized) chiefs, headmen, and tribal councillors. The 1959 Bill did not enlarge the role of election, nor did it restrict the power of the government to consider unacceptable any member of any Bantu authority or to veto any action. The Bill itself did not define self-government, nor did it indicate the steps to be taken or any timetable to be followed.

Like earlier legislation, the Bill gave extraordinarily wide powers to the government to rule by regulation and to delegate power. But the Bill itself gave Bantu authorities no important new powers. It was a Bill that could be described as containing "nothing but promises," according to Walter Stanford, one of the Native Representatives, or as one creating "a future of hope and expectation," according to De Wet Nel. The list of "powers, functions and duties" ranged from a statement that the territorial authority "shall maintain the closest possible contact with the commissioner-general" to the granting of "power" to invite the Minister of Bantu Administration to attend a popular conference and "power" to impose taxes (subject to veto) on Africans under its jurisdiction. One clause provided that "by-laws" in the 1951 Act should be construed to mean "enactments"; and the word "enactments" was used in the Bill itself. Territorial authorities were being given new "status," said De Wet Nel. For example, "formerly the Governor-General could dismiss or appoint any chief [or headman] at will." As a result of the Bill's amendment of the Native Administration Act of 1927, "he will now be obliged to consult the Territorial Authority."

In short, the Bill was "positive," according to the government, and not "negative." In January, 1959, Dr. Verwoerd asked the opposition not to concentrate their attention on "the apparently negative aspect" of the removal of the Native Representatives but on the "supremely positive" provisions of the rest of the Bill. This attitude explained the undercurrent of rumor in Pretoria during late 1958 that the government

4. For an analysis of the proclamations and notices implementing the 1951 Act and their relation to the pending Bill, see Muriel Horrell, *Second Interim Report on the Establishment of Bantu Authorities* (Johannesburg: South African Institute of Race Relations, May 11, 1959).

in the New Year would embark on a policy in the field of race relations that would enable major Western powers to support South Africa in the United Nations. In March, De Wet Nel pointed out that Clause 15, providing for removal, was only one of sixteen clauses. "The other and the good clauses are the positive clauses," he said, to the accompaniment of laughter. But the essence of the Bill was Clause 15, said Mrs. Margaret Ballinger, the senior Native Representative. On the last day of debate in June, De Wet Nel looked back upon the opposition's frequent description of Clause 15 as a negative element and provided his own reassessment. The sixteen clauses, he declared, were "all positive clauses and one of the most positive of them is Clause 15. . . ."

During the debate, Nationalist speakers conformed closely to the party's line of argument. Basson's defection marked the only break in Nationalist ranks. He was "a young man, a theoretical idealist, a person who is motivated by emotional factors," declared Dr. Verwoerd. But Basson himself, as an active member of SABRA (the South African Bureau of Racial Affairs, composed largely of philosophically inclined Afrikaners), strongly supported "the experiment of territorial separation." The idea of development, he said, repeating the words of De Wet Nel, had "gripped the imagination" of the Bantu. De Wet Nel carried the main burden of debate for the government, although Dr. Verwoerd spoke for one hour and forty minutes of the eighteen hours devoted to the second-reading stage. Of thirteen Nationalists who spoke during that stage, eight were ministers or deputy-ministers and two (J. H. Abraham and S. F. Papenfus) were future commissioners-general.

Opposition to the Bill reflected, characteristically, a wide range of approaches. Within the United party, Sir de Villiers occupied a middle position. On his right were such conservatives as Douglas Mitchell, who stressed the dangers to the Whites of a policy of enlarging and consolidating African areas, especially in Natal. Another conservative, Dr. L. S. Steenkamp, declared that South Africa had not produced "a bigger negrophilist in the past 100 years" than De Wet Nel, whereas the United party looked at the Bill in the first place from the standpoint of the White man rather than the Bantu.

On Sir de Villiers' left was a group of over a dozen members who had argued, unsuccessfully, at a United party caucus a few days before the second-reading stage began, for the presentation of a more progressive alternative to Nationalist policy.[5] With a few exceptions, members of this group were to resign from the United party in August, 1959, and later to form the Progressive party. Contributing to the debate were Harry Lawrence, Dr. Jan Steytler, Helen Suzman, Colin Eglin, R. A. F. Swart, John Cope, and C. B. Van Ryneveld. They emphasized the United party's commitment to a common South African patriotism in

5. *Press Digest,* May 21, 1959, p. 187.

an undivided, multiracial country, but they were careful not to go beyond the party's policy regarding non-White representation, as expressed by Sir de Villiers. This policy of the United party, while less liberal than that subsequently enunciated by the Progressive party, formed a sharp contrast to Nationalist policy. The United party, said Sir de Villiers, favored extension of the system of African representation in the House of Assembly to all provinces and the enlargement of the number of elected Native Representatives in the Senate from four to six. But these and other changes should be made only after agreement by "a decisive majority of the existing electorate, and . . . adequate safeguards for the maintenance of White leadership." "A strong body of opinion" favored making non-Whites eligible for membership in Parliament, he admitted, but current United party policy limited membership to Whites. In August, 1959, the United Party Congress voted that the maximum number of Native Representatives elected to the Assembly from all provinces should be eight.[6]

The participants in the debate upon whom attention was most dramatically focused were the Native Representatives themselves: Mrs. Margaret Ballinger, one of the original Representatives; Walter Stanford, representing the Transkei; and L. B. Lee-Warden. Mrs. Ballinger and Stanford spoke at greater length and more frequently than anyone in opposition except Sir de Villiers. Although the leader of the Liberal party since its founding in 1953, Mrs. Ballinger was a moderate among South African liberals but an "ultra-liberal" to the Nationalist chief whip. Stanford was also a Liberal, though late in the year he left that party to join the Progressives. He found it difficult, he said during the debate, to speak "vehemently enough" and was described by De Wet Nel as "really embittered . . . proof again of the feeling of guilt in his heart" for his failure to help the Bantu. Lee-Warden, addressed at one point by Minister Paul Sauer as "you silly ass," spoke less frequently and apparently with less passion than Ballinger and Stanford but epitomized for the Nationalists the dangers of African involvement in parliamentary elections. He was the successor to two Communists who had been expelled from the House, and was involved in the publishing of the left-wing *New Age*. He had been arrested in 1956 on charges of high treason, but was discharged a year later. Meanwhile he had been allowed to continue attending Parliament while on bail.

Mrs. Ballinger had sat on the cross-benches for over twenty years, subjected to frequent badgering by the Nationalist back-benchers. Her parliamentary skill and devotion to her constituency received many tributes from United party speakers and also from Basson; De Wet Nel himself declared, "I am not one of the persons filled with hatred to-

6. Muriel Horrell, *A Survey of Race Relations in South Africa: 1958–1959* (Johannesburg: South African Institute of Race Relations), p. 3.

wards her." On the eve of her retirement, however, she displayed no mellow resignation. The Bill, she declared, was "pernicious and dishonest in itself and a disaster for the whole country." She agreed that Sir de Villiers' description of future dangers was "perfectly logical" if one assumed that the government really intended to establish territorial apartheid. But, she declared flatly: "I know that they are not capable of it and that they do not intend to do it."

Did the government, in fact, sincerely intend to develop the Bantu areas and to promote Bantu self-government? The opposition was not united or consistent in its attack on the Bill, treating it sometimes as a sham but more often as a serious move toward eventual partition. Sir de Villiers agreed with Dr. Verwoerd that South Africa was at a final crossroads. According to Sir de Villiers, the choice was between "the continued existence" of the Union or "a system of colonialism . . . which will lead to the destruction of the Union"; according to Dr. Verwoerd, it was between movement toward "a common political society" or "total separation in the political sphere."

Accepting the direction of the government's policy at face value, at least for the sake of argument, Sir de Villiers warned of the great dangers that independent Bantustans could pose for the Whites in "the remaining rump of South Africa . . . a multiracial state in which the White people will be outnumbered . . . by a politically rightless proletariat." He pictured a situation in which South Africa's economy would become dependent on foreign labor, and its military security endangered by a horseshoe of Black states, extending from Bechuanaland to most of the eastern seaboard, able to have direct relations with African and Communist states, and likely to become "springboards for the propagation of foreign ideologies." But the greatest danger, he said, would be from

the existence in our White areas of a gigantic potential fifth column consisting at the end of the century of at least 6,000,000 Natives, and possibly supported by millions of Coloureds and Indians.

Sir de Villiers was attempting to scare the people, answered De Wet Nel; whereas the result of United party policy would be "a bloodbath." Dr. Verwoerd agreed and warned that a common political society would mean

A South African army and a South African police force under Black generals; an air force under a Black air-marshall; a Government with Black Cabinet Ministers; a Parliament with Black Members of Parliament; administrators and mayors, all Black! . . . If the Leader of the Opposition wants to come along with alarmist stories about imaginary eventual consequences of our policy then I can do the same in respect of his! [Laughter]

Nevertheless, the political and military dangers of independent Bantustans seemed so obvious to the United party that its speakers did not hide their belief that promises of eventual independence were a sham. Disbelief was strengthened by the opposition's interpretation of the policy of encouraging White industry to locate near the borders of Bantu areas: "economic integration" was being "moved from one urban area to a new urban area." There was no willingness, said Sir de Villiers, to endure the economic sacrifices involved in "total territorial separation," which both SABRA and the Dutch Reformed churches believed was "the only morally justifiable alternative." After reviewing the political and military dangers and also the high economic cost, including the cost of developing the Bantu areas into "Black Belgiums," Dr. F. J. C. Cronje, one of the United party's financial experts, concluded, "That is why I do not really think this state of affairs will ever come about."

The opposition's assessment of the government's motives was largely cynical, as one would expect. "For the sake of argument," said R. A. F. Swart, "you must accept that the Prime Minister means what he says" when he talks about "separate independent sovereign states" (in Swart's words). But the "complete lack of sincerity" in the so-called positive provisions of the Bill was demonstrated by the Bill's history, he said. These provisions and the Prime Minister's "new vision" speech early in the year came in the wake of criticism by supporters of the government as well as by those opposed to the negativism implicit in the removal of the Native Representatives. "The real reason" for their removal, said Sir de Villiers, was that the government had found it necessary once again to inflame color prejudice. But he believed that the other provisions of the Bill represented Dr. Verwoerd's "reaction to the march of events in Africa."

Dr. Verwoerd left no doubt that the government hoped the Bill would decrease external pressures on South Africa. "The choice of separate Bantu development," he said, was "in line with the objects of the world at large." The Bill's enactment would enable the government to "tell the world and Africa with even more justice: Also give us, the White people, the right to retain and to govern our own area."

The Bill had already been received favorably in the United States, said Eric Louw, the Minister of External Affairs, though he produced no evidence on this point during the debate. Louw also quoted the liberally inclined *Rand Daily Mail* as saying that the government rather than the opposition was seeking to adapt itself to "the post-Accra situation in Africa" and had acquired "a new sense of moral justification."

Dr. Douglas Smit, a former United party Secretary of Native Affairs, agreed that the provisions for self-government were "an attempt to placate world opinion"; but he saw as the Bill's central feature the shortsighted ending of representation in Parliament. Many in Africa and abroad had already criticized this feature, said Basson, speaking as a

Southwest African who was "in the front line," and the position of South Africa's few friends in the West had been made more difficult. "How can we be so out of touch spiritually and intellectually," asked Marais Steyn, one of the United party's most skilled debaters, "with the facts of this world in the second half of the twentieth century?"

In response, the Nationalists insisted that they, and not the United party, were realistic in their appreciation of African expectations. Their recognition that "the demand for self-determination on the part of the non-White nations" could not be suppressed, had greatly impressed a number of foreign sympathizers of the Bantustan policy. Since 1936, when Prime Minister Hertzog thought a final solution had been reached, said Dr. Verwoerd, "tremendous developments" had occurred in the granting of independence and "tremendous changes" had taken place among the South African Bantu themselves. As experience elsewhere had shown, he said, the Bantu would be satisfied within a partnership with nothing less than "equal rights . . . in order eventually to dominate South Africa." Did Sir de Villiers "really expect," asked Dr. T. E. Dönges, the Minister of Finance, "that in the long run political rights can be withheld from the majority of the population?" The United party's aim of "White leadership with justice" was "so unrealistically and childishly naive," said De Wet Nel, that it amused him.

Sir de Villiers admitted that the Whites could be swamped but insisted that the government's course was far more dangerous. Was it more realistic, he asked, to think that permanently urbanized Africans —"the crux of South African politics in the future"—would be satisfied with political rights in the Bantu areas "where they have never lived, which they have probably never visited and about which they possibly have no knowledge?" Under the Bill, it was true, urban Africans could state their grievances to a tribal representative appointed by a Bantu authority; but his appointment was subject to the Minister's approval, Sir de Villiers pointed out, and there was no assurance that the grievance would reach the ears of the parliamentary opposition or the press.

The Nationalists claimed that they were not only more realistic but also more idealistic than the United party. De Wet Nel, in particular, reached for heights—"typical ecstacy," said R.A.F. Swart—of commitment to selfless promotion of Bantu interests. He seemed vulnerable, therefore, to Steenkamp's charge of "Negrophilism" and placing the White man in second place. On the day before Steenkamp spoke, De Wet Nel had listed White survival as an aim of the Bill but had not listed it first. Two days later, he was categorical in listing "the future and safety of the White Man" as the government's first aim. But the listing of pragmatic priorities is misleading, at least in the case of De

Wet Nel, who saw a subtle interrelation of realism and idealism in the Bill. His rationale had "a sort of mystic foundation" related to religious beliefs, said Sir de Villiers, beliefs that would surprise the Christian world. Indeed, De Wet Nel spoke of South Africa's "divine task" before the final vote was taken on the Bill.

The calling of this small White nation [he said] is to give the world the basis and the pattern on which different races can live in peace and safety in future, each within its own national circle. That is the prescription for the solution of the racial problem not only in Africa, but throughout the world. . . . Western civilization, and particularly Christian civilization, is one of the great powers in the world. In this southern corner of Africa we are one of the strongholds of that Western civilization. It is our duty to see that that civilization is not destroyed. Therefore we should legislate in such a way that our civilization will be preserved and that it will be a source of power not only to the White people but also to the Bantu population.

That self-preservation was a Christian obligation was a "religious heresy," retorted Mrs. Ballinger. And Major Picter van der Byl, a former Minister of Native Affairs, who had just heard J. E. Potgieter speak of "the cross" as "a mighty anchor for national preservation," described such arguments as "nauseating." Like De Wet Nel, Potgieter saw no conflict between national preservation and "Christian White guardianship," since he believed that the former was necessary if the latter was to be carried out. But Christian guardianship also required being "just toward the guardian," said Dr. Dönges. Putting the problem differently, he said that two ideals had to be reconciled: "the ideal of Black nationalism for our Bantu" and "the ideal" of White political control in White areas. This argument was dismissed by Harry Lawrence, however, as "oligarchic sophistry."

The philosophical argument could be drawn from the Nationalists' reading of South African history. "Perverted history," said Mrs. Ballinger, a former professor. More time was spent by Nationalist and United party speakers—both sides quoting Botha, Hertzog, and Smuts—in debate, it seemed, on the correct meaning of the past than in speculation about the future consequences of each other's policies. The traditional policy of South Africa, according to the United party, was to encourage non-White workers to move into White areas and to accept the development of a single, multiracial country. The traditional policy, the Nationalists replied, was to reject multiracialism, to recognize Bantu homelands, and to endorse separate development.

The Nationalists insisted that the people of South Africa—the Whites, both Afrikaans-speaking and English-speaking "as a nation," and the vast majority of Africans—had chosen apartheid despite "the sickly humanism of people overseas."[7] The philosophy of apartheid, said De Wet Nel, was "not a mere abstraction which hangs in the air" but "a conviction the roots of which have been anchored in the historic processes of South Africa for 300 years." Apartheid "was only the crystallization of the will of the people" and, in a formulation that combined the most commonly used words, he declared the Bill was "the logical and positive development of the traditional policy of South Africa. [Laughter]"

The White nation had never, for example, accepted the principle of representation of Natives, said De Wet Nel. With obvious exasperation, a number of United party speakers asked, in effect, how such a statement could be made. General Hertzog and over two-thirds of Parliament had supported the 1936 Act, they pointed out. Nationalist speakers replied that the legislation was a compromise forced by liberals who opposed an earlier bill that did not provide for Native Representatives. That bill did provide for them in the Senate, said Harry Lawrence. Hertzog's earlier bill, said De Wet Nel, was the one "which came from his heart."

De Wet Nel, it must be added, conceived of apartheid as something more than a widely accepted traditional policy, and of South African history as having an inner, teleological dynamic: "Apartheid is the ideal which is systematically being realized." Thus, in commenting on an article published in March, 1959, written by Dr. W. W. M. Eiselen, the Secretary of Bantu Administration and Development, stating that there was "no prospect" that the Bantustans would become sovereign, De Wet Nel explained that the article had been correct when it was written at the end of 1958. But apartheid was "always growing," he said (presumably in response to its own dynamic and not to external pressures), and there had been "progress" since 1958.[8]

Because of the Nationalists' preoccupation with the symbolism and direction of policy, the opposition's historical arguments were treated as largely irrelevant; and because of Nationalist expectations that the achievement of African self-government would require a long time, perhaps a century or more, demands for precision regarding the territorial boundaries of the Bantustans were considered unrealistic and premature. In seeking to demonstrate that the building up of territorially com-

7. C. R. Swart, Minister of Justice, supported the Nationalist argument by quoting from *The Black Problem,* a collection of papers by D. D. T. Jabavu, a well-known African professor in South Africa. (2d ed.; Lovedale, Cape Province: [Lovedale Institution Press], 1921.) Jabavu was quoted as speaking sorrowfully of the loss of some tribal values. The quotation was from an address delivered in 1919 in which Jabavu also warned against tribal division and said that since all Natives were under White rule the time was ripe for Native unity.

8. *House of Assembly Debates* (May 27, 1959), col. 6784. See Dr. W. W. M. Eiselen, "Harmonious Multi-Community Development," *Optima,* March 1959, p. 8. Dr. Verwoerd commented on the article on May 20 (*Debates,* col. 6221).

pact Bantu homelands was not traditional policy, several United party speakers went back to 1916, when the Beaumont Commission had said:

It is in fact too late in the day to define large compact areas or to draw bold lines of demarcation; for . . . lands solely occupied by Natives are, with the exception of the Transkeian Territories, scattered in all directions and hopelessly intermixed with the lands owned and occupied by Europeans. . . .

But such argument missed the Nationalist point that what was being promoted was in the main not territorial but political apartheid. "It makes no difference where a member of . . . [an] ethnic group finds himself . . ." said Dr. L. I. Coertze, the Nationalist expert in constitutional law. "It has nothing at all to do with borders . . . He can be governed wherever he is."

In reply to charges that territorial consolidation would require the uprooting of people, De Wet Nel declared that over a long period of time the Bantu heartlands would gradually be "embroidered" by the addition of land still to be purchased in accordance with the 1936 legislation. After that, however, no land would be purchased. Meanwhile, he believed that Bantu national units were becoming concentrated "from the psychological point of view."

Government spokesmen affirmed the primacy of politics and the potentialities that are created by the control of political institutions, convictions confirmed for them by the political success of Afrikaner nationalism. "We do not regard politics only as the science of government," said J. E. Potgieter, the chief whip, "but as the most important sphere for determining all the other spheres of your national life." What Dr. Verwoerd called "the beginning of an emancipation movement" would be created through the "dynamic link" (presumably the tribal "ambassadors" to urban areas) between African forms of government in the Transkei and Africans anywhere in the country. Sir de Villiers, however, turned the metaphor to the system eliminated in 1959 and said the Native Representatives had been "the vital link" between the Africans and Parliament, one which "symbolized" the democratic system for millions of Africans.

That symbolism, countered De Wet Nel, had disrupted "Bantucentric" development, created false hopes, and caused "human erosion" when able Bantu deserted their communities. The Native Representatives, in particular, had abused their positions in his view by creating false impressions. They had "access" to the Natives, Dr. Verwoerd said; they were among the few persons, agreed Mrs. Ballinger, who could enter the Native reserves without official permission. The conclusion that Dr. Verwoerd drew, however, was that the Native Representatives must be eliminated at that point. He insisted that

For the sake of clarity in the mind of the Bantu and of the world, in Africa and amongst our own population, a definite choice should be made, and one of the greatest symbols of this choice is the removal of the Native Representatives from this White Parliament.

What did the speakers believe was in "the mind of the Bantu"? There probably was not a single White man who could answer that question, said Douglas Mitchell. Other United party speakers, however, did not hesitate to generalize about the wishes of "the Bantu," "a people just emerging from barbarism," said Henry Tucker, leader of the United party in the Transvaal. "He wants to retain the guidance of the guardianship of the White man," said Dr. Steenkamp. But the main United party argument, as expressed by Sir de Villiers, was that the "real crux" of the African problem was "the vast numbers" who had lost their tribal affiliation, were "integrated in the economy of multiracial South Africa," and permanently settled in the urban area. Among them, the greatest demand for political expression came from

. . . the most evolved section of the Native population, the section which has been longest in contact with civilization, the section which includes professors, lawyers, doctors, clergymen, teachers, many skilled workmen . . .

Agitators [interjected G. F. H. Bekker].

This interjection by Bekker, a back-bencher, expressed a prevailing Nationalist conviction that the Africans who demanded representation in Parliament were a small minority who had turned their backs on their own communities. Both Dr. Verwoerd and De Wet Nel compared these Africans to anglicized Afrikaners in the 1880's who had refused to work for Afrikanerdom. They were not inspired by "racial nationalism," said De Wet Nel, meaning tribal nationalism or the nationalism of South African Whites. Historically, throughout the world, nationalism was "one of the forces which had led to the most beautiful deeds of idealism and sacrifice and inspiration." Fortunately, tribal nationalism was still possible for 80 per cent or more of the Africans in the cities, including those who had been city-dwellers for two or three generations, since they had retained their ties to tribal areas. Discussion of what constituted a detribalized African was lengthy and inconclusive, and De Wet Nel himself was not consistent in his estimate of their number.

The government's approach, De Wet Nel said at one point, was "jubilantly approved of by easily 98 per cent to 99 per cent of the Bantu population throughout South Africa." Only African National Congress agitators and a small number of "denationalized" Africans were opposed. The statement was consistent with that of a back-bencher who had said earlier in the day that he doubted that even 2 per cent of the Africans could be regarded as detribalized. Proof was the fact, he declared, that when they visited the tribal areas from which they came, they reverted immediately to tribal custom.

Disagreement regarding the attitudes of Africans in the reserves was as wide as that regarding urban areas. "I make bold to say," stated De Wet Nel, "that 95 per cent of the Native people in the reserves support this Bill." In answer to a question in April, as we have seen, he had said that no steps had been taken to consult Africans regarding the Bill since it was "the logical outcome" of the Bantu Authorities system that they had favored. During the debate, however, he wondered whether the Bantu had ever been more "informed and consulted about a Bill." His frequent references to spontaneous and congratulatory telegrams—"crawling telegrams," said Van der Byl—received during the debate from tribal chiefs and others caused some merriment among the opposition who referred to the Minister's susceptibility to the flattery of stooges.

De Wet Nel rose to the defense of the chiefs and attacked the injustice of calling them stooges. The majority were neither cowardly about expressing their views, he maintained, nor men who would accept bribes. "Those people may be Black but behind their Black skin the majority of them have a noble soul." De Wet Nel challenged the opposition to cite a single case of anyone against whom official steps had been taken because he had differed with the government. A short while earlier, Lee-Warden had referred to chiefs and headmen who had been deported "because they were not prepared to play ball with the Administration."[9] But steps were taken, De Wet Nel declared, only against persons, particularly those under leftist influence, who encouraged strife or undermined "the whole policy of the country."

Dr. Verwoerd was less disposed than was De Wet Nel to demonstrate that Africans had been informed and consulted and that, as De Wet Nel said, telegrams had been received "from Bantu organizations which represent millions of people." Since the Bill was essential to White survival, Dr. Verwoerd said, its enactment could not be made subject to consultation. Nor was consultation necessary for purposes of ascertaining the Native will.

We know what type of Native is in favour and what Natives are against the measure and we also know why some of them are in favour and some against it. But we also know that the great mass of the Bantu are not able to decide on a matter of this nature.

Whether or not the White government as guardian foresaw an extension among Africans of the electoral procedures of liberal democracy within the Bantu "nations" was not stated by Dr. Verwoerd. The Bantu system of government had developed over centuries and was "engraved

9. On February 3, 1959, in answer to a question by Lee-Warden, De Wet Nel listed the names of 34 chiefs or headmen who had been deposed and three who had been deported during 1955–58. The reasons cited appear to be political in only two cases: the deposition of one chief for "agitation against the administration and unsatisfactory conduct," and the deporting of an acting chief because, in part, he "became a tool in the hands of agitators from the towns." (*House of Assembly Debates*, cols. 324–28.)

in their souls," he said. At any rate, as applied in the Bantu Authorities scheme, the system was one in which tribal leaders were recognized or appointed by the government, with the elective principle retained only in the Transkei and only for the selection of a small minority in tribal authorities. Elections, in fact, had been the bane of the Transkei's political experience, said Dr. Verwoerd.

. . . when the former Bunga was still there, it was an incontrovertible fact that the Bantu representatives attached so much value to re-election that they were not prepared to govern properly, that they were not prepared to levy taxation and that they were not prepared to do anything concrete for their area. They just concentrated on talking and all their actions were aimed at being popular so as to be re-elected. . . . They will under their own system in future have authority without fearing that they will lose it if they do unpopular things which are in the interest of their people. As has been said over and over, the Bantu system is very suitable for the expression of the co-authority of the people, for the inherent democracy.

The descriptions of recent Transkeian history presented by Dr. Verwoerd and De Wet Nel and their expectations regarding the responsibilities of the Transkeian Territorial Authority produced heated and obviously troubled reactions. Stanford reviewed the "intrigues and pressures" that had been brought to bear upon the Africans since 1956, the evidence of popular African opposition to the Bantu Authorities system, and the support of the Bunga councillors, as recently as 1958, for the continuation of Native Representatives. Looking toward the future, both he and Mrs. Ballinger also warned against the surrender of responsibility for the development of African areas. If handed over to African authorities, said Dr. Douglas Smit, the lands would be "irretrievably ruined" within a few years by overstocking and bad farming methods. In reply to such fears, De Wet Nel declared—"with a sob in his throat," said Van der Byl—that he had more faith in the African.

On May 26, a few days after the Bill had passed the second reading by 102 votes to 58, De Wet Nel attended the formal opening of the Transkeian Territorial Authority in Umtata. Coincidentally, on the following day Albert Luthuli, President-General of the African National Congress, was banned from meetings for five years and confined to his home district. The restrictions upon him were unquestionably necessary from the Nationalist standpoint because of the marked impression he was making in White areas. It was apparently believed that removing Luthuli from his active political life could aid in curbing African nationalism, especially if accompanied by positive policies of domestic colonialism. J. H. Abraham, soon to be appointed commissioner-general at Umtata, did not believe, in fact, that African nationalism was a genuine and spontaneous phenomenon. Two kinds of agitation—"communist . . . and British-American"—he said, had inspired its rise in Africa. But other domestic obstacles also existed: ". . . if the Opposition and its Press and the liberals who oppose this peaceful neighborly development would stop their venomous attacks," said Dr. Verwoerd, there would be "great hope for South Africa." It seemed clear that dark days were yet to come before his new day could dawn.

THE TRANSKEI CONSTITUTION ACT OF 1963

The turbulent period of 1960–61 has already been described (Chapter 1, pp. 23–29). One consequence was the announcement by Dr. Verwoerd on January 23, 1962, of an accelerated timetable of development in the Transkei. During the preceding year, African leaders of the Transkeian Territorial Authority had renewed their demands for self-government, and during the remainder of 1962 they were involved in the preparation of the Transkeian Constitution, which, according to Dr. Verwoerd, was to be in operation by the end of 1963. The interplay between the Transkeian leaders and government officials is discussed in Section IV, which describes also the electoral campaign conducted under the Constitution. Before this new phase of activity could begin, however, parliamentary enactment of the Transkeian Constitution was necessary. (Provisions of the Constitution are discussed in Chapter 6.)

The United party opposed the Bill as a further step toward balkanizing the country and repeated many of the arguments made in 1959. Again it followed the uncommon procedure of objection to the first reading, on January 28, 1963, and promised to fight the Bill at every stage. The Bill's eventual enactment was never in doubt, however, since the government enjoyed a majority of 50 in the House and of more than three to one in the Senate.

Before the government could proceed with the Bill, the opposition raised an unexpected constitutional objection that was of some embarrassment to the government, or that, at any rate, caused a diversion which delayed action for several weeks. Early in February, Sir de Villiers Graaff told the press that enactment of the Bill by ordinary procedures would violate the entrenched language provisions of the Republic of South Africa Constitution Act of 1961. That Act provided that English and Afrikaans were the official languages of the Republic. Moreover, the equality of the two languages was entrenched, and could only be amended through a bill passed by both Houses of Parliament sitting together and by two-thirds of all members at third reading. The problem was that Section 6 of the Transkei Constitution Bill made Xhosa the official language of the Transkei, although English, Afrikaans, and Sesotho could be used for official purposes in addition to, or instead of, Xhosa.

On February 14 Minister de Wet Nel acknowledged that the language clause of the Transkei Constitution might be in conflict with the Republican Constitution and said it would be redrafted. During February 25–28 a joint sitting of both Houses of Parliament considered and approved the Constitution Amendment Act of 1963 by 146 votes to 64. The Act allowed Parliament to recognize for such Bantu areas as should become "self-governing" one or more Bantu languages as additional official languages or as languages for use for specified official purposes. Although in its original form the Constitution Amendment Act would also have allowed Parliament to recognize a Bantu language as the sole official language within a "self-governing" Bantu area, this provision was dropped at the request of the opposition.

On March 5 a new Transkei Constitution Bill was introduced in the House of Assembly. It passed the third reading on May 10 and, after passing the Senate, became law on May 29. The Bill differed from the earlier version only with respect to section 6, which as rewritten now provided that Xhosa would be recognized within the Transkei as an additional official language. Sesotho might also be used for such official purposes as were determined by the Transkeian Cabinet. It is worth noting that the Republican government had not felt it necessary to have the Transkeian Territorial Authority approve the revision.

During the debate, the opposition claimed that Africans of the Transkei had not been properly consulted regarding the proposed constitution and did not understand the self-government which the government now asked Parliament to bestow upon them. Nevertheless, it was apparent that the opposition's foremost concern was the potential impact of Transkeian self-government upon White interests, both inside and outside the Territory. In particular, United party spokesmen pointed out that the plan made no allowance for the protection of the more than 14,000 White residents within the Territory, while Steenkamp charged that it constituted a giving away of part of South Africa "for which our grandfathers fought and made sacrifices."[10] The claim, as in the 1959 debate, was that a self-governing Transkei would jeopardize the military security of South Africa and offer a base for Communist subversion of the Republic; indeed, it was said, the Transkei could become a South African Cuba. Moreover, since the Prime Minister had agreed to negotiate the boundaries of the Transkei, they charged that White landowners in border areas had no security of property. Fears were also expressed that the Transkeian government would endanger the economy of the rest of the country by forcing Transkeian laborers to return to the Territory.

The government, from its side, claimed that its plan for the Transkei

10. The source of all statements about the 1963 debate and of quotations from it is in one or more of the following columns of the *House of Assembly Debates:* Jan. 28—292 (Botha); March 5—2152 (Steenkamp); March 18—2961 (Botha); March 21—3162 (Schoeman); April 1—3806 (Faurie); May 2—5273 (De Wet Nel); May 7—5463 and 3476 (De Wet Nel); May 10—5802 (Froneman).

was the logical, indeed the necessary, continuation of South Africa's "traditional" policy of racial separation. "Every Prime Minister who sat in this House," said Deputy-Minister Botha, "made the same statement . . . that he undertakes, sooner or later, to give self-government to the Bantu in their own areas." De Wet Nel maintained that Whites with freehold tenure in the Transkei had always understood that the Territory was "a Bantu area." At the same time he assured the opposition that Port St. Johns would remain a White area and anticipated that Whites would live in Umtata for "many years."

The Minister also denied categorically that Transkeian self-government would diminish the sovereignty of the South African Parliament. In the event of the South African State President receiving contradictory advice from his Republican and Transkeian cabinets, he would be obliged (not surprisingly) to accept the advice of his Republican Ministers. Another Nationalist member, Froneman, pointed out that Parliament could unilaterally amend and even repeal the Transkeian Constitution. The House was also assured that the boundaries of the Transkei could not be altered without the prior consent of Parliament.

Government spokesmen conceded that the Transkei would probably evolve to greater autonomy and possibly even to eventual independence. Minister de Wet Nel spoke warmly of "modern development" taking place on "evolutionary lines." Faurie said the "granting of self-government to the Bantu" in their own areas was "traditional policy." However, the government obviously expected the process to be gradual and its consequences distant. Asked when the Transkei might gain independence, B. J. Schoeman, Minister of Transport, replied: "How politically naive that question is! After all, history has taught us that the road to independence in our case took more than a full century."

In the end, the government obviously counted on the "common bonds" between the Transkei and the Whites of the Republic to reduce, if not eliminate, the risks of constitutional advance for the Territory. These bonds, as enumerated by Deputy-Minister Botha, were: Christianity; the good will of Transkeian Africans toward Whites; economic interdependence; and the links in transportation and communications. Once its "national" and cultural right to exist was assured, government spokesmen contended, the Transkei would want to cooperate closely with the Republic.

Section III
Testing Ground: The Transkei

4

The Transkei:
Land, People, and Administration

APPROXIMATELY 700 miles east of Cape Town, one of the largest rivers in the Eastern Province winds its way across a thorn-tree-covered coastal plain and flows quietly into the Indian Ocean. This river is called the Kei, a Hottentot name meaning "sand water," and has contributed its name to the area of the Transkei on its eastern bank and the Ciskei on its western bank. The Kei is not a large river, but it has carved a deep and rugged gorge in the surrounding plateau country which effectively forms a boundary between the Transkei and the rest of the Cape Province.

EARLY HISTORY

The Bantu-speaking tribes of South Africa—the so-called southern Bantu—are usually classified into four main divisions: Nguni, Sotho, Venda, and Tsonga. Of these, the Nguni now occupy the fertile country between the Drakensberg range and the Indian Ocean and extend from Portuguese East Africa to the Cape. They include the Swazi, the Zulu, and a group of people known as the Cape Nguni.

In the eighteenth century, the Cape Nguni were the outriders of large, southwardly migrating groups moving ever onward with their herds in search of fresh grazing lands. By 1700 they had already reached the Kei

River. Here the Cape Nguni met the easternmost Hottentots and engaged in a series of bloody skirmishes with both Hottentots and Bushmen. As a result, the Bushmen were practically exterminated. By 1750, the Xhosa tribe of the Cape Nguni had reached the Keiskamma River and its tribesmen had become the first Africans to come into sustained contact with the westward-moving Dutch farmers.

Contact between White farmers and Africans, both pastoralists, inevitably engendered conflict. Their skirmishes and raids caused the government at Cape Town considerable concern. Its reaction was to promulgate a series of boundary proclamations which attempted to fix a clear separation between Black and White. In 1743 the boundary was fixed on the Great Brak River, but already some farmers were near the Gamtoos River to the east. In 1770 the Gamtoos, in turn, was made the eastern boundary of the Colony. Later the boundary was moved to Bruyntjes Hoogte. But Cape Town, the center of government, was 500 miles away and had little control over the land-hungry stock farmers. In 1775 the government again moved the frontier, this time to the Fish River. Here the colonists met the Africans in force. The stage was now set for the struggle for land which has been a basic factor in Black-White relations ever since.

Annexation and Union of the Transkeian Territories

The region now known as the Transkei is the result of a series of annexations which began with proclamations relating to Fingoland and East Griqualand in 1877 and culminated in the annexation of Pondoland in 1894. These annexations were partly a response to the appeals by traders and others, in the Cape Colony, London, and beyond the frontier, who sought the annexation of additional territory in the interest of land hunger, frontier security, and of trade which had been disrupted by frequent intertribal wars and cattle raids.

Despite the sporadic attempts by the colonial government, over more than a hundred years, to prohibit trade and intercourse between the White settlers and the African tribes, tension between the two groups exploded periodically in open conflict, known in South Africa as the nine "Kaffir wars." A series of treaties proved fruitless in stopping the westward expansion of the farmers and traders. By 1865 the tribes south of the Kei River had been incorporated into the Colony. Official policy was reluctant, however, to accede to the colonists' request for further annexations of land, and this action had to await, first, the establishment of responsible government in the Cape Colony and, second, evidence that the territories beyond the Kei were financially able to support their own administration.

The Cape achieved responsible government in 1872 under Prime Minister Molteno, and one of its first acts was to establish a Department of Native Affairs under Charles Brownlee. Both Brownlee and his successor, William Ayliff, were enthusiastic protagonists of an expansionist policy, and in this they were supported by most of the missionaries and also by some government agents, such as Captain Matthew Blyth, the Fingo agent. Their hand was strengthened when in 1874 the people of Fingoland began to pay a hut tax of ten shillings a year. The revenue from this source exceeded expenditures, thus proving that Fingoland could support the burden of administration. Heartened by this fact, the Cape Legislature passed a bill in 1875 providing for the annexation of Fingoland and Idutywa Reserve. By Act 38 of 1877, both these districts and the area between Umtata and the Natal border and between Pondoland and the Drakensberg, now known as East Griqualand, were annexed to the Colony. But in fact, as W. B. Campbell points out, "The Acts of annexation only legalized a gradual process of more and more direct rule which had been continuing since the end of the sixties."[1]

The next Transkeian area to be annexed to the Cape Colony was what is known today as Gcalekaland. This was the territory of the Xhosa, the southernmost group of African tribes who, since 1702, had been at varying times in contact and conflict with the White farmers. At one time the Xhosa tribes extended as far west as Queenstown but much of their former territory was depopulated by the Cattle Killing of 1857. In that year a young prophetess, Nongqawuse, announced that if the Xhosa destroyed all their cattle, the dead would arise on a certain day and drive the White man into the sea. Most of the Xhosa tribes obeyed her commands and, when the expected millennium failed to materialize, thousands of destitute Xhosa fled into the Cape Colony. Xhosa power was effectively broken forever.

Part of the area depopulated by the Cattle Killing was restored to the Xhosa chief, Sarili (usually referred to by Europeans as Kreli), in 1864 and was not immediately annexed to the Colony, for the Gcaleka, the senior Xhosa tribe, desired to remain independent. The government was represented among the Gcaleka, but by an agent who had no power to interfere in tribal affairs. This arrangement lasted for thirteen years, until August, 1877, when war broke out between the Xhosa and the Thembu. The colonial troops supported the Thembu chief, Ngangelizwe, and Sarili and his impis were decisively beaten. In September, 1878, this newly conquered territory, known as Gcalekaland, was divided administratively into the districts of Willowvale and Kentani, and these, with the already-annexed Idutywa Reserve and Fingoland, became known as the Transkei, a defined administrative area under a

1. "The South African Frontier, 1865–1885: A Study in Expansion," *Archives Year Book for South African History* (Office of the Chief Archivist, 1960), I, 124.

chief magistrate.[2] At the same time East Griqualand, which comprised the districts of Elliot, Maclear, Mount Fletcher, Qumbu, Tsolo, Matatiele, Kokstad, Umzimkulu, and Mount Frere, was also constituted a chief magistracy.

The Transkei and East Griqualand were separated from one another by the countries of the Thembu and the Pondo, and these, in turn, were also annexed to the Cape. Tembuland was annexed partly because of internal troubles between the young, inexperienced, and temperamental Thembu chief, Ngangelizwe, and the so-called Emigrant Thembu. The latter had crossed the Kei River in 1828 after the Thembu country had been subjected to raids by the warlike Ngwane, and had constituted themselves as a separate Thembu tribe under their own chief, Matanzima. (This feud revived, it should be noted, in the contemporary rivalry between the Paramount Chief of the Thembu tribal cluster, Sabata Dalindyebo, and Chief [now Paramount Chief] Kaiser Matanzima of Emigrant Tembuland, the first Chief Minister of the Transkei. This rivalry has been apparent both in connection with the establishment of Thembu Tribal Authorities and in the Transkeian political development.)

Ngangelizwe also had a feud with the Gcaleka Chief Sarili, and this developed into open war. Matters became so serious that, under pressure from his own people as well as from the local British official and missionaries working in the area, Ngangelizwe and other minor Thembu chiefs asked Britain for protection. In June, 1876, the Molteno Ministry in the Cape passed an annexation bill and magisterial rule was at once established in Tembuland. In the following year Emigrant Tembuland was also annexed and divided into the districts of St. Marks and Xalanga.

It was inevitable that Pondoland would be made to follow suit, but seventeen years elapsed before it conformed to the general pattern. Pondoland was by then the last independent native territory between the Cape and Natal. Cecil John Rhodes was Prime Minister of the Cape at this time, and his aims for a united South Africa made it inevitable that he should attempt to annex the territory. There had been some unrest in Eastern Pondoland, resulting from trouble between Chief Sigcau and his half-brother, Mhlangaso, and Natal made overtures for annexation. Major Henry Elliot, British Resident in Western Pondoland, met Sigcau with a small party, on March 8, 1894, and demanded that he submit to colonial rule. Sigcau considered the matter with his councillors for several days before formally signing the deed of submission on March 17. Two days later, Nqwiliso, the Western Mpondo chief, signed

2. Formal annexation of Gcalekaland was postponed until 1885, when the Colonial Office attempted unsuccessfully to use the issue to force federation of the Cape Colony with Natal. Formal annexation of Tembuland and Emigrant Tembuland also waited until 1885.

a similar document. In September, 1894, both Eastern and Western Pondoland were annexed to the Colony.

The annexed territories now consisted of three chief magistracies: the Transkei, with its capital at Butterworth; Tembuland, with its capital at Umtata; and East Griqualand which, with Pondoland, was administered from Kokstad. In 1903, all these areas were incorporated as the United Transkeian Territories under a Chief Magistrate who had his seat at Umtata, which was made the capital of the whole region. The Transkeian Territories were divided into twenty-seven districts, each under the control of a magistrate *cum* native commissioner, who with his staff was directly responsible to the Chief Magistrate for both administrative and judicial matters. The districts themselves were divided into areas known as locations, each under the control of a government-appointed headman who was directly responsible to the magistrate, and, indeed, was a paid official of the Department of Native Affairs.

THE LAND

The area thus brought under White rule as the Transkeian Territories, and now known as the Transkei, covers a total of 16,554 square miles, lying in the comparatively well-watered eastern seaboard of South Africa between the Drakensberg Range and the sea and stretching from the Kei River in the southwest to the borders of Natal in the northeast. Approximately 13,000 square miles of this area were reserved under the 1936 Native Land Act for African occupation. The remaining 3,554 square miles are occupied by the European centers of magistracy and a few European farms, the latter mainly in the Mount Currie (Kokstad) district. These areas did not fall under the jurisdiction of the new Transkei government.

Topographically the area divides into four main physical regions: the costal belt, the midlands, the highlands, and the great escarpment. The costal belt occupies the area from the seacoast to about 2,000 feet above sea level. Characteristic of this area is the fact that the grain of the land lies toward the sea. As a result the land is deeply dissected, trenched by the precipitous canyons of the rivers that flow eastward from the Drakensberg. Progress along the coast is extremely difficult, as the survivors of early shipwrecks found when they tried to reach the Cape Colony by foot. The shoreline is extremely regular, and there are no good natural harbors. Generally, agriculture and cultivation are difficult in the coastal area.

Between the coastal strip and the highlands lies a corridor of plateau country that extends from the 2,000-foot to the 4,000-foot contour. This part of the Transkei is gently undulating and, since it is cut by the upper courses of the rivers that flow into the Indian Ocean, is a region also of countless hills and valleys, mesas, and sharply pointed peaks. Toward the north the corridor becomes progressively more mountainous in the Tabankulu, Mount Ayliff, and Mount Currie districts, and here considerable afforestation projects have been initiated by the administration.

The highlands occupy the area between the 4,000- and the 6,000-foot contours and form a region of considerable variety. There are great mountain masses in the districts of Mount Fletcher and Matatiele, which are part of the foothills of the Drakensberg. The country is generally barren, with narrow valleys of shallow alluvial soil, but there are also areas of grass-covered flats, particularly in the Matatiele and Umzimkulu districts.

Finally, in the northwest are the mountain fastnesses of the Drakensberg, which mark the outer marches of Basutoland.

There are six perennial rivers—Kei, Bashee, Umtata, Tsitsa, Thina, and Umzimvubu—which all take their rise in the uplands and flow eastward toward the sea. The climate is fairly equable. The average rainfall is more than thirty inches, and precipitation is never less than twenty inches, but the rainfall is unreliable, and frequent droughts make life hazardous for the peasant farmer using age-old, inefficient methods of agriculture. The indigenous cultivation is dryland farming, that is, entirely dependent upon precipitation, and extensive droughts mean that large quantities of grain must be imported into the area on occasion to prevent widespread starvation. Typically, the vegetation is grass, which originally grew man high but has been cropped by the thousands of cattle and sheep to a lawnlike shortness.

On the mountain ranges and in the southward-facing mountain ravines there were once large stands of yellow wood, stinkwood, and other hardwoods. Although these have been substantially destroyed by native cultivation, there are still patches of forest, particularly in the coastal strip and on the slopes of the escarpment. Vegetation changes in the river valleys, where it is predominantly thorn scrub dotted with aloes, which color the slopes in winter.

Criticism that this reserve land is one of the poorer areas of South Africa cannot be sustained. On the other hand, the broken nature of the country means that only about 11 per cent is comparatively flat. The use of mechanized agricultural methods is, therefore, seriously restricted. The country provides excellent grazing in most areas and is able to support a large cattle population, but because of the ritual place cattle occupy in African social life, the whole of the Transkei is greatly overstocked, in some areas rising to at least 40 per cent in excess of normal carrying capacity. Overgrazing plus poor agricultural methods and occasional torrential downpours have caused much of the soil of the Transkei to be badly eroded.

THE ECONOMY

The African economy of the Transkei, like the economies of the other African reserve areas of the Republic, still rests in practice almost entirely upon subsistence farming, mostly carried on with inefficient methods on uneconomic-sized plots. Since the land is not sufficient, under present conditions, to support most of the people of the Transkei, a high proportion is forced to seek wage employment. There are few such jobs within the Transkei. In 1963 industries in the Transkei included only the small Vulindlela factory near Umtata, which makes furniture and prefabricated houses; a clothing firm; a cane and wicker works; several factories making soft drinks; three bakeries; several building contractors; twelve motor garages; and a number of dairies. The Vulindlela factory is the only enterprise of note among these and employs less than 200 people. In addition, there were some 160 African contractors erecting fences, about 72 small agricultural plantations, 316 African traders, and about 300 Africans operating one or more buses. Moreover, apart from building hotels for Africans (who cannot at present use those in Transkeian towns since these are reserved for Whites) and establishing some shops and other service structures, there are few enterprises in which African businessmen can invest.

While admittedly there are man-made obstacles to the economic development of the Transkei, as we have seen, what is more important is that, under any foreseeable circumstances, the economic prospects for the Territory are exceedingly dim. Within the Transkei African capital available for investment is so scarce as to be virtually nonexistent. The Transkei has no known power reserves of significance, and few mineral resources. In the Mount Ayliff and Tabankulu districts there are quantities of copper, nickel, and cobalt, and there is known to be low-grade coal in the Mount Frere district, but none of these deposits occur in economically significant quantities. Farmland is the Transkei's only obvious natural resource, but even this cannot be fully exploited because of overpopulation on the land, the widespread communal basis of land tenure, and the engrained conservatism of tribal Africans, especially regarding the traditional importance of cattle.

The infrastructure of the Transkei is also limited. A single-track railway winds its way from East London northeast to a terminus at Umtata. The Territory has few good roads for such a vast area, and only one of these, the so-called national road from East London to Natal, has an all-weather surface. The Transkei's most likely port,

Port St. Johns at the mouth of the Umzimvubu River, has long been silted and, in any case, lies within a White area outside the present jurisdiction of the Transkei government.

Finally, the local manpower resources of the Transkei, while not insignificant, are limited. About 250 or more university graduates live in the Transkei; many of them are among the 3,000 or more teachers in the Territory. There are a few African doctors and attorneys. African businessmen—traders and small entrepreneurs—probably number not more than six to seven hundred. Numerous Africans work as clerks. But most of the Transkeians who have developed professional and commercial skills are outside the Territory and seem more likely to remain where they are than to return to an area offering so few specialized or rewarding opportunities.

THE PEOPLE

The population of the Transkei stands at approximately 1,500,000 persons of whom the only non-Africans, according to the 1960 census, are 10,000 Coloureds, 30 Asians, and some 14,000 Whites. The Asians are almost all Indians and reside in the Umzimkulu district, which borders on the province of Natal. Indians are prohibited from owning land in the Transkei. The Coloureds are found mainly in the Umzimkulu, Umtata, Lusikisiki, and Matatiele districts, but there are also some in each of the twenty-six White towns. The total figure does not include the large number of Coloured descendants of the Griqua who settled at Kokstad, as the Mount Currie district is no longer considered part of the Transkei. The White population of the Transkei consists of those persons in the various villages, or so-called White spots, centered in each district, who are engaged in administration, law, and trading. Formerly there were a few White-owned farms in the Umtata district but these have been progressively acquired for Africans by the South African Native Trust.[3]

The average density of population for the Transkei as a whole is 89.4 persons per square mile, but there is considerable variation between districts. For example, Willowvale has 134 persons to the square mile; Mount Frere, 82; Umtata, 100; and Tsolo, 75. These figures notwithstanding, one's first impression of the Transkei may be of areas of emptiness and of large tracts completely devoid of people. This impression results from the scattered nature of settlement. The Africans live largely in homestead groups of four or five huts that dot the country,

3. The White areas are enclaves within the so-called Bantu areas of the Transkei and were excluded from African jurisdiction by the Transkei Constitution Act of 1963. In 1963, 3,233 Whites (including 660 traders, whose stores form a network throughout the Territory, and about 26 farmers) and 2,550 Coloureds were living outside the White enclaves of the Transkei. Since they are not Africans, however, they cannot be Transkeian citizens. (*House of Assembly Debates* [April 3, 1963], cols. 3947–48.)

but tend to concentrate in river valleys, along the tops of escarpments, and on the sides of mountain slopes. Substantial areas of cultivation and grazing usually separate such settlements, thus allowing the Transkei to appear to be a thinly populated region.

The area of the modern Transkei coincides almost exactly with the traditional country of the Cape Nguni, occupied before contact with White farmers, although a considerable number of Cape Nguni themselves live in reserves and on White farms in the Ciskei, a closely allied and still more densely populated area lying west of the Kei River and closer to Port Elizabeth and East London. The Transkei includes, however, a few Sotho chiefdoms in the northwestern districts of Matatiele and Mount Fletcher, people who have spilled over, as it were, from Basutoland (now Lesotho) into the highlands.

The tribes of the Transkei and the Eastern Cape are commonly spoken of as the "Xhosa." This is incorrect usage. Although, save for the Sotho, all tribes in the region speak dialects of the Xhosa language, the Cape Nguni are divided among a number of mainly unrelated tribal clusters, each with its own history, customs, and strong sense of identity. There are twelve of these clusters: the Xhosa, Thembu, Mpondo, Mpondomise, Bomvana, Bhaca, Hlubi, Bhele, Zizi, Mfengu (usually known as the Fingo, a group descended from refugees and remnants of various shattered tribes), Xesibe, and Ntlangwini. Each of these clusters is divided into a number of independent chiefdoms, whose chiefs are related to one another through membership in a royal patrilineage. Thus the Xhosa cluster comprises the independent chiefdoms of Gcaleka, Ngqika, Ndlambe, Dushane, Qhayi, Dange, Gasela, Ntinde, and Hleke; the Thembu cluster contains four independent Hala tribes: the Jumba, Hlanga, Tshatshu, and Ndungwana, and so on. Only the first group of tribes may correctly be called Xhosa. Some of the other tribal groups, notably the Thembu and the Mpondo, greatly outnumber the Xhosa, who were decimated, as has been indicated, by the Cattle Killing of 1857. All, however, are Xhosa-speaking, and Cape Nguni culture shows a remarkable uniformity. Van Warmelo, a distinguished government ethnographer, estimated the total number speaking Xhosa at the 1946 census as 2,354,000, practically all of whom were domiciled in the Cape Province.[4] Today their number is probably over 3,000,000 and, as already noted, they form the largest Bantu-language group in South Africa: 31.8 per cent of all Africans in the Republic.

Social Organization

Cape Nguni social organization, particularly its settlement pattern, is distinctive and differs considerably from that of the neighboring Sotho and the Venda. The latter have true villages whereas all the

4. N. J. van Warmelo, *Language Map of South Africa* (Ethnological Publications No. 27 [Pretoria, 1952]), p. 6.

Xhosa-speaking tribes live in homesteads scattered over the tribal territory. A homestead consists of a number of huts grouped around a cattle enclosure of stone, planted aloes, or brushwood. In the past the huts were hemispherical, but today all are of the cone and cylinder type, made from sun-dried brick and thatched with grass. The homestead is the basic unit of settlement and is occupied typically by a family—a man, his wife, and their dependent children, and often a widowed parent or some other relative as well. Families are ideally polygynous among non-Christians, and a man's status is enhanced if he has more than one wife; but today not more than 5 per cent achieve this ideal. Formerly, and in some cases still, the family is extended to include married sons of the homestead head. But with the increasing individualism engendered by migrant labor and the ability to earn an income at a comparatively early age, sons tend to set up their own homesteads when they marry, and the size of the extended group is therefore decreasing. Typically, a homestead contains a main living hut and also a private hut and a kitchen hut for each wife.

Highly important relationships are those of the various kinship structures. Most basic is the *family*, either monogamous or polygynous. Where polygyny exists, it involves a special structuring of the family. Among all the tribes except the Bhaca, the first wife married by a commoner is considered the great wife (*indlunkulu*), or the wife of the great house, and the second wife (*ekunene*), the wife of the right-hand. Any other wives married subsequently are allocated, usually alternately, as "supports" to one or another of these houses. Each house has its own field and stock which are inherited by the eldest son in that house. The same pattern is found among the chiefs, a fact which, as we shall see, has important repercussions in the political sphere by giving rise to problems of succession.

There is a tendency for kin to settle near each other, and this larger group of relatives, whether so settled or not, forms the *lineage group* of people descended from a common grandfather in the male line. The lineage is an important social and ritual grouping, much more so than the *clan*, which is a widely dispersed group of presumptive kin who, although they cannot actually demonstrate their relationship in genealogies, believe themselves to be related because of their possession of a common clan name. The clan is important socially, however, because it is exogamous, i.e., its members must marry outside the group. Friendship and hospitality are expected among clan members.

Political Organization

The basic political unit among the Cape Nguni is the *chiefdom* or *tribe*, which still retains a large degree of social and cultural cohesion.

THE TRANSKEI: LAND, PEOPLE, AND ADMINISTRATION

Like other southern Bantu, their well-defined administrative structure is centralized with the chieftainship forming the pivotal institution. Tribes, then, are political communities, and each owes allegiance to a chief who is independent of other chiefs. This factor of independence, more particularly independence from the senior or paramount chief, is crucial and is defined by the fact that, in the traditional system, no appeal lies from the court of a chief to any higher court.

A distinctive feature of Nguni political units has been their instability, their tendency to split. This tendency is common to all southern Bantu groups, but among the Cape Nguni it has been institutionalized, as it were, in the system of the great house and the right-hand house. As the Nguni say, "The chieftainship is like the horns of a bull: there is a great house and there is a right-hand house." This means that there is a presumptive right for the right-hand house to establish its own chieftainship. It has thus been theoretically possible for a tribe to split once in every generation. Whether this occurred or not has depended on several factors: the personality of the chief and his heirs, pressure on tribal lands, and the presence or absence of external pressure from other tribes.

This built-in fissiparous tendency is common among all Transkei tribes. The present division between Eastern and Western Pondoland is a consequence of a split which took place even before the death of Chief Faku in 1867, and occurred with his sanction and without fighting. In this case there was considerable friction between Ndamase, son of Faku's right-hand house, and Mqikela, the heir. Ndamase was advised by Faku to cross the Umzimvubu River and occupy the territory which is now Western Pondoland, the area under Paramount Chief Victor Poto (who was the original titular head of the official opposition in the Transkei Legislative Assembly, the Democratic party). In another case, the chieftaincy of Kaiser Matanzima, recently made Paramount Chief of Emigrant Tembuland (and first Chief Minister of the Transkei), had its origin in the breaking away of his ancestor, who was of the right-hand house of the Thembu chief, and his establishment of the tribe in 1828 in its present area of the southwestern Transkei.

The origin of the present day tribal clusters is due to this splitting tendency. Most of the constituent tribes of the tribal cluster can be placed on a genealogical tree showing their relationship to one another, and it is possible to arrange them in order of seniority, the chief of the senior tribe being paramount. There can be only one paramount chief in a tribal cluster, for example, Paramount Chief Sabata Dalindyebo among the Thembu. As is obvious, however, the tribal clusters themselves cannot be arranged in order of seniority. Thus any leadership of local governmental structures above the paramount chiefdom level

must be based on other than genealogical (and traditional) criteria—
usually on White control established through annexation or on African
control through delegation of power by the White authorities to nominated or elected bodies.

TRANSKEIAN ADMINISTRATION
AND LOCAL GOVERNMENT

The policy governing the administration of Africans in the Transkei
has passed through a number of phases. The earliest attitude toward the
chiefdoms of what was called British Kaffraria (today the Ciskei) was
characterized by a desire to avoid close interaction between Black and
White. An attempt was made to control relations through treaties with
the chiefs which aimed at the establishment of boundaries and spheres
of influence. The interest of both Whites and Blacks in the same grazing
land and an increasing desire of Whites for trade among the Africans
caused the consistent failure of this early policy, however, and the so-
called treaty system was finally renounced by Sir Harry Smith in 1847.

After this date the area southwest of the Kei River came progressively under what may be best described as "magisterial" or "direct"
rule. In 1848 the chiefs were allowed the "reasonable exercise of their
authority" under the supervision of White magistrates; after the war
of 1850, full authority was again restored to the chiefs, the magistrate
reverting to the role of political agent. This position proved temporary,
however, and from 1855 colonial control was again imposed.

While chiefs were allowed to try cases under traditional law, they
were "assisted" by the magistrates and received an annual stipend in
lieu of the court fees and confiscations that traditionally formed the
basis of their wealth. Later the magistrates assumed sole authority, and
in the Ciskei the chiefs were reduced to mere figureheads with judicial
and administrative authority passing wholly out of their hands. As the
Transkei was progressively annexed—from 1877 to 1894—the chiefs
were similarly reduced to stipendiaries. The government felt that the
chiefs were the focus of tribal resistance, or at least had been so in the
past, and it pursued a definite policy at that time of limiting their
powers. To all intents and purposes, chiefs were excluded from direct
participation in local government. Chiefs did continue to hear civil
cases under native law, but appeals from the courts of headmen could
bypass entirely the court of a chief and go directly to the court of the
magistrate, who was also the native commissioner. In fact, even the
headman's court could be bypassed, as there was free access to the court
of the native commissioner. This was, in effect, a system of direct rule.

THE TRANSKEI: LAND, PEOPLE, AND ADMINISTRATION

Administrative Structure

Although settlement is scattered, homesteads usually cluster in well-defined, named areas, separated from other similar clusters by a stream or fields or a stretch of grazing land. These areas of settlement are the *location sections*, each under a subheadman who is appointed by and directly responsible to the location headman (described below) for peace within his area, but who has no official status. Members of a location section are often related to one another, that is, there is a strong lineage core to the group; but substantial interlocation movement means that in the majority of cases the population is very mixed. A location section tends to have all its fields together in one area and grazes its stock on the same stretch of pasture. Living together naturally engenders a strong feeling of neighborliness and a community of interests which impart to the location section a quality of life similar to that of a typical village.

Four or five sections make up a *location*, with an average extent of perhaps six or seven square miles. A location and its subheadmen are under the control of a government-appointed headman, who is an African employee of what is today called the Department of Bantu Administration and Development. These locations have no traditional base, having been originally demarcated by the administration soon after annexation during the last quarter of the nineteenth century, but over the years they have emerged as the crucial administrative units, capable of arousing a high degree of loyalty on the part of their members.

Above the locations are two larger and commonly intersecting administrative units: (1) the magisterial district, under the control of a Bantu Affairs Commissioner, who is a White official of the Republic's Department of Bantu Administration and Development, and (2) the chiefdoms, which as we have noted, have been effectively under the control of the White bureaucracy since annexation. A number of locations, averaging perhaps thirty to forty, comprise a magisterial district, and there are twenty-six such districts in the Transkei. Until the establishment of the Transkei Legislative Assembly in 1963, their administration was coordinated by the Chief Magistrate and Bantu Affairs Commissioner for the Transkeian Territories, who had his headquarters at Umtata, the capital.

The chiefdoms, each under a chief with his council, partly coincide with, but sometimes cut across, the territorial administrative structure. Some chiefdoms coincide exactly with a magisterial district. A few include more than one district, but this is unusual. Most are composed of a smaller number of locations, so that a district frequently contains more than one chiefdom. The locations themselves are never divided between chiefdoms, and they compose the irreducible building blocks of the whole administrative system.

The pattern is thus one of a largely traditional territorial administrative system which includes progressively widening areas of authority from the homestead, location section, and location, to the chiefdom. On this structure is superimposed the bureaucratic magisterial district system.

Despite the changes instituted under the Bantu Authorities system (accepted in the Transkei in 1955) and the Transkei Constitution Act (implemented in late 1963), the magistrates remain the centers of power within the system. They continue to perform dual roles in the Transkei, depending on which segment of the population is concerned. To the White population the magistrate functions as such, thereby justifying his official designation. At the same time, his responsibilities for administering the comprehensive body of laws and regulations that govern the life of the African inhabitants of his district go far beyond those of his Department of Justice colleagues in the so-called White areas of the Republic and are in effect equivalent to those of Bantu Commissioners elsewhere. The magistrate is ultimately responsible for everything that occurs in his district—for its peace, prosperity, and still, to a degree, for its good government. Local engineering and agricultural experts, although technically employees of the new Transkei government and thus responsible to their respective departmental heads in Umtata, work in close collaboration with the magistrate. The magistrate is also inspecting officer for the jail that is a feature of every Transkei village. He is the fiscal officer who is responsible for collecting taxes. Until recently his office handled all welfare services such as poor relief, old-age pensions, and invalidity grants. All land matters are ultimately his responsibility, although the actual allocation of lands, originally left to the location headman, is under the Bantu Authorities system handled by the chief. The magistrate is frequently called upon to settle boundary disputes, both between locations and individual landowners. Although court work takes up much of his time, his administrative duties are many and varied.

There has always been some delegation of authority by the magistrate, first to his immediate staff, but more particularly in the past to the location headman. Although a criminal code, drawn up by the 1883 Commission on Native Laws and Customs and based on the Indian Penal Code, is in operation in the Transkei and effectively excludes traditional authorities from handling criminal cases, chiefs handle most minor civil cases, such as those concerned with family law, trespass, and land disputes. Minor criminal cases are heard by the magistrate with an appeal to a Circuit Court which sits twice a year, once at Kokstad and once at Umtata.

In noncriminal cases, traditional customary law is recognized,

provided that such Native law shall not be opposed to the principles of public policy or natural justice; provided further that it shall not be lawful for any court to declare that the customs of *lobola* or *bohadi* (i.e. bridewealth) or other similar custom is repugnant to such principles.[5]

Since about 1930 some of the more important chiefs have been officially accorded civil jurisdiction, and their courts then keep written records. All chiefs and headmen, however, regularly settle disputes and give judgments within their areas, as they have done since time immemorial. It is a type of limited self-government, an ordering of one's own affairs, that has been going on quietly and has been comparatively independent of the bureaucratic superstructure. These courts are not recognized, however, by the administration, and, in cases of appeal to the magistrate's court, all evidence is given *de novo*.

Administratively, headmen have had a wide range of functions. As laid down in the *Government Gazette Extraordinary* of December 21, 1928, they must "carry out such lawful orders and instructions as may from time to time be given to them," and assist all responsible government officials in the registration of taxpayers, the collection of taxes, the dipping of stock, and the eradication of noxious weeds, to name only some of the more important matters. They cannot be members of any political party, nor can they absent themselves from their area of jurisdiction for more than seven days without the authority of the magistrate. Their duties were and are time consuming and often irksome, and the pay is paltry. It is not surprising, therefore, that some men avoid office if possible, especially, as we shall see, since the Bantu Authorities system limited their powers and prestige in favor of that of the chiefs. Some headmen have been known to seek to supplement their meager income by accepting bribes. The post of headman is theoretically elective by all taxpayers in the location, but in practice it is almost invariably inherited through the male line. Sometimes headmen are of the royal lineage but more often the original incumbent was an outstanding commoner, placed over the location by the chief.

Local Representation

A third strand in the government of the Transkei, unique to it and the Ciskei, was the council or Bunga system, providing for a measure of direct election and representation. This important development in local government occurred in 1894 with the Glen Grey Act, which made effective the recommendations of the 1883 Cape Native Laws and Customs Commission's report. Of the two main provisions of the Act, namely, the introduction of a form of individual land tenure and the

5. Native Administration Act, 1927, Sect. 11(1).

establishment of a system of *local district councils*, only the latter need be considered here.

In 1894, by Transkeian Proclamation No. 352, the so-called Bunga system (from the Xhosa word meaning "a discussion," "a meeting") was applied tentatively to four districts and then extended until, by 1926, the system applied to the whole of the Transkei, with the exception of the White farming district of Mount Currie. For some years the areas of Eastern and Western Pondoland had a separate Pondoland General Council, but in 1931 all district councils in the Territories were federated in the United Transkeian Territories General Council, meeting annually in the imposing Bunga building in Umtata.

Each of the 26 Transkeian magisterial districts (that is, all except Mount Currie) was divided into four electoral areas or wards, with the landowners and taxpayers in each ward electing one member to the local district council. Two additional members were nominated by the magistrate to complete the six-member district council, which met under the chairmanship of the magistrate every second month. The strongly tribal nature of Pondo sentiments resulted in a modification, however, in their area. In Pondoland two members were elected by the taxpayers, two were nominated by the magistrates, and two were nominated by the paramount chief.

The United Transkeian Territories General Council (UTTGC), or Bunga, consisted of the Chief Magistrate of the Transkei, who acted as chairman, the 26 district magistrates, and three members appointed by each district council from among their number. The three paramount chiefs of Eastern Pondoland, Western Pondoland, and (after 1932) Tembuland (the Xhosa paramount chief was not officially recognized until after the Bantu Authorities system was introduced in 1956) sat on the Council ex officio, making 108 members in all. The function of the Bunga was originally confined, at least in theory, to discussing and expressing opinion on matters affecting the local population; but in 1932 its scope was extended to the discussion of any proposed legislation affecting Africans. Its resolutions were reviewed by a conference of official members—that is, the magistrates—before being submitted to the Governor-General for his information. The Bunga had limited control over certain locally raised funds, which were allocated mainly for road-building and other public works, agricultural improvements, and scholarships.

Summary of Transkeian Local Government to 1956

Until 1956, then, the interaction of bureaucratic, traditional, and elective advisory bodies formed the pattern of Transkeian local government. Despite the existence of the ultimately dominant magisterial bureaucratic structure, with its auxiliary bodies of police and agricultural staff, the informal moots and courts of headmen still functioned. And even the chiefs, the attempts of earlier administrations to curb their powers notwithstanding, still performed some administrative and judicial functions. Alongside these two structures operated the council system, based largely on popular elections and providing a third mechanism of local government. The distribution of authority among these structures—the traditional tribal system, the White administrative bureaucracy, and the local councils—was, however, uneven. Legitimized by the processes of outright conquest or of more or less peaceful annexation, ultimate authority at every level was vested in the government in Pretoria. In the Transkei the government was represented by the magistrates of the Department of Native Affairs, which was subsequently renamed the Department of Bantu Administration and Development.

The Bantu Authorities System

In 1955, as we have seen, the Bunga, at a special session, voted that the system of Bantu Authorities, provided for by Act No. 68 of 1951, be applied in the Transkei. This was effected by Proclamation No. 180 of 1956. The Bunga was then replaced by a Territorial Authority consisting entirely of chiefs (or councillors), and the structure at the lower levels was made to conform to the Bantu Authorities system.

To recapitulate, the Bantu Authorities system provided a three-tier— in the Transkei, a four-tier—structure of authority which emphasized the role of the chief under overall White control. The lowest level consisted of tribal authorities, each under a chief. In the Transkei (but nowhere else), the next level was the district, which grouped the relevant tribal authorities. Above this was the regional authority, which associated such tribal authorities, communities, or their combination as was determined. At the apex was a territorial authority consisting entirely of chiefs. It was the territorial authority that was principally affected by the Promotion of Bantu Self-Government Act of 1959, and the Transkei Constitution Act of 1963.

The tribal authority under the Bantu Authorities system is chosen partly by the chief and partly by the government. Under tribal custom, some persons choose themselves through their prestige or influence or relation to the chief; others are selected by the chief because of their particular usefulness to him. However, since the chief's councillors must, in effect, be approved by the Bantu Affairs Commissioner, those opposing the Bantu Authorities system have felt that it inhibits, if not prevents, the selection of independent-minded men.

As far as administration is concerned, the most significant change in the Transkei at the lowest level of administration was the shift in power from the headmen to the chiefs. Under Proclamation 110 of 1957, commonly known as the Jansen Proclamation, headmen lost independent authority in the allocation of land and also their judicial functions. Complaints were henceforth to be reported to the chief. The chief also assumed control over the allocation of land, which previously had been only his technical right.

This new division of authority between chiefs and headmen had wider consequences than might be expected from a cursory consideration. The headmen, most of whom, as we noted, were hereditary, now found themselves restricted to the administration of almost universally unpopular laws concerning the rehabilitation or betterment of land. Thus they tended to come into constant conflict with the villagers and to epitomize the dilemma of the African who is expected to direct his people toward useful but unpopular actions and who will gain the disapproval of the government if he does not succeed. With most of his powers removed, the headman ceased to carry his traditional prestige, while the limited remuneration, approximately £5 ($14) a month, was little enough recompense for the disfavor in which he found himself.

In the Transkei, as elsewhere, headmen have tended to divide into two categories. Some have definitely pitted themselves against the villagers and have been very strict in enforcing regulations. Feeling threatened by the antagonism of the villagers, they have sought the protection of progovernment chiefs and the native commissioner. Those who, on the other hand, have not accepted government policies and have attempted to maneuver on behalf of the villagers have been popular—the common phrase is "he is a man"—but they have walked a veritable tightrope. In a meeting of six or seven men participating in the selection of a headman, the latter was warned that his fate was likely to be either "fire or imprisonment." Fire would mean having the thatch of his hut burned by the villagers because they were angry at the way he carried out his duties; alternatively, imprisonment might be ordered by the chief or a government official if it were thought that the headman was not loyally carrying out his orders.

The other major change in the structure of government in the Transkei through acceptance of the Bantu Authorities system was at the territorial level. The Bunga, as we have seen, was replaced by the Territorial Authority, which was composed entirely of chiefs. Thus from 1956 until the Promotion of Bantu Self-Government Act of 1959 and, in particular, the Transkei Constitution Act, 1963, there was no elective element in the Transkeian structure above the district level— and only a modicum of election below that level.

The structure established as a consequence of the 1963 legislation reintroduced the practice of elections, as we shall see, for a limited number of representatives in the Legislative Assembly but on a much broader franchise. Moreover, the Transkei Legislative Assembly (TLA) gained some specific powers not possessed either by the Bunga, which was an advisory body, or by the Transkeian Territorial Authority. Like the TTA, the TLA is wholly African. The office of chief magistrate was abolished by the 1963 law, and contact between the TLA and the Republican government is now technically maintained through the resident commissioner-general for the Xhosa National Unit, who reports directly to the Minister of Bantu Administration and Development.

Conclusion

Thus the Transkei remains in a situation not unlike that of British colonies in their late preindependence stage. An exclusively African legislature, still only partially chosen by election, manages a limited number of subjects under the overall control of the Republican government. Moreover, at the district level power remains in the hands of magistrates who function as did district commissioners in British and French colonies.

What does not fit the colonial pattern are the double switches in the composition of the top territorial organ: at first in the mid-1950's away from the use of popular elections, and then in the early 1960's back to the use of elections but on a more direct basis. The first change, as we have seen, was from the quasi-representative and largely advisory body, the Bunga, meeting under a White chairman, to the Territorial Authority, which had a few more responsibilities and had an all-African membership but was composed wholly of chiefs. The second move was to establish the Legislative Assembly, an all-African body, composed partly of chiefs and partly of elected members, with some increased responsibilities and potential powers, although only for the rural areas of the Transkei and under the controls noted earlier.

The expressed and other reasons for these changes have been discussed earlier with reference to White-African political relations and the enactment of the 1951, 1959, and 1963 legislation. But it is also important to see how far back the Transkeian political tradition extends, and what issues most exercised its elected representatives in the Bunga.

5

The Bunga, 1920-1956

T HE BUNGA, or, as it was more officially termed, the
United Transkeian Territories General Council (UTTGC) was the major platform for self-expression in the Transkei from its establishment in
1931 until it transformed itself into the Transkeian Territorial Authority in 1956. Its forerunner was the Transkeian Territories General
Council (TTGC). This latter body, first established in 1894, as noted,
for the four districts of Butterworth, Idutywa, Nqamakwe, and Tsomo,
gradually expanded with the extension of the Bunga system to include
representatives from the new local district councils. Both councils, the
TTGC and the UTTGC, were quasi-popular bodies, but both were
chaired and directed by White officials. Neither ever had more than advisory powers. Both discussed the distribution of a small budget, consisting of funds raised within the Transkei to meet their limited local
responsibilities. An overwhelming proportion of the considerations in
the two councils focused on purely local and practical issues like cattle
dipping to combat disease, the building of minor roads, and markets.

Unless the government specifically asked for an opinion, the councils
were not supposed to concern themselves with political matters. Yet
every so often their members raised such issues. Particularly in regard
to the franchise, the strength of their feelings was obvious. On current
developments the councillors were acquainted to a striking degree with
discussions and developments in the central Parliament in Cape Town,

and also with comments in the press and other publications.

Three general topics received fairly constant consideration both in the TTGC and its successor, the UTTGC, and these comments cast a good deal of light upon the thinking of their members and their constituents. The first topic, and the one by far the most frequently raised, involved the general issue of African political representation within South Africa as a whole. This was hardly surprising since Africans who met the Cape-wide literacy and economic qualifications had voted on the common roll with Whites since the Cape received responsible government in 1854. By 1884, in fact, African voters numbered 47 per cent of the electorate in the five border constituencies of the Eastern Cape and over 50 per cent in two of them. Fearful of their political influence, a majority of the Whites in the Cape Legislative Assembly passed the Parliamentary Legislation Act in 1887, removing communal tenure of land as a qualification for the franchise. As a result 30,000 African electors were struck off the rolls. Five years later, property qualifications were raised, and an educational test was added. Even so, African voters held the balance of power in seven constituencies between 1896 and 1910, when South Africa became a self-governing Dominion of the British Commonwealth of Nations and thus in full control of its own internal policies.

The price paid for English-Afrikaner cooperation in the new Union of South Africa, which succeeded by only eight years the end of the Anglo-Boer War, was largely paid by non-Whites. They were denied seats in the national legislature under the South Africa Act of 1909, and their franchise remained almost wholly restricted to Cape Province. Nevertheless, in keeping with Cecil Rhodes's maxim of "equal rights for all educated men," the non-White franchise in that area was made the subject of one of the entrenched clauses of the Constitution, and hence could be amended only by a difficult procedure. Those interested in, as well as those opposing, non-White—and in particular African—political influence were well aware that the character of the existing franchise was crucial in determining its future extent.

The two other issues of a general character that were raised from time to time reflected the essentially conservative nature of the members of the Bunga. One was the fear of movements in the Transkei that might stir up the people and threaten both established authority and social conduct. The other was the attempt to define the status of chiefs. This latter issue interacts, naturally, with the ultimate establishment of the Bantu Authorities system and is of particular interest in this regard.

THE FRANCHISE

The conviction of councillors that the franchise is an essential and natural right pervades all their discussions on political representation.

TESTING GROUND: THE TRANSKEI

The earliest expression of aspiration and concern indicates both a naively optimistic hope of achieving equality with Whites within the Transkei and a preference for British, as compared to South African, administration. The latter is reminiscent of the abortive appeals made to Great Britain in 1914-15 by the newly organized South African Native National Congress (renamed the African National Congress in 1923), which fruitlessly sought through British action a reversal of the exclusion of Africans from seats in South Africa's national political institutions and of the restriction on African settlement outside the reserves embodied in the 1913 Land Act. Subsequently the Africans sent an unheard delegation to the Versailles Peace Conference. Transkeian discussions reflected this universal and continuing aspiration.

In 1920 one councillor moved in the TTGC that:

In the event of the Republican propaganda at present being prosecuted by a certain section of the people of this country materializing, the Imperial Government [will] take over the Natives of this country under its protection as was done in the case of Basutoland.[1]

This motion was apparently stimulated by General Hertzog's deputation to the Versailles Peace Conference to ask for a South African republic. In the debate in the Council, strong pro-British sentiments were expressed, and the treatment of Africans in the Cape Province was compared favorably to that in the Free State and the Transvaal. If separated from Great Britain, it was feared there might be a reversion "to the old state of the sjambok [a heavy, rhino-hide whip]." The motion did not go unopposed as one councillor, Chief S. Lehana, felt the issue was not pressing, but on a vote the motion was carried.

In the following year, 1921, the Council requested the government, to grant to Native voters all rights that were possessed by Whites in the Transkeian Territories. Those who supported the motion asserted that to be able to buy liquor and to travel without passes would create a sense of freedom, dignity, and responsibility. The one African critic of the motion argued that people might seek to qualify as voters in order to get rights, and then commit offenses such as being drunk. But the strongest opposition was put forward by a White magistrate who, though sympathetic to the Africans' feeling against "a badge of servitude," suggested that the seeming indignities—such as the restriction on buying liquor—might in fact promote their well-being. He compared the pass system to the passports which Whites in South Africa needed in order to go to England. Though he advised the Africans to be patient under their existing hardships and to hope for the future, and suggested

1. The references are in Transkeian Territories General Council, *Proceedings and Reports of Select Committees at the Session of 1920* (Umtata: The Territorial News, Ltd., 1920), pp. 92–93. All subsequent references will similarly be grouped together by year and debate.

that the motion be withdrawn, it was pushed through to a vote and carried.[2]

When the General Council next discussed voting rights, it was in a very different context. By 1926 attention focused on Prime Minister Hertzog's proposal to eliminate the Cape native suffrage. Alarmed by this proposal, the councillor from Xalanga, Elijah Qumata, moved that,

in view of the restlessness of native public opinion of this province caused by the Prime Minister's proposal to take away the Cape Native suffrage, a sacred right which has not been abused since the granting of responsible government in the Cape in 1854, the Transkeian Territories General Council should make representations to the Union Parliament to consider the advisability of affecting no change in the present system of direct representation.[3]

Interest in this issue in 1926 was evident and sincere; the speeches were long and the opinions outspoken. There was a general agreement that the right to vote was the right of the individual, a symbol of the justice of the British government and a mark that the Africans were the children of Britain. Less optimistic than five years before, the councillors now clearly sensed danger to the Africans' most effective means of exerting influence. It was agreed that a deputation of three members should proceed to Cape Town to present their resolution to Parliament, a rare instance of an attempt to make direct contact with the national government. The Council also set up a committee on the Prime Minister's native bills, and it is clear that the franchise question dominated its discussions.[4]

The major part of the debate took place in a committee of the General Council composed only of Africans, because of the restrictions on the discussion of political questions in a mixed group of Africans and officials. In its report, the committee claimed that the vote was a sacred inheritance, essential to native development. It urged the retention of the franchise and the right of direct voting for ordinary representatives in the House. In fact, so convinced was the committee of the paramount importance of voting privileges that it was prepared to forego all other legislative rights rather than part with the franchise. Only Chief Scanlen Lehana from Mount Fletcher and Jacob Manelle from Xalanga objected to this blanket proposal, and the report was adopted.

Though first raised by Prime Minister Hertzog in 1926, the so-called Hertzog settlement was not consummated until 1936, after the depression and political maneuvers had led to the formation of the United party. In the new party General Smuts agreed to serve under General Hertzog to provide a common front in the face of the economic crisis. As the price of unity, Smuts sacrificed his opposition to Hertzog's native bills. The Hertzog settlement involved three interrelated pro-

2. TTGC, (1921), pp. 92–94.
3. *Ibid.* (1926), pp. 119–26.
4. *Ibid.* (1927), pp. 44–45, 118–24.

posals: (1) to remove the Africans from the common roll in Cape Province (the only part of South Africa in which they could vote for the same representatives as did Whites); (2) to establish the Natives' Representative Council as a national advisory body composed of prominent Africans; and (3) to buy more land to consolidate current African holdings and bring them up to 13 per cent of the land area of South Africa.

Already in 1935, the Bunga, clearly alarmed about the threat to the franchise, agreed to the recommendations of its Select Committee on Laws and Native Customs that a special deputation should be sent to the central government to represent African views on the proposed legislation.[5] Ruling the issue a political matter, however, the chairman (a White magistrate) refused to permit discussion. In 1936 the story was different. The government itself sought the reactions of the Bunga to the native bills. The Secretary for Native Affairs explained the legislation to the Council and then retired to leave its members to discuss the subject. "It is on record," said the mover of the subsequent motion of disapproval,

that we decided that we would have nothing that would shake our franchise, and we would not sell it for anything. We are willing to take what Government offered us in the way of Council and land but those two things are not in any way to interfere with our franchise.[6]

The motion presented by Councillor J. Moshesh disapproved the government franchise plan in strong terms. He moved:

that this Council views with grave concern the Government's intention by its proposed legislation to abolish the existing form of franchise to natives and thereby tamper with the rights of citizenship and that this can only have the effect of undermining the good feeling between European and native which has hereto existed. This Council therefore expresses its profound disapproval.

Harking back to the 1920 differentiation between the British government and the South African legislature, Councillor Moshesh asked his fellow members "to bear in mind that we are here today dealing with the great gift that was given to us by our beloved Queen Victoria the Good, and that now the Union Parliament wishes to abolish it."

Although on an earlier occasion (described later in relation to the Council's reactions to outside movements), the Transkeian Territories General Council had expressed itself critically in regard to the African National Congress, this crisis over the removal of Africans from the common roll saw the Bunga align itself with urban protests. This is best described in Moshesh's own words:

5. United Transkeian Territories General Council, *Proceedings and Reports of Select Committees at the Session of 1935* (King William's Town: The King Printing Co., Ltd., 1935), p. 214.
6. *Ibid.* (1936), pp. 281–86 for the debate.

Our views then expressed were, I believe, placed before the Government. We were not satisfied with that. A meeting [the national meeting of protest called by the newly constituted All African Convention under Dr. D. D. T. Jabavu] was again called by the Natives themselves which met at Bloemfontein, and there were Natives there from all parts of South Africa. I am glad to say that all parts were represented and I must here thank the three Northern provinces who said that they would not accept anything which would tamper with the Native franchise existing in the Colony though they were quite willing to take anything else the Government offered them. The resolution passed, was taken to Cape Town by the delegates appointed by that meeting and was presented to General Hertzog himself. His replies are well known. He refused to listen to anything that was suggested to him by these delegates of ours, and told them he would push on with the bill.

Moshesh, in the same speech, and with the evident approval of the Bunga, also dissociated himself from the compromise they thought Professor Jabavu had accepted, though he was finally to regret it. Under this so-called compromise, the Africans taken off the common roll were to be grouped into three constituencies, each of which was to elect one White to sit in the House of Assembly. Moshesh described to the members how he believed this compromise had been reached. He said:

The delegates came home and told us what had happened. After they got home they were recalled to Cape Town. They were not then sent down by us who sent them originally; they were called by a quite different body of people. A compromise was suggested in Cape Town which was put to the Natives who were down there. The money which took these delegates there was not ours; they were not sent down by us. We therefore do not recognize them.

Moshesh continued by reading a letter from Mr. L. D. Gilson, member of Parliament for Griqualand, in which the latter said that he and two or three others had met Jabavu "and other representative Cape Native voters" and had found them "in full agreement with our suggestion that we should try and effect a compromise" along the lines finally decided.

Speaking with scorn of this action, Moshesh asked rhetorically:

Is it possible that they could make such a suggestion knowing very well that this compromise was going to take away our franchise, for they have been laboring all these years in order to obtain this? Is it possible for us Natives to say we are represented by these gentlemen? I say the compromise is not ours and that the people who agreed to it were not sent by us. . . . I therefore call this a white compromise not a Native compromise, and this will bring about misunderstanding between European and Native. The one will not be able to trust the other, and whose handiwork is it? We are not willing under any circumstances to hand over our franchise to anybody. . . . I therefore call upon you Councillors when dealing with this subject to know that the most sacred gift that we have is about to be taken away.

Others were no less forceful in their criticism. Seconding the motion of Moshesh, Councillor L. Bam declared:

Today, with the franchise being taken away from us it means that the door is being closed against us. We think that a great privilege is being tampered with for the first time in the history of the British Government.

Shrewdly analyzing the political realities, Bam declared:

We are now told that there are 150 members of Parliament altogether, and I would ask what three members will avail against 150 men? There is no provision made for an increase in the number of members to represent Native interests as the number of Native voters increases. That is why I say we are satisfied with the little we have had.

Another councillor, G. Dana, commented sarcastically:

Natives are in a majority compared with Europeans. This Union Government is known as a democratic government. If that is true it is strange that we should be represented by three members when the Europeans are represented by a hundred and fifty. That could never satisfy the Natives of South Africa.

In this stringent criticism of the government action of removing Africans from the common roll and replacing this representation with what the councillors clearly felt was a much less adequate means of expressing their opinions, the Bunga members were aware of the government's proposals for the Natives' Representative Council and for buying more land. They considered both to have been already promised to them. Councillor P. Xabanisa pointed out that, under Act 23 of 1920, it had been stated that councils would be introduced in all the provinces of South Africa. As for land, he cited the 1913 Act, and the work of the Beaumont, Scully, and Stanford commissions, all of which were designed to divide the land between Africans and Whites. "What sort of man would he be who came to buy an ox and gave you in payment a horse that was already yours?" he commented scornfully. This he followed by saying that "the government must know our natural right in the land as being the Native People of this country." It is likely there would have been still further speeches had not the chairman, a White official, brought the discussion to an end. It should be noted that the motion proposed by Councillor Moshesh was approved unanimously. The significance of the debate lies in the sentiments expressed, for there is no indication that the motion had any effect on those in the White-controlled Parliament who were able to determine policy.

Thwarted in their efforts to retain their franchise on the common roll, Bunga members did not renounce their aspiration to possess the full political rights of citizenship. A 1943 motion opposing segregation, and a warning the same year that insecurity of land tenure (under section 5 of the Native Administration Act, No. 38 of 1927) might open the way to a fifth column, by promoting insecurity and discontent, made it clear that there was continued consideration in the Bunga of African disabilities. In 1945, and in the succeeding years, such consideration gave rise to a series of forcefully discussed motions centering around the denial of civil rights to Africans; discrimination on the basis of skin color;[7] and lack of citizenship rights.[8]

More positively, Bunga members expressed their desire for extension to the other provinces of the franchise rights under the Representation of Natives Act (that is, the right of Africans in the Cape to elect three Whites to represent them in the House of Assembly in Cape Town) and an increase in the members elected to the House of Assembly under this Act from three to thirty.[9] They also sought an amendment of the law that would allow Africans to represent Africans in Parliament.[10]

In 1952 the Bunga members repeated their desire for direct representation by Africans in the legislative body of the Union of South Africa,[11] and the next year they added a request for the calling of a national convention to ease "racial tension by the review, repeal, or amendment of such laws as are irksome to the majority of South Africans of all races."[12] Also in 1953, they voted "that the Government be respectfully requested to grant Natives in the Union of South Africa representation in Parliament by their own people in proportion to their number." Thus, almost every year saw a motion in the Bunga referring to the restoration of the Cape African vote on the common roll, or for representation of Africans by Africans in Parliament.

At the end of World War II, the framework within which civil rights were requested was "the declared aims of Allied nations." (These aims are similarly referred to by the African National Congress in its *Atlantic Charter from the Africans' Point of View,* which was incorporated with the *Bill of Rights,* adopted at the 1945 ANC Annual Conference, and published as *African Claims in South Africa.*)[13] The civil rights specified by the Bunga were "freedom of occupation, freedom of movement and the rights of free nations under the British flag so that people can discuss their matters freely."[14]

The immediate reference was to a proclamation[15] under which the African people of Natal, the Transvaal, and the Free State were not to hold any meetings except religious ones. In seconding a motion of Councillor Dana criticizing the denial of civil rights to non-Whites, T. Ntintili from Tsomo asked:

7. *Ibid.* (1945), pp. 100–1.
8. *Ibid.* (1946), pp. 60–61.
9. *Ibid.* (1947), p. 53.
10. *Ibid.* (1948), pp. 54, 57.
11. *Ibid.* (1952), pp. 125, 135–36.
12. *Ibid.* (1953), pp. 54–58.
13. Congress Series No. 11, Johannesburg: ANC, (1945).
14. UTTGC, *Proceedings* (1945), p. 100.
15. No. 31 of 1945, in the *Government Gazette,* March 2, 1945.

that the freedom of all nations, which were the last words in the mouth of the late President Roosevelt, should come and reign in this country so that those white South Africans who are wedded to the principles of race separation and race segregation should now abandon those principles.[16]

This motion was carried. Immediately thereafter, Councillor Dana introduced a second motion criticizing discrimination on the basis of skin color. Speaking to his motion, Dana warned that "the Union legislation is driving the natives to Communism . . . [for] Communism knows no color bar." This motion was also passed.

NATIONAL REPRESENTATION

Though the issue of the franchise on the common roll remained constantly to the fore in the Bunga, a good deal of attention was also directed toward the Natives' Representative Council. Whether or not prominent Africans should accept membership in this government-established advisory body had been hotly disputed among Africans represented in their two national organizations existing after 1936: the All African Convention, which continued in existence despite its failure to prevent the Hertzog-Smuts legislation removing Africans from the common roll; and the longer established, and ultimately more influential, African National Congress. The former, the AAC, was to give rise in the 1940's to the Non-European Unity Movement, an association of like-minded Coloureds and Africans in a program of noncollaboration with any government-endorsed organization until full political and civil rights were granted to non-Whites. The African National Congress was stimulated in the same period by the rise of its dynamic Youth League, which similarly claimed full rights in the South African society and which late in the 1940's endorsed noncollaboration. On the other hand, older ANC members were prepared to work through the Natives' Representative Council until 1946, that is, as long as it appeared to offer a channel of influence on the White-controlled government.

It was not these issues, however, that originally concerned the Bunga in relation to the NRC, but objections raised by Councillor G. Dana to the presence of chiefs and headmen on that body. These comments can be better considered in relation to the issue of the status of chiefs, and they have an obvious relevance to the establishment of the Bantu Authorities system, the Transkeian Territorial Authority, and, ultimately, the Transkei Legislative Assembly.

The Bunga was not unaware, however, of the broader issues with which the NRC was concerned. When the NRC ceased its sessions in 1946 in protest at the failure of the government to consult it at the time

16. UTTGC, *Proceedings* (1945), pp. 101–2.

of the Witwatersrand strike by African miners, the Bunga endorsed its action. The Bunga also approved a lengthy proposal by Councillor Dana that the NRC'S African membership be increased, and that the Council should be given legislative powers with respect to African affairs so that it "shall become an impressive instrument in South African native administration."[17] A year later, however, the Bunga proved strangely reluctant to discuss the proposals of General Smuts to provide quasi-legislative powers for the NRC in relation to African areas—the Prime Minister's final though abortive effort to ease the breach between himself and that body. This suggestion, in any event, had no chance of being implemented, as we have seen, since the Smuts government was replaced by the Nationalists in May, 1948. That the Bunga's predominant concern remained its opposition to the 1936 Hertzog laws was reasserted in its rejection of a motion of regret in 1949 at the abolition of the Natives' Representative Council. Realistically, its members recognized that there was no substitute for the right to vote on the common roll.

ATTITUDES TOWARD POLITICAL MOVEMENTS

Though alert to the importance of national representation through which to try to secure rights and some measure of equality for Africans, the Bunga showed itself essentially conservative concerning political activities within the Transkei itself. Strongly conscious of their own dignity and sense of responsibility, they reacted to political movements brought to their attention with a sense of the need for order and respect for governmental authority, and a fear that Africans might discredit themselves in White eyes. Only on rare occasions was there discussion in the Councils of movements which might disrupt order. These were primarily regional issues, raised by representatives of the areas concerned and not by aspiring leaders using the matter in order to promote their own interests. At least until the 1940's the Transkei seems to have been little touched directly by the ferment of African urban-based political movements—the African National Congress and the All African Convention. This relative political quiescence of the Transkei throws into sharp relief the constant and vehement discussions in the Bunga concerning the loss by Africans in the Cape of the franchise on the common roll.

Indeed, an outspokenly critical comment on the African National Congress occurred in the Transkeian Territories General Council in 1925, a comment referring with obvious irritation to what was looked on as an anti-British move on the part of the Congress. Councillor

17. *Ibid.* (1947), p. 53.

Moshesh, who, as we have seen, later took a leading role in protest against the Hertzog laws, declared in an unopposed motion that:

this Council, representing the natives of the Transkeian Territories disassociates itself absolutely and entirely from the action of the African Native Congress in issuing a manifesto to native organizations directing them to refrain from participation in the festivities incidental to the visit of His Royal Highness, the Prince of Wales.[18]

Moshesh continued by commenting that "of late people from all parts of the world, people whose character is known to be bad in their own parts, have gone to Johannesburg and organized a Native Congress." (The Congress had, in fact, been organized in 1912.) He felt that this Congress was trying to upset the country. In relation to its attempts to get higher pay for mine workers, he added: "The members of the Congress pretended they were the voice of the people whereas they were only there for their own benefit and for the benefit of nobody else." Two other councillors also criticized the Congress and the motion was carried unanimously. It is not without relevance, however, that at the same session Councillor Sakwe from Butterworth moved that a petition should be presented at the bar of the House of Assembly protesting the color bar provisions of the Mines and Works legislation, a motion that was carried unanimously. There was also a motion against the proposed segregation policy in the Union, showing that however much the councillors might be suspicious of the actions of the Congress, they felt impelled toward the same kind of protests.

Stronger emotions appear to have been roused by two movements inside the Transkei itself which the councillors felt might threaten the area's stability. Even so, the so-called Wellington Movement, which began in 1921 when Wellington Butelezi went to the Transkei and claimed that American Negroes would soon come in planes to free the Africans, did not attract the Council's attention until 1927. In that year, however, Peter Malandu from Mount Fletcher proposed that the government take immediate steps to check the movement, and he received firm and vociferous support in his opposition to the influences Wellington typified. The councillors, rather than concerning themselves with the local grievances the movement built upon, argued that the movement threatened to undermine the loyalty of the people to the government, and feared the native people might easily be misled. They felt that it was essential, therefore, that some action be taken immediately. There was some attempt to blame the government for the delay in taking action against the ferment raised by the Wellington Movement, and suggestions were made by several councillors that chiefs and headmen be given authority to deal with people who called "strange meetings." From another side, Elisha Mda from Umtata argued per-

18. TTGC, *Proceedings* (1925), p. 202.

suasively that the fault lay not with the law nor with the administration of the law, but with the people themselves for not reporting disturbances quickly enough.[19]

In 1935, the Select Committee on Laws and Native Customs of the Bunga made recommendations for controlling unauthorized meetings in native locations. This proposal may well have been related to concern over the Wellington Movement. The Committee recommended that headmen report unlawful or undesirable meetings, and that chiefs and headmen be empowered to disperse or arrest leaders of such meetings. The proposal sought to avoid the delay that was possible under the Riotous Assemblies Act whose procedures could only be set in motion on the direction of a Minister.[20] This recommendation was followed the succeeding year with a motion by E. C. Bam from Tsolo requesting a law prohibiting meetings by a group called "Americans." It was charged that this group withdrew their children from, and therefore hurt, the schools; refused to pay taxes or respect chiefs; and appeared not to want to live peacefully. Other districts, which did not experience these influences directly, supported the Tsolo councillor and the motion was carried.[21]

The only other mention of a political movement came as a warning from the White chairman of the Bunga in his opening address on April 16, 1941. Noting that there was an increasing number of semipolitical societies, but not identifying them, the chairman recommended that councillors use their influence to check the formation of such societies.[22] Although he suggested that discussions be held in the Bunga, where they would relate to the general welfare, councillors did not raise the issue implied in this warning.

THE STATUS OF CHIEFS

Highly relevant to the future acceptance of the Bantu Authorities system was the spasmodic but fairly frequent consideration in the Bunga of the status of chiefs. This subject reflected the increasing awareness of the councillors that there was a potential and probably real role conflict confronting the chief in his dual position as representative of his tribe and as an administrative official of the government.

Before this role conflict had crystallized in the minds of the councillors, however, deep concern was expressed regarding the effects of the government's policy of limiting the chiefs' power for fear that the chiefs might take an antigovernment position. The earlier governmental policy

19. *Ibid.* (1927), pp. 45–56.
20. UTTGC, *Proceedings* (1935), pp. 211–12.
21. *Ibid.* (1936), pp. 27–78.
22. *Ibid.* (1941), pp. 48–49.

of systematically smashing the independent power of the chiefs was a legacy of the long series of cattle wars in the eastern Cape that ended only in 1877. The government's position had also been influenced by the Zulu rebellion of 1906. Chief S. Lehana, councillor from Mount Fletcher, made the first direct appeal for clarification of the status of chiefs and headmen on April 7, 1913.[23] This appeal was followed by motions in 1916 and 1917 and by a motion of May 16, 1921, that the Council should send a delegation to interview the Native Affairs Commission on the status of hereditary chiefs in the Territories.[24] The burden of Lehana's complaint was that hereditary chiefs were losing the respect of their people because of lack of clarity over their powers and that as a result damage was being done to the administrative system. In a distinction of particular significance in view of the subsequent establishment of the Bantu Authorities system, Lehana pointed out that only the duties of the headman were officially defined, whereas Africans had always seen a distinct difference between a chief and a headman. Interestingly, in the light of later developments, there was apparently little general concern for the subject of Chief Lehana's motion in 1913, and no comments upon it, although—like most other proposals—it was carried unanimously.

The government's main concern over the position of chiefs as potential centers of disaffection appeared in a 1921 debate. Citing the government's 1914 reply to his motion, "that if the present practice was to be altered there would be wars among the natives," Lehana claimed that there were chiefs who did not fight against the government but yielded to all its proposals, such as levying taxation. His concern was principally for the prestige and ceremonial role of the chief: "To the native people, the chief is like the sun—a sacred thing, there to give life to the world." Africans, he said, "were quite willing to live under the Government but it should not destroy the nation by cutting off its head." Again councillors expressed little concern, but they agreed to appoint a deputation to raise the matter with the government.

When the question of the role of the chiefs came up again in 1927, it was largely debated by the White magistrates; African members appeared surprisingly indifferent to the outcome. Underlining the unprecedented responsibilities of a "new era" (presumably the Hertzog proposals that ultimately, somewhat modified, were acted on in 1936), Magistrate Barrett from the Nqamakwe district suggested that the government had gone too far in trying to abolish old customs and to substitute new ones. The main point discussed by the magistrates, however, was that of allocating further responsibilities to native administra-

23. TTGC, *Proceedings* (1913), pp. 37–39.
24. *Ibid.* (1921), pp. 46–48.

tors, and little distinction was made either by Whites or Africans between traditional chiefs and government-appointed headmen.[25]

Not until 1930 did the councillors make a serious effort to clarify their attitude toward the role of traditional chiefs.[26] When they did so, there emerged on the floor of the Council for the first time a recognition of the difficulty of maintaining the traditional role of the chief in the face of a White-defined legal system. With Chief Lehana again leading the way, the councillors debated a motion requesting authority for recognized chiefs in the Transkei to hear civil and criminal cases. Arguing that "what God created should not be disregarded," Chief Lehana and his supporters declared that this expansion of chiefly authority was essential for maintaining tribal custom and good administration. Although all the councillors obviously felt that chieftainship was important for maintaining order, both Josiah Mlokoti from Tsomo and Charles Sakwe argued that once the government's legal system had been established, untrained chiefs could not administer it. In the end the motion was carried, although the chairman pointed out that in any case criminal and civil jurisdiction would not be accorded to the chiefs.

That there was no notion of chiefs exercising an independent authority was clearly reflected in two debates in 1931. When W. D. Cingo of Flagstaff moved for closer consultation between chiefs and White magistrates, he emphasized that the objective was to enable a chief to learn the current method of administration, not in any way to challenge the authority of the magistrate.[27] There was also no challenge to the statement by R. D. H. Barry, magistrate from Umtata, that the government was the sole authority. On the contrary, as E. Pinyane of Tabankulu phrased it: "We admit we are all the children of the government. The chiefs themselves are the government's children." Cingo's motion was, in fact, withdrawn in belated recognition of the impossibility of establishing equality in the relations between the councillors and the magistrates.

While primary concern in the Bunga was focused on the 1936 Hertzog legislation, the councillors showed renewed and persistent interest between 1935 and 1939 in the status of chiefs. The first of the motions on the subject, raised by Saul Mabude of Lusikisiki on April 4, 1935, sought to refer certain disputes, those concerning the allocation of land by headmen, to the appropriate chief before referring them to the magistrate.[28] By this time the government's position in regard to the chiefs had become somewhat more sympathetic; the official response was that "there is not the slightest intention on the part of the Administration to shut the Chief out altogether, but to invite his advice on large matters

25. *Ibid.* (1927), pp. 155–56.
26. *Ibid.* (1930), pp. 131–36.
27. UTTGC, *Proceedings* (1931), pp. 178–84.
28. *Ibid.* (1935), pp. 133–34, 137–38.

rather than trivial land matters." Despite the earlier rebuffs, W. W. Dana, the articulate councillor from Lusikisiki, moved in 1936 that all authorized chiefs in the Transkeian Territories, regardless of their education, be authorized to hear and determine civil claims arising out of native law and custom.[29] This motion was repeated in 1939 under the same sponsorship and with the justification that a chief without such powers did not gain respect.

In the meantime, the Bunga had also agreed that there was a clear distinction between a headman (who was only a paid servant), a constable, and a chief, since the last could not be pensioned off because there was no end to his term.[30] A further distinction was later sought by Councillor W. W. Dana in a motion seeking to prohibit "subsidized chiefs and headmen on account of their function and status from being eligible for nomination and election as members of the Natives' Representative Council." In this debate there appears a clear notion of potential role conflict, for Dana justified his motion by saying that "our people look upon the chief as an infallible person—one who never makes a mistake." Thus he found it unsuitable "that in the Natives' Representative Council, to which they may be appointed, the works of a leader are not above criticism."[31]

The distinction that was emerging was between the ceremonial and the administrative roles of the chief. In the first of these roles the chief was looked on as the head of his people, its guide and high priest, and one above criticism because of his representational role on behalf of the tribe. In the second, he had administrative and quasi-political responsibilities which would inevitably lead him as a person into consideration of policy and to decisions which were necessarily subject to criticism. Not only was there a potential conflict of roles but also a fear that participation in a particular institution, in this case the Natives' Representative Council, would impair, if not destroy, the traditional, ceremonial, and representational role felt to be so important for the cohesion of the tribe.

Rather surprisingly, it was not the 1941 and 1942 reports of the Bunga Select Committee on the Privileges of Chiefs and Headmen, but a debate in 1943 on the same issue of prohibiting chiefs and headmen from being eligible for membership on the Natives' Representative Council that precipitated the most searching discussion on the role of chiefs.[32] In 1941 the Select Committee's report concentrated primarily on the abuse of the custom of receiving presents—in effect, on bribery and corruption. The 1942 report attempted to outline in some detail the status and financial needs of the chief, but did not delineate his duties or

29. *Ibid.* (1936), pp. 89–91.
30. *Ibid.* (1936), pp. 209–11.
31. *Ibid.* (1939), pp. 114–15.
32. *Ibid.* (1941), p. 169, and (1942), pp. 125–27.

responsibilities. In 1943 when Councillor Dana again introduced his motion opposing the selection of chiefs and headmen for the Natives' Representative Council, the basic issues and differences of opinion became apparent. The discussion is the more significant because for the first time Chief Douglas Ndamase—the nephew of Chief Victor Poto, who was a member of the NRC from 1937 to 1951, and subsequently titular head of the opposition Democratic party in the Transkei—entered into the discussion.

Dana stated his position well at the beginning of the debate. He declared that:

We are living in critical days. We have chiefs in the Native parliament [the Natives' Representative Council], and they are liable to be attacked by newspapers and other people. And that is not in accordance with our custom. They are attacked even by commoners, a sort of democracy's criticism, but it is not nice to see our chiefs being criticized, and I do not like to hear nasty things said about them. They should not be treated like commoners.[33]

Dana added another reason why he believed that chiefs were not appropriate members of such bodies as the NRC:

Whenever our chiefs go around on their tours as representatives of the Natives Representative Council, I am always ashamed to put questions to the chiefs. I do not like asking why this, that or other is done. When it comes to my equal, I ask as many questions as I like.

Still another aspect of role conflict was brought out by his seconder, Councillor Mlandu, when he asked: "Can one expect chiefs who are government servants to have the courage to criticize the Prime Minister?" Mlandu continued, saying, "Whether the chief goes as Government nominee or as elected representative of the people, he cannot freely express his views." The opposition to the presence of chiefs in what was looked on as a political body, the Natives' Representative Council, thus rested on two main arguments.

The contrary position, that chiefs and headmen were leaders of the people and as such should "lead the people to civilization," was raised in this debate by Chief Douglas Ndamase of Western Pondoland. It was the basic argument which later would be used to justify the Nationalist government's Bantu Authorities system, namely, that it is the "natural leaders of the Africans, i.e., the chiefs" who should assume administrative direction under White control. In the long run, Douglas Ndamase was to change his position under pressure from his people and as the Transkei assumed its Bantustan status. In this later period he came to endorse the distinction between the traditional leader, who should have an honorary and upper-house role, and the elected representative, who should have power. In 1943, however, Ndamase's opposition led to the defeat of Dana's motion.

33. *Ibid.* (1943), p. 102.

Relative to the Bantustan status achieved by the Transkei in 1963, by far the most significant motion made in the history of Bunga came in 1944 when Councillor Qamata from Emigrant Tembuland, possibly with the knowledge and approval of Kaiser Matanzima, future Chief Minister of the Transkei, proposed that:

as a post-war reconstruction measure this Council requests the Government declare the Transkeian Territories a Union Native Province or State with sovereign rights in the administration of government and its affairs and people.[34]

Both the clear request for a self-governing state and the fact that it came from Emigrant Tembuland are significant, showing as they do that persons in this area held this idea at least as early as 1944.

Particularly striking were the reasons given to justify so radical a proposal. Pointing out that the African problem had existed from the day the first White set foot on the coast of South Africa, and that various governments had tried to solve it, Qamata seized on Smuts's 1942 comment that segregation had been a failure. Qamata pushed the point to one of its logical terminations: that the application of segregation had not been carried to "its legitimate conclusion." If "we are allotted our own part of the country in which to reside, with the Europeans in a separate area," he said, "the position will be solved." The Whites would "protect us from the enemy outside and they will be our trustees in every way." He went on to argue:

Let us have an opportunity to stand on our own two feet. This country is large enough and rich enough. When you regard the extent and wealth of the country you will find there is no place for the Native. . . . There is no hope that we will ever be anything under existing circumstances under the policy of the Union Government.

Then with unusual frankness he declared:

It is not always true when we affirm our love towards the Union Government, and we say we like our Government. We say these things because we hope the Government will be persuaded and take us into its confidence.

TOWARD THE BANTU AUTHORITIES SYSTEM

Of the issues that have been considered so far in this chapter—and they are the only issues of a general nature that exercised the General Councils during their respective lifetimes—by far the greatest amount of attention and concern was directed against the removal of Africans from the common roll. There is no question but that the councillors were fully aware of the significance of the franchise and of the fact that

34. *Ibid.* (1944), p. 81.

Africans had considerably more influence when they voted along with White people for the same representatives than they had when they were placed on a separate roll to elect their own White representatives. This concern over the loss of common voting rights did not diminish with time. It is significant in this regard that when D. D. P. Ndamase spoke favorably of the Bantu Authorities system in the 1955 session of the Bunga, he coupled his remarks with requests for local self-government that "will ultimately lead to direct representation in Parliament."[35] No objective was ever held so firmly and so consistently as restoration of the common roll franchise.

One may wonder why the leaders of the Transkei, a relatively undeveloped area without adequate resources even to feed its own people, should have been so concerned about a political right. The discussions in both General Councils show considerable sophistication, a knowledge of what was being discussed outside the territory, particularly in Parliament, and an awareness of trends of opinion in the urban areas (although there are extremely few direct references to these developments). Yet, even with much less sophistication, it would not have been difficult for the councillors to appreciate the loss involved in the African removal from the common roll. They could easily see that politics were paramount in the decisions affecting their present conditions and their future. Without means of political pressure, they knew they were at the mercy of the White policy-makers in Cape Town and the White administrators in Pretoria. They were shrewd enough to recognize that no alternative means of pressure existed for them.

The insistence of the councillors upon the loyalty, obedience, and respect of the Africans for the government no doubt had a genuine basis in the friendly relationship that has nearly always existed between Africans and White administrators and residents within the Transkei itself. But whether or not they had been outside the Transkei, the councillors well knew the conditions of racial segregation imposed there. They passed resolution after resolution regretting this imposed segregation. Only in the one motion by Councillor Qamata from Emigrant Tembuland in 1944, and in a couple of comments during the same session, was there any acceptance of the view that since segregation was inevitable it might be ameliorated by reducing the degree of control by Whites within the limited African areas. Persistent opposition to discrimination based on race and continued awareness of the significance of political power form the general context within which the Bantu Authorities system was accepted for the Territory by the Bunga in 1955.

In the 1951 debate on the Bantu Authorities Bill, the Minister of Native Affairs had made it clear that he had no intention of forcing the Transkei or Ciskei to accept the Bantu Authorities system.[36] Why then

35. *Ibid.* (1955), p. 33.
36. *Ibid.* (1953), p. 67.

did the Bunga accept the principles of the Bantu Authorities Act in 1955 and, in effect, vote itself out of existence?

Part of the appeal to the Bunga members was that, unlike the situation in most other African areas in the country, there already existed in the Transkei a structure extending to the top level. Thus the transformation into the Bantu Authorities system would not involve losing their four-tiered structure, and, they were assured, not many of them would be eliminated from political responsibilities. These responsibilities, in turn, were outlined as being more substantial than the purely advisory ones to which the Bunga was limited. In essence, therefore, it probably appeared to the members of the Bunga that the Bantu Authorities system would provide more power for Africans and that they themselves would be the people to exercise this power.

This view is borne out by the comment of Councillor H. H. Masebe, who moved the acceptance of the Bantu Authorities Act, when he said:

I take it that the purpose of the Act is to enable the Bantu people to integrate themselves, to control and administer their own affairs, so that all matters concerning them will be handled exclusively by them.[37]

He was seconded by Councillor D. D. P. Ndamase, who endorsed the move as "a limited opportunity for self-help." One of the more articulate of the councillors, C. K. Sakwe, commented that "the Bantu Authorities Act is not in opposition to the Bunga." Since there was no further room for expansion of the functions and provisions of the Bunga he was ready to work through the Bantu Authorities system. This view was also endorsed by S. Mabude. The secretary, C. B. Young, declared that there is "little difference between the function and duties of a system based on the Bunga or under the Bantu Authorities Act," but suggested that there was a wide difference in regard to their constitutions since "one is based on a system of Westernization. The other is based on the traditional Bantu ideas." From the reactions in the Bunga, it may have been still more important in their decision that he noted that various revenues from White traders, fines, and so forth, would now come into "your coffers if the matter is properly arranged."

Although a special Research Committee of the Bunga was appointed in 1955 to investigate the introduction of the Bantu Authorities system into the Transkei—with special concern that the central integrity of the Transkei would not be adversely affected—the crucial decision had been taken. In the following year the draft proclamation was discussed, but with little comment of interest. For better or worse, the Transkei had adopted the Bantu Authorities system. Although it could not be foreseen at that point, it had already started on the road toward becoming the first Bantustan.

37. *Ibid.* (1955), pp. 32–36.

Section IV
A Bantustan in Being

6

Constitution-Making for the Transkei

THE LOCAL ACTION sparking the process of constitution-making for the Transkei was unexpected and surprisingly orthodox, at least in form. On April 21, 1961, during a session of the Transkeian Territorial Authority, Lingham Maninjwa, a commoner of Port St. Johns, Western Pondoland, rose in the Bunga building in Umtata and moved "That . . . this Territorial Authority in session respectfully requests the Government to declare the Transkei Territories as a whole a self-governing state under the control of the Bantu people."[1]

This motion sparked a lively debate. Chiefs and headmen, some of them well known for their support of the South African government, now challenged the government to prove the sincerity of its previous declarations regarding separate political advance for the African. Members rose to demand nothing less than complete freedom and independence for the Transkei, and an amendment called for the inclusion of the neighboring Ciskei in a self-governing Transkei.

Despite the fact that Maninjwa had tabled his motion two days earlier, White officials in Umtata appear to have been unprepared for the consequences of its introduction. During the midafternoon tea ad-

1. Transkei Territorial Authority, *Proceedings and Reports of Select Committees at the Session of 1961* (Umtata: Territorial Printers, 1961), pp. 49–52. Here and subsequently references to the same debate are found within the pages cited.

113

journment, Hans Abraham, Commissioner-General for the Xhosa National Unit and Umtata "ambassador" of the Union Cabinet, unexpectedly appeared outside the debating chamber and held private conversations with two White officials and Chief Kaiser D. Matanzima, the presiding officer of the Authority and an open sympathizer with government policy.[2] Shortly after the TTA session reconvened, Chief Matanzima adjourned the debate and declared that the matter would be postponed indefinitely.

RECESS COMMITTEE

Five days later, the question of Transkeian self-government was raised again. M. D. C. de Wet Nel, Minister of Bantu Administration and Development, in the meantime had let it be known in Cape Town that the government had no objection to the devolution of power to Africans to rule themselves in the Bantu "homelands." All the signs are there," he said, "that self-government will come soon in the Transkei."[3] Maninjwa withdrew his motion, and the TTA unanimously resolved "to appoint a recess committee of 27 members, . . . to go into the implications of the granting or otherwise of self-government to this Authority during the next session."

Fourteen chiefs and thirteen ordinary councillors, including Maninjwa and Chief Matanzima, were chosen by the TTA on April 28, 1961, to be members of the Recess Committee. In ending the debate, Matanzima had declared that the decision of the TTA was an "unequivocal rejection of the policy of a multiracial society." Though unchallenged then, this was a conclusion which many were to oppose thereafter.

Despite the obvious importance of its mandate the Recess Committee did not meet for nine months, not until January 31, 1962. In December, 1961, however, the executive committee of the TTA and some others traveled to Pretoria to meet with Minister de Wet Nel. During their visit they had an unexpected interview with the Prime Minister, Dr.Verwoerd, who, as we know, was a former Minister of Native Affairs. Dr. Verwoerd told the Transkei delegates that the government was prepared to cooperate with the TTA in obtaining self-government for the Transkei. He explicitly excluded, however, the possibility of a multiracial government elected by a multiracial electorate. The Prime Minister suggested that within these limits delegates would and should decide what sort of constitution they wanted.[4] On January 23, 1962, as

2. *The Cape Times,* April 22, 1961.
3. This statement was reported in the press and read to the TTA by Paramount Chief Sabata Dalindyebo on April 26. (TTA, *Proceedings* [1961], p. 84. Quotations from pp. 82–85.)
4. *State of South Africa: Economic, Financial and Statistical Yearbook for the Republic of South Africa, 1963* (Johannesburg: Da Gama Publications Ltd., 1963), p. 90.

we have seen, the Prime Minister told the House of Assembly that self-government would be in operation in the Transkei before the end of 1963, a statement given wide circulation overseas by the South African Department of Information.

In view of the government's commitment to Transkeian self-government, the Recess Committee went well beyond its original terms of reference and set about framing a constitution. The deliberations of the Committee were conducted in camera, and *The Cape Times* reported that when it met in Umtata police guards surrounded the room and the members were sworn to secrecy. A Department of Information pamphlet later revealed that the Committee had decided to base its discussions upon a preliminary constitution drafted by its chairman, Chief Matanzima.[5] That there was also another contrasting proposal is suggested by a comment of an unnamed member of the Committee that "an alternative constitution providing for a multiracial Transkei was not even permitted to be discussed."[6] This particular point was not, in fact, contradicted by the denial in the report of the Recess Committee of "certain newspaper reports to the effect that the committee had received proposals for a multi-racial parliament."[7] Moreover, the report's expression of the Committee's "appreciation of the patient, valuable and friendly assistance" rendered it by various officials of the Department of Bantu Administration and Development suggested that there was considerable official influence on the formulation of the document.

OPPOSITION

At his December meeting with the TTA delegates, the Prime Minister had suggested that the Recess Committee should canvass the views of Transkeian Africans residing in urban areas outside the Territory. To make this easy, he promised that the government would pay the travel and accommodation expenses of those urban Africans who wished to go to the Transkei to give evidence regarding the new constitution. A special five-man subcommittee of the Recess Committee was appointed to get together with these urban delegates, and meetings were arranged in Umtata for the third week of April.[8] Before this time, however, the Recess Committee, after a second visit to Pretoria and another meeting with the Prime Minister on March 19, completed its report on March

5. *The Transkei: Emancipation without Chaos,* n.d., p. 10.
6. *The Cape Times,* February 2, 1962.
7. TTA, *Proceedings* (1962), p. 55.
8. The subcommittee submitted its report on April 30. It was accepted by the Recess Committee, but not discussed. At the opening of the 1962 session of the TTA two days later, the subcommittee's report was tabled. Its findings were thus available to members of the Authority as they proceeded on the following day to discuss the draft constitution prepared by the Recess Committee.

30.[9] There are conflicting stories about what happened thereafter. The government claimed that more than 40 urban representatives were received by the subcommittee,[10] but a press account maintained that when 64 urban delegates arrived in Umtata, they were handed a fully drafted constitution and merely asked their opinions on it. Their response, it was said, was to term Transkei self-rule a "mockery" and to boycott the meetings with the subcommittee.[11]

Further criticism appeared before the TTA session opened on May 1. Copies of the draft constitution had been circulated among members of the Transkei's nine regional authorities in order to elicit popular reactions to its provisions. Whatever the response elsewhere, members of tribal meetings both in Western Pondoland and in Tembuland rejected the document.[12] Indeed, a meeting of 400 Thembu tribesmen called to discuss the draft constitution ended with most of those attending shouting, "We do not want this scarecrow."[13]

The session of the TTA might thus have been expected to provide an open and critical review of the Recess Committee's constitution-writing and an expression of popular sentiment regarding Transkeian self-government. The presence on the opening day of a considerable number of officials, academics, and foreign diplomats in the public gallery attested to the significance of the meeting. However, no critical review was forthcoming, and popular views received no hearing. The keynote was struck by Mr. C. B. Young, Secretary of Bantu Administration and Development, who expressed the government's belief that the constitution was already an accomplished fact and, in any case, was really a unilateral decision by the government. Disparaging "eleventh-hour constitution makers," Young declared that

it rests in the hands of the Government of the Republic of South Africa to decide what it will concede to the Transkei in the form of self-government. The committee has been consulting with the Government for a long time and *the basis of agreement, you might say, has already been reached.* [Italics added.]

He advised the members to "accept what has been offered to you and be thankful for this great step forward in the historical and constitutional development of the Transkei Territories."[14]

It was difficult indeed for critics of the draft constitution to express their opposition. At the beginning of the TTA's consideration of the report of the Recess Committee, Chief Matanzima declared that the

9. South African Information Service, *The Transkei: Major Steps on the Road to Self-Determination, Fact Paper 102,* Supplement to the *Digest of South African Affairs,* June 1962, p. 4.
10. *The Transkei: Emancipation without Chaos,* p. 10.
11. *The Cape Times,* April 19, 1962.
12. *Contact* (Cape Town), May 17, 1962.
13. *The Cape Times,* April 30, 1962.
14. TTA, *Proceedings* (1962), p. 33.

"committee was unanimous in arriving at the decision placed before you now, and all the members should abide by their signatures."[15] The Committee's deputy-chairman, C. W. Monakali, later suggested that an amendment offered by Committee-member Chief D. D. P. Ndamase (nephew of the Paramount Chief of Western Pondoland, Victor Poto) would be "more in order" if it were moved by one who had not been on the Committee.[16]

A few members refused to be silenced. Paramount Chief Sabata Dalindyebo of Tembuland, in particular, felt that he had a mandate from his Thembu tribesmen to express dissatisfaction with the constitution. Though a signatory of the report, he explained that he had "had to sign because I am a Government man," which was to say, a chief appointed and paid by the government. But Chief Sabata failed to understand the procedure employed by the TTA in its consideration of the draft constitution. Believing that he would have the authority to bring forward the "views of the people" after the Authority had completed discussion of each constitutional provision separately, Chief Sabata held his fire until that moment, only to be told by the Deputy-Chairman to resume his seat when he began to speak. "The Thembus do not want to hear anything about this constitution," Sabata blurted out in awkward confusion. But he had lost his chance to express their opposition.

Less than three days were used to consider the draft constitution. Each section was introduced and moved by Chief Matanzima and seconded by Councillor Columbus K. Madikizela, later to become the first Transkeian Minister of Agriculture and Forestry. All but one of the constitution's seventy sections were adopted either automatically or without significant discussion. Only two amendments were voted on, and both were defeated. In the end, the draft constitution was adopted without change.

The only controversy of the debate centered on Section 24 to which both amendments were offered. This section provided that the Transkei Legislative Assembly (TLA), the new and unicameral parliament of the semiautonomous Transkei, would consist of 109 members, of whom 64 would be chiefs sitting ex officio and the remaining 45 members would be popularly elected. Two issues were involved: whether or not chiefs should be permitted ex officio membership in the TLA; and the proportion of ex officio to elected members. It may be noted that at the time of the March, 1962, Pretoria meeting with the Prime Minister, the Recess Committee was prepared to recommend a TLA in which ex

---

15. The report of the Recess Committee was signed by all but five of its members, excepting two who had died. Nevertheless, it was said by the government that the Committee had approved its report unanimously. It does appear that no particular significance may be attributed to the fact that five members did not sign the report.

16. TTA, *Proceedings* (1962), pp. 48–53.

officio members would enjoy an even greater predominance—95 of 131—than that which ultimately obtained. Dr. Verwoerd had then suggested a proportionate increase in the number of elected members.[17]

George M. Matanzima, Chief Matanzima's brother, argued that chiefs had to be included in the membership of the TLA since the Committee's terms of reference stipulated that "self-government . . . shall not in any way tamper with the present set-up of chieftainship in these Territories."[18] An amendment to have 105 members popularly elected was only withdrawn in favor of a later amendment to increase to 60 the number of elected members, thereby raising the total membership of the TLA from 109 to 124. This latter amendment was defeated, however, and section 24 was adopted unchanged by 70 votes to 3.

Having adopted the Recess Committee's report in its entirety, the TTA then carried a motion introduced by Chief Matanzima:

That the Republican Government of South Africa be respectfully requested to draft the necessary legislation embodying the proposals contained in the Recess Committee's report and to take such other steps as are necessary to expedite the formulation of the Government of the Transkei.

Before the constitution bill, drafted by a small constitutional branch of the Department of Bantu Administration and Development, was presented to the TTA at a further session in December, 1962, a mass meeting of Thembu tribesmen had again voiced their dissatisfaction. At Chief Sabata's "Great Place," Bumbane, on August 11, 1962, they declared it "unacceptable." Thereupon the Thembu appointed their own committee of fifteen persons to draft a new constitution which would be without "racial discrimination in the electoral system" and would be "for all the people of South Africa and not for the Transkei alone." In early November this committee recommended that (a) Transkeian citizenship "embrace all persons domiciled in the Transkei regardless of race"; (b) that the TLA consist of four paramount chiefs (or their representatives) and an unspecified number of elected members; and (c) that the object of Transkeian self-government be total independence from the Republic of South Africa within a space of two years.[19] According to one report, the government repeatedly postponed giving the necessary permission for a Thembu tribal meeting at which these recommendations of the committee could be publicly reported. The reason given for postponement was that such a meeting was unnecessary since the Dalindyebo Regional Authority had already rejected the committee's constitutional proposals.[20]

The Thembu proposals were never submitted to the TTA. When the Authority met on December 11, 1962, it was to consider a "Bill to

17. *House of Assembly Debates* (April 12, 1962), col. 3804.
18. TTA, *Proceedings* (1962), p. 55.
19. "Draft Constitution Proposals," typewritten.
20. *New Age*, November 15, 1962.

Confer Self-Government on the Bantu Residents in or Deriving from the Transkei and to Provide for Matters Incidental Thereto." This Bill had been prepared by the Department of Bantu Administration and Development and copies had been circulated among TTA members about a week earlier. Curbing comment, Secretary Young declared at the opening session that:

The Government could have introduced the Bill into Parliament without further consultation with the Territorial Authority. In view, however, of the fact that there had been the closest consultation and harmonious relations, at a high level, between representatives of the Government and the Territorial Authority since the inception of these negotiations, it was decided to give this body an opportunity to see each clause of the proposed Bill to be introduced into Parliament.[21]

He suggested, however, that the chairman rule out of order any discussion of principles decided upon by the TTA in May. It is "your duty to scrutinize the draft," said Chief Matanzima in his capacity as presiding officer, ". . . and to find out whether your requests which were made at the last session have been met or not."

Nonetheless, opposition to the principles inherent in the bill was not wholly stifled. Indeed, Chief Sabata, the foremost opponent of the preponderance of chiefs in the TLA and of the exclusion of Whites from representation in the Transkei Legislative Assembly, appeared somewhat more effective in expressing the dissatisfaction of the Thembu than he had been in May. In part this may have been due to advice given, although under severe handicaps, by Liberal party well-wishers.[22]

There was, however, only one real challenge to the Transkei Constitution Act as it stood at the December meeting of the TTA: an amendment to change the membership of the new Transkei Legislative Assembly to 109 elected members or, alternatively, to 64 ex officio chiefs and 64 elected persons. This amendment was only narrowly defeated by 48 votes to 43.

In addition, members queried numerous provisions, such as the exclusion of Kokstad and Port St. Johns from the jurisdiction of the Transkeian government. But only two minor amendments were proposed, and both were defeated. The TTA thus adopted the bill without change.

The government of the Republic of South Africa contends that the idea of self-government for the Transkei originated with the Africans

21. Transkei Territorial Authority, *Proceedings. Special Session called to consider Draft Bill for the Granting of Self-Government to the Transkei* ([Umtata]: Territorial Printers, 1963), pp. 5-6.
22. On the third day of the special session, the TTA agreed to expel from its meeting Mr. Randolph Vigne, representative of the newspaper *Contact* and Vice-Chairman of the Liberal party of South Africa. Mr. Vigne had been accused by a White official before the House of having passed notes from the visitors' gallery to members of the floor advising them on various matters (TTA, *Proceedings [Special Session]*, pp. 31-32).

of the Transkei; that they drafted the Transkeian Constitution; and that they were consulted by the government at every stage of that Constitution's enactment. These contentions minimize the crucial role of the government at all stages of the constitution-making process and are misleading if they suggest wide African participation in the process, or wide popular support. To be sure, opponents both of the government's Bantustan policies and of the draft constitution were members of the Recess Committee and signed its report, and the report was reviewed twice by the TTA. In addition, the government made special provision for members of the TTA to learn the views of Africans in the cities before the TTA considered the draft constitution in May, 1962—though the record is not clear regarding the efforts made to canvass urban opinion and to hold hearings for urban delegates.

While Secretary Young discouraged a critical review of the draft constitution, it is clear that some opposition was expressed. Despite government reports to the contrary, popular opposition to the Transkeian Constitution did exist, although its extent is difficult to gauge. It failed to manifest itself effectively in the Recess Committee, or later within the TTA, because of the ineptness and isolation of its leaders, especially Paramount Chief Sabata Dalindyebo; the determination and parliamentary adeptness of the opponents, principally Chief Matanzima; and the susceptibility of ex officio members of the TTA to official suggestion and direction.

Consideration of the Transkei Constitution Bill shifted in January, 1963, from Umtata to Cape Town. Parliamentary passage of the Bill has been discussed in Chapter 3. We may now analyze its main provisions.

PROVISIONS

The Transkei is declared to be "a self-governing territory within the Republic." Among the Constitution Act's distinctive features is the description of the territory itself: it includes only the African areas in what is known as the Transkei. Thus it provides for a kind of extra-territoriality in the White enclaves of Umtata, the administrative capital; 25 other towns that are seats of magisterial administration; certain White farming areas; and Port St. Johns, the only harbor. However, the Republican government may "zone" these areas for African occupation and ownership; and if both houses of Parliament and also the Transkei Legislative Assembly approve, the State President of South Africa may add such areas or other African areas in the Transkei or may excise any area.

The Constitution provides for a Transkeian flag, to be flown side by side with the Republican flag, and a national anthem, "'Nkosi

Sikelel'i-Afrika!" which is the traditional anthem of the African National Congress, and has also been adopted as a national anthem by Zambia and Tanzania. Provision is made for a Transkeian citizenship of Africans only, thus excluding those Whites and Coloureds who live permanently in the territory. Citizens include Africans born in the Transkei or domiciled there for at least five years, Africans living outside the Transkei who speak a dialect of Cape Nguni even if they were not born in the Transkei and have never resided there and who owe no allegiance to another "Bantu homeland," and others outside who derive from a Sotho-speaking tribe resident in the Transkei. Citizens are not to be regarded as "aliens" elsewhere in the Republic and internationally are to be regarded as citizens of the Republic. The franchise is open to all Transkeian citizens—men and women—over twenty-one years of age, or, if taxpayers, over eighteen years of age. As already noted, Xhosa is recognized as an additional official language, and Afrikaans, English, and Sesotho may also be used for official purposes.

The Transkei Legislative Assembly, as we have seen, consists of four paramount chiefs (or their representatives), a maximum of 60 additional chiefs, and 45 elected members. (Provisions regarding the holding of elections are discussed in the next chapter.) Thus, the Assembly is indirectly controlled by the central government, since under existing legislation the government either recognizes or appoints all chiefs and may remove them from office and consequently from the Assembly.

The Constitution expressly excludes certain subjects from the Assembly's legislative power—for example: the control and presence of the South African Police "charged with the maintenance of public peace and order and the preservation of internal security"; military operations and factories that manufacture arms or explosives; communications, railways, and national roads; the entry into the Transkei of persons other than Transkeian citizens; currency, public loans, and banking; customs and excise; foreign affairs; and amendment of the Transkeian Constitution. Legislative power on all these important matters is reserved for the South African Parliament. Another control over the Transkei's legislative power is the requirement that bills passed by its Assembly be approved by the President, who acts on the advice of the Republican government. In effect, the President has the power to veto, although the Constitution does not expressly give him that power. If he does not assent to a bill, he refers it back to the Assembly for further consideration. Furthermore, the President retains his powers under the Native Administration Act of 1927 and earlier Cape laws to legislate by proclamation except with regard to the Assembly's scheduled powers.

What powers, then, does the Transkeian Assembly have? The Constitution Act gives it power to make laws on subjects listed in twenty-

121

four paragraphs in a schedule to the Act. The subjects range from direct taxation on Transkeian citizens, residing outside as well as inside the Transkei, to "generally all matters which . . . are of a merely local or private nature in the Transkei." (The full text of the schedule appears in the Appendix to this book.) These subjects include more than those with which the Republic's four provincial councils are now concerned. Of particular importance to Africans is the Transkei's responsibility for so-called Bantu education, which had been removed from provincial to national control in 1953. As Chapter 8 relates, the Assembly displayed notable independence during its first year in reversing certain aspects of Nationalist policy under the Bantu Education Act.

Other subjects of TLA concern include agriculture; soil and water conservation; roads and bridges (excluding national roads); "protection of life, persons and property"; control of police personnel who may be transferred to the Transkeian government by the Republic's Minister of Justice; establishment and control of inferior courts; "labour matters"; welfare services; intoxicating liquor; and so on. The Assembly also has authority over African local government, that is, over the structure of Bantu Authorities below the level of the Transkeian Territorial Authority (which was disestablished when the first Transkeian cabinet was constituted late in 1963).[23]

The Constitution provides that the President, with the approval of both houses of Parliament, may add to the subjects listed in the schedule, except for the matters already set down as being expressly excluded from the Assembly's power. On the other hand, the Constitution also provides that future acts of Parliament relating to the scheduled subject matter shall not apply in the Transkei or to Transkeian citizens. There is no provision, furthermore, as there is in the Republican Constitution, with reference to provincial ordinances, rendering an act of the Assembly void if it is repugnant to an Act of Parliament. Indeed, the Transkei Constitution Act goes still further. Although the Assembly may not amend the Constitution, it may provide "for the amendment or repeal" of any parliamentary act relating to the subjects listed in the schedule insofar as the act affects the Transkei or Transkeian citizens outside the territory.

In short, the South African Parliament appears to have given exclusive competence to the Assembly in certain limited matters. Donald

23. The Act does not alter the existing judicial machinery within the Transkei. It does permit the Transkeian Minister of Justice to establish new inferior courts and to appoint judicial officers to them. It allows for the eventual transfer of existing inferior courts to the Transkeian government, and for the creation of a "High Court for the Transkei" to replace any provincial or local division of the Supreme Court of South Africa. Appeals would lie to the Appellate Division of the Supreme Court. The Republican government retains power to establish courts to hear cases in which one of the parties is not a Transkeian citizen.

Molteno, a former Native Representative and an eminent lawyer, has asked (in a talk that has not been published) how Parliament itself can amend the Transkeian Constitution if, in doing so, it legislates regarding subjects assigned to the Assembly. The question, he has said, is "one of the major puzzles" of the Bill.

Finance

Crucial to developing local independence of action is the extent to which the TTA can depend on local sources of funds. It has the power to tax its citizens, including those residing outside, and this income enters the Transkeian Revenue Fund along with revenue from a variety of other sources, such as property taxes within the Transkei, death duties, license and other fees, and fines. In 1964, Chief Matanzima estimated that R1.2 million ($1.68 million) of the R3.1 million ($4.34 million) derived from the Territory's "own sources" would be raised from the general tax. Nearly R1 million ($1.40 million) of the R1.2 million, he said, would come from Africans outside the Transkei.

This revenue covers only a small proportion of the expenditures needed to maintain local services, however, and the balance has to be made up by subsidies from the Republican government. These subsidies include an annual grant to the Transkei government approximately equal to the Republican government's expenditure on behalf of the Transkei in the 1962–63 fiscal year.

The Assembly may not impose customs and excise duties, as we have seen. Also, there is no provision for borrowing on the credit of the Transkei; for a parliamentary appropriation to provide an advance of loan funds to meet capital expenditure; or (as in the case of the provincial governments) for short-term borrowing with Republican Treasury approval to cover temporary deficits. These provisions, taken in conjunction with the Territory's poverty and heavy dependence upon the meager earnings of migrant labor, clearly leave the Transkei's economic development dependent upon the uncertain will of future Parliaments.

Cabinet

In carrying out its policies, the Assembly acts through a Cabinet that is elected by the Assembly but is apparently not collectively responsible to it. The Assembly elects a chief minister by secret ballot from among its own members. Five other ministers are elected in the same way (rather than selected by the chief minister) after at least one day has elapsed following the chief minister's election. The chief minister holds the portfolio of finance and allocates the other portfolios to members of the Cabinet: at first, Justice, Education, Interior, Agriculture and Forestry, and Roads and Works. The limited number of departments is said to have been by choice of the Africans, to whom such responsibilities were new. The number of ministers may be increased to a maximum of nine (three more were added in 1966—Minister of Posts and Telegraphs, Minister of Transport, and Minister of Information) and additional departments may be created by the President.

In order to overcome the difficulties anticipated because of the lack of a party system, the Constitution stipulates that the Cabinet is to decide questions by a majority vote of members present. In case of a tie, the chief minister has an additional or casting vote. Later practice has shown that these provisions have not been of importance because of the rise of political parties and the dominant position of Chief Matanzima.

The Cabinet holds office during the life of the Assembly, which may continue for five years. The Assembly may be dissolved by the President, acting—if so advised by the Republican government—on the recommendation of either the Transkeian Cabinet or the Assembly itself. Another and curious provision empowers the Assembly to request the President to remove one or more members of the Cabinet. The President, "if he deems fit," may accede to such a request. If he did not, a Cabinet, or one or more ministers, would remain in office even though they did not command the confidence of the Assembly.

SOUTH AFRICAN "COLONY"

The Transkei Constitution Act placed the Transkei in the same constitutional position that had been occupied by most British and French colonial territories in the early 1950's. The fact that government-appointed chiefs held a majority of the seats in the Assembly was comparable to the official majorities that were commonplace in those colonies then. Indeed, the British Crown still retained as great reserve powers in 1963 in Basutoland as the South African government held in respect to the Transkei. Moreover, the Executive Council of Basutoland was not responsible to the Basutoland National Council, and no member of the Basutoland National Council had as yet been seated as a result of direct popular election. In this context, South Africa's "domestic colonialism" for the Transkei might be looked on as the first step toward full self-government. How the development in the Transkei was, in fact, to compare with that in former British and French colonies and in neighboring Basutoland—which by 1966 was to be independent Lesotho and a member of the United Nations— remained to be seen.

7

The 1963 Elections

AFTER the State President signed the Transkei Constitution Act, only seven months remained to fulfill Dr. Verwoerd's pledge of limited self-government for the Transkei before the end of 1963. These months were filled with electoral activity. Moreover, in this period the Transkei became a subject of nationwide and, indeed, international attention.

Electoral activities fell into three phases. The first, a considerable task, was to compile a voters' roll. While this effort was essentially an administrative problem, it also carried possible political overtones, inasmuch as voter registration was voluntary. Phase two began with the nomination of candidates on October 2, continued through the ensuing campaign, and ended on November 20 with the election to the Transkei Legislative Assembly of the 45 popularly chosen members. This campaign was marked by a fair measure of political activity in the Transkei itself and some, though considerably less, among Transkeian Africans, elsewhere. The election also involved much administrative organization.

The third phase of electoral activity was distinguished by "caucus politics," the lobbying for support among the members of the TLA by the two aspirants for the post of Chief Minister of the Cabinet. These two, Chief Kaiser Matanzima and Paramount Chief Victor Poto, and their supporters were at work even before the November election, soliciting the support of the chiefs, who were automatically ex officio members of the Assembly, and of the candidates for popular election. The pace of their efforts quickened after the results of the election were known at the end of November, and continued up to the very moment of the election of the Transkeian Cabinet in December.

REGISTRATION OF VOTERS

The Transkeian Constitution opened the franchise, as has been seen, to all citizens of the Territory over twenty-one years of age, and to tax-payers over eighteen years of age. (It may be noted that the voting age of Whites in the Republic had been lowered to eighteen years in 1958 with no property requirements.) How many persons could qualify as Transkeian voters can only be estimated. A journalist's calculations, based on the detailed returns of the 1960 South African census, suggested that approximately 1,150,000 Africans were eligible in 1963 for the Transkeian franchise. Some 500,000 of these persons were thought to be residing outside the Territory,[1] and thus 650,000 inside.

Registration of voters began on June 17 and continued until August 17. Responsibility for enrolling voters rested with the Department of Bantu Administration and Development, while the Republic's Department of Information dealt with publicity. Registration was voluntary, as has been said, but it was clearly the hope of the officials—consistent with the desire of the South African government that Transkeian self-government be seen as a popular development—that a maximum registration be achieved.

No effort was spared to publicize the importance of registering to vote. Both departments committed a considerable number of their regular personnel to the registration drive, and more than 1,000 Africans were employed temporarily to serve as registration agents. Mobile registration teams traveled to the more remote areas. One million pamphlets in Xhosa and Sotho were disseminated to inform prospective voters both when and how to register. Registration appeals were issued over the Xhosa transmission of the South African Broadcasting Corporation.

In addition, administrative pressure to register was reportedly applied to individuals having dealings with officials and to those employed by the government. One informant alleges that the Regional Director of Bantu Education, subsequently the (White) Secretary of the Transkeian Department of Education, personally informed teachers in the Idutywa and Willowvale districts that they were expected to register and that the names of those who failed to do so would be noted and action taken against them. Teachers are important opinion leaders in the Transkei

---

1. *Eastern Province Herald*, (Port Elizabeth), September 4, 1963.

and, when such organization was permitted, were heavily enrolled in the Cape African Teachers' Association, an affiliate of the All African Convention and the Non-European Unity Movement. (The chief tactic of these organizations was to boycott government-sponsored political organizations for non-Whites.)

In the end, this determined administrative effort was remarkably successful, particularly in the light of some known fears that registration might be linked to new taxation. Approximately 630,000, or 97 per cent of those deemed eligible, registered within the Transkei, while outside the Territory about 250,000 registered, or 50 per cent of those thought to be eligible. Total registrations, 880,425, constituted 77 per cent of the possible total, always assuming the estimated population figures were correct. Fifty-three per cent of all those registered were women, a likely consequence of the lower rate of registration in the urban areas outside the Transkei where migratory labor means that African men outnumber African women by a large margin.

The success of the registration drive, especially within the Transkei, owed much to its support by chiefs and headmen. The latter commonly assisted the registration agents, who explained the mechanics of registration, and they encouraged their tribesmen to register. Some chiefs and representatives of chiefs also traveled to their tribesmen in the African townships outside the cities to offer further support for the registration drive; at least in some instances, this support was probably important in determining the degree and character of voting. That there was, in general, a considerably lower rate of registration in the cities than in the Transkei itself is hardly surprising. Three main causes were apathy on the part of the Transkeian citizens in the cities toward happenings in the Transkei; the greater influence in the cities of the banned African National Congress and Pan-Africanist Congress; and the administrative difficulty of identifying and contacting a dispersed population.

Tribal leaders gave considerable support to the registration of voters not only because they were government employees but also, in some measure, because of political self-interest. The Transkeian Constitution provides that each of the nine regions that comprise the Territory will serve as a single multimember constituency, and the number of members to be elected from each region will be in the same proportion to 45 (the total of elected members) as the number of registered voters in that region is to the size of the total electorate. Thus, tribal leaders, anxious that their particular region should enjoy the maximum possible influence within the new Assembly, naturally supported efforts to build the size of their region's electorate. The result of registrations and the number of elective seats for each region are shown in Table 1.

TABLE 1
ELECTED AND EX OFFICIO SEATS IN THE TRANSKEI LEGISLATIVE
ASSEMBLY AND THE NUMBER OF CANDIDATES AT THE FIRST
TRANSKEIAN GENERAL ELECTION, 1963

REGION	MEMBERS		CANDIDATES
	Ex officio (chiefs)	Elected	
Fingo	3	4	23
Gcaleka	5	7	29
Dalindyebo	11	7	20
Qaukeni	15	8	33
Emboland	8	5	20
Maluti	8	4	24
Em. Tembuland	6	4	10
Umzimkulu	4	2	11
Nyanda	4	4	10
TOTAL	64	45	180

NOMINATION OF CANDIDATES

Nomination of candidates for the 45 elected seats in the TLA took place on October 2 at the nomination courts established within each of the nine regions of the Transkei. The procedure was similar to that for Republic elections. A prospective candidate had to be a registered voter within the region in which he or she sought election, and each nomination had to be proposed and seconded by two other persons similarly qualified. Though each candidate had to provide an electoral deposit of R20 ($28)—a sum forfeited if he obtained less than half as many votes as that candidate within the same region who was elected by the smallest number of votes—this requirement failed to prevent a superabundance of candidates.

One hundred and eighty nominations were filed, an average of 4 per seat; and in three regions—Fingo, Maluti, and Umzimkulu—the number rose to about 6 nominations per seat. This large number of candidates threatened to confuse the subsequent campaign even more than is common in multimember elections.

Of the 180 candidates, approximately one-fifth were headmen, one-fifth farmers, and nearly one-fourth teachers or retired teachers. Apart from two clergymen, there were only two professional men among the candidates: one an attorney and the other a medical practitioner (both were elected). Two (one of whom was elected) of the candidates were women. Only 8 of the 180 candidates resided outside the Transkei, and only one of these was elected.

Data on age, education, and experience outside the Transkei was obtained by the authors in 1964 from about half the successful candidates, and nearly half—28 of 64—the chiefs. Of the 22 elected members who filled out questionnaires, nearly all had some secondary education;

over half had matriculated; and over one-third had some university training. Only 9 per cent were under 40 years of age, and three-fourths had spent at least three years outside the Transkei. Only slight differences between followers of Poto and of Matanzima were revealed by the questionnaire, namely that Poto's followers as a group were somewhat younger than Matanzima's and, perhaps surprisingly, had spent somewhat less time away from the Transkei.

The major differences, as one would expect, were between the elected members and the chiefs. The chiefs as a group were somewhat younger than the elected members. The latter had markedly higher levels of education and had spent more time outside the Transkei than the chiefs. Chiefs who followed Poto generally had more formal education and were older than followers of Matanzima. Detailed data appear in Table 2. The breakdown regarding followers of Poto and Matanzima is shown under the names of their respective parties, which were organized in 1964: DP (Democratic party) and TNIP (Transkei National Independence party).

As far as is known, no candidate was nominated as the representative of a particular occupational or economic interest group, as, for example, teachers. In two regions, however, Dalindyebo and Emigrant Tembuland, the candidacies of certain nominees had been previously agreed to at public meetings convened by their senior chiefs, Paramount Chief Sabata Dalindyebo and Chief Kaiser Matanzima, respectively. These candidates thus constituted, in effect, the endorsed slate of the tribe within their region. Elsewhere, individual candidates, and groups of candidates, frequently claimed—with varying degrees of validity—that they, too, carried the blessing of their tribes and their chiefs.

Political parties were not a feature of African politics within the structure of Bantu Authorities in the Transkei, although the ANC, the AAC, and even the PAC had earlier been active in the Transkei and may well have had some influence in this election although they were under ban. The ANC was reported to have decided at a meeting in Bechuanaland not to take any role in the election, but there is speculation that the Congress had a hand in promoting a local body known as the Eastern Pondoland People's party, which was founded in August, 1963. On October 2, the secretary, M. S. Mdingi, and seven other members of this People's party were nominated as candidates in Qaukeni, which, as previously noted, had been the scene of widespread anti-government demonstrations and disturbances in 1960. Shortly thereafter, Mdingi was taken into custody by the South African Police on undisclosed charges and was held through the course of the campaign. With this government action, the Eastern Pondoland People's party passed out of sight. Whether it ever had much popular support is not known.

TABLE 2
BIOGRAPHIC DATA ON FIFTY MEMBERS, TRANSKEI LEGISLATIVE ASSEMBLY, 1964

	ELECTED MEMBERS			CHIEFS			ALL DP MEMBERS	ALL TNIP MEMBERS	ALL MEMBERS
	DP	TNIP	ALL	DP	TNIP	ALL			
Numbers for whom data are available	13	9	22	4	24	28			
	%	%	%	%	%	%	%	%	%
AGE:									
Under 40 years	15*	8	9	0	33	29	12	24	20
40 to 60 years	69	67	68	75	37	43	71	46	54
Over 60 years	15	33	23	25	29	29	18	30	26
FORMAL EDUCATION:									
None	0	0	0	0	8	7	0	6	4
Some primary	100	100	100	100	92	93	100	94	96
Some secondary	92	100	95	75	37	43	41	55	66
Matriculant	54	56	55	25	4	7	47	18	28
Some university	31	44	36	0	4	4	24	15	18
Univ. graduate	23	22	23	0	4	4	18	9	12
TIME AWAY FROM TRANSKEI:									
None	31	22	27	50	50	50	35	42	40
Up to 3 years	0	0	0	25	25	25	6	18	14
Over 3 years	69	78	73	25	25	25	59	39	46

*All percentages have been rounded-off to the nearest whole percent.

With this single exception, no African political party emerged in the Transkei to play a public role either in the nomination of candidates or during the six-week campaign that followed. The electoral regulations did not provide for the appearance on the ballot of any party or other designations, but there was no formal and legal proscription either of the creation of parties or of their activities. Had there been parties in the Transkei to contest the election, however, they would have been hampered, as were the individual candidates, by Proclamation 400, which requires the permission of the local Bantu Affairs Commissioner for all meetings of ten persons or more.

Parties having roots outside the Transkei were strongly discouraged from participating in the campaign. In September the executive committee of the TTA, of which Chief Matanzima was an important member, warned that participation in the elections by "European [that is, White] led and organized parties" would be a "transgression" of the Transkeian Constitution.[2] At one point the Transvaal Congress of the Progressive party, which endorses the extension of the parliamentary franchise to all non-Whites who meet high qualifications, resolved in favor of participation in the Transkeian election.[3] Subsequently, however, the National Executive Committee of the party decided that participation would imply acceptance of the principle of separate development that underlay the Transkeian Constitution—and this it could not countenance. Nonetheless local members of the party provided advice during the campaign, and a member of the Transvaal executive committee, the Rev. B. S. Rajuili, stood as a candidate in the Maluti region and was elected.

The position of the Liberal party was still more difficult. Well before 1963 it had adopted a program of universal adult franchise; and by then the number of Africans who were members appears to have exceeded the number of Whites, though its major leaders were still White: Alan Paton as President and Peter Brown as Secretary. The periodical *Contact*, owned and managed by Patrick Duncan, was in an unofficial sense an organ of Liberal party expression; and both Duncan and Randolph Vigne, its editor, had close personal links in the Transkei. Although the national Liberal party executive committee, like that of the Progressive party, renounced official participation in the Transkei election, individual White liberals were still active at various points in the campaign.[4] They probably also extended some financial aid, particularly to candi-

2. *Territorial News* (Umtata), September 12, 1963.
3. *Daily Dispatch* (East London), August 12, 1963.
4. This assistance was offered despite the obvious dangers involved in being caught by the South African police on reserve land more than 100 yards from the national highway, an offense under Proclamation 400. The difficulties of advising political leaders in the Transkei were partly circumvented by meeting such leaders and delegations in cities of the Eastern Province and even as far away as Cape Town.

dates in the southwestern Transkei who were believed to be members of the party.

One prominent Liberal party member, Hammington Majija from Cape Town, announced his intention to seek election as a Thembu, not as a Liberal, but was prevented from running. Appearing at a tribal meeting at Sabata's Great Place, at which Commissioner-General Hans Abraham was present, Majija was seized for a moment by police officers but released on Sabata's outraged demand that he be freed before the enraged Thembus precipitated a further incident. Subsequently, by an order of October 1, Majija was confined to the Cape Town area for a period of five years, making his candidacy impossible.

THE CAMPAIGN

The period between October 2 and election day seven weeks later comprised two major types of political effort. One was the campaigns of the only two announced candidates for the post of chief minister of the Transkei—Chief Kaiser Matanzima and Paramount Chief Victor Poto—for the support of the 62 other chiefs who with them would hold ex officio membership in the Legislative Assembly. In fact, as already mentioned, these campaigns had commenced even before the last meeting of the TTA in May. After nomination day both candidates also sought the support of the candidates for election to the TLA. This aspect of the campaign resembled the struggle between two presidential aspirants for delegate support at an American party's national nominating convention.

The other major activity was the campaign by candidates for election to the TLA for the support of the electorate within their respective regions. Some candidates in certain areas tried to link themselves to one of the two chiefs seeking to become chief minister, and some of these candidates were in turn assisted by these chiefs. These relationships helped to make the election throughout part of the Transkei a test of popular support for Poto or Matanzima rather than an electoral "free-for-all." To this degree, even in the absence of organized political parties, the election became a contest between two recognized groups.

The Republican government clearly favored the election of forty-eight-year-old Chief Matanzima as chief minister. Its support was probably the deciding factor in his eventual election. For a number of years, the Chief had been an outspoken supporter of cooperation with the government's Bantu Authorities policy. His election manifesto had pointed out that his entrance into the Bunga in 1955 had been followed by the successful reversal of the Bunga's rejection of that system in 1954. He had been the chairman of the Recess Committee which prepared the first draft of the Transkeian Constitution, and he had presided at the special session of the TTA which approved the Transkei Constitution Act in December, 1962.

Matanzima would be, moreover, one of the best-trained and ablest members of the new Assembly. A graduate in law and politics in 1939 from Fort Hare University College, he had been articled to an Umtata law firm in 1944, and four years later admitted to practice as an attorney in the Cape Province. In 1958 Matanzima was recognized as senior tribal chief over the 88,000 tribesmen of Emigrant Tembuland. His chiefly rule is reputedly harsh. His considerable unpopularity in the Transkei in 1963 stemmed more particularly, however, from his close identification with the Republican government and his prior association as a leading member of the TTA with such unpopular administrative measures in the Transkei as land reclamation. Visitors to Matanzima have commonly found him haughty, ambitious, highly articulate, and bitter about White domination in South Africa.

Particularly noteworthy is Matanzima's reputation among African nationalist leaders as intelligent, crafty, ruthless, and unpredictable. Their judgments are based upon personal contacts extending over many years. Matanzima himself was closely and sympathetically associated with the anticollaborationist AAC until about 1951 and emphasized then the dangers of a revived tribalism; unlike his brother George, however, he was never a member. Later, according to AAC leaders, Matanzima attempted to destroy all vestiges of AAC influence in the Transkei, particularly in his own district.

Matanzima has also attacked the PAC, as well as Communists and Liberals, but seems to have been more circumspect regarding the ANC. At any rate, he has known many ANC leaders, who are largely Xhosa in tribal background.[5] Matanzima's political associations with the younger leaders began at Fort Hare University College, but he has also known some of the older ANC leaders, for example, Dr. A. B. Xuma, also a Transkeian and President-General of the ANC during 1940–49; Dr. James Moroka, Xuma's successor; and Professor Z. K. Matthews, his teacher at Fort Hare. A particular friend is Nelson Mandela, whom Matanzima visited at the treason trial and who is the son-in-law of Columbus K. Madikizela, a member of Matanzima's Cabinet. Matanzima's secretary for several years was T. E. Tshunungwa, formerly Cape Provincial Secretary of the ANC, who was suspended from that position when he joined Matanzima some months before December, 1956, when, ironically, he was arrested for treason.

5. Among ANC leaders whose tribal ties, like Matanzima's, are Thembu are Nelson Mandela (the son of a prominent chief and related closely to Paramount Chief Sabata Dalindyebo and more distantly to Matanzima), Walter Sisulu (a member of the Thembu council), Govan Mbeki, Duma Nokwe, and Robert Resha. Oliver Tambo, a Pondo who attended Fort Hare on a Bunga scholarship, is also Xhosa-speaking.

A BANTUSTAN IN BEING

Sixty-six-year-old Paramount Chief Victor Poto lacked the university training of his younger rival, but his experience in government in the Transkei had spanned nearly 45 years. He had been a paramount chief since 1918 and was a member of the Natives' Representative Council from 1937 until the Council was abolished in 1951. The popularity of the dignified, unassuming, gray-haired chief of the 138,000 tribesmen of Western Pondoland was undoubted. Poto's very moderate attitude toward Transkeian Whites, whom he asserted should share in local political rights, awakened neither particular enthusiasm nor particular opposition. In the election campaign his role appeared to be more that of elder statesman than of the leader of anti-Matanzima or anti-Republican government feeling and groups in the Transkei.

While the candidacies of both men for the post of chief minister had been obvious for a number of months before, they waited until late October before issuing their formal election manifestoes. Set side by side, these manifestoes pointed up two important differences between the positions of the two men. The issues involved were highly significant: the future of the more than 14,000 Whites and 10,000 Coloureds who resided in the Transkei; and the place and role of the tribal chiefs in the legislative process.

Poto declared that the "non-Africans" of the Transkei who were prepared to "serve" under an African government should always be welcome in the Territory, and that he stood for "Government which is truly representative of the population comprising the inhabitants of the Territory over which it has authority." Poto also stated his belief that the "dignity and traditional leadership" of the chiefs would best be served by creating a bicameral Transkeian parliament consisting of a lower house of elected members and an upper house of chiefs, the second having power to review proposed legislation.

Matanzima, in contrast, maintained that the full participation of the chiefs in the "body that makes the laws"—the Legislative Assembly—was necessary for the preservation of the principle of chieftainship. Matanzima asserted, moreover, his support of the policy of separate development and his belief that all land in the Transkei, including the "White spots," should be owned only by Africans. He maintained that the Transkei's civil service should become "entirely Black," and while he agreed with Poto that the Territory should be industrialized, he also insisted at that time (and in so doing again followed Republican government policy) that "no European private enterprise should be allowed."

Little more was said about the chiefs' place in the legislative process as the campaign proceeded. The attention of the press focused instead on the matter of race relations within the Transkei. Visiting newsmen pressed Poto to expand upon his race policy as incorporated in his manifesto, a policy that they termed "multiracialism." After some initial hesitation, Poto eventually agreed to their description of his views.

The foremost issue of the campaign thus appeared to become— somewhat unrealistically, many thought, in view of the largely rural electorate and the limited powers of the Transkeian government— multiracialism versus separate development. Observers noted that in this issue were implied at least three important subsidiary questions: (a) acceptance or rejection of the race policy of the Republican government; (b) acceptance or rejection of the personnel as well as the institution of the "old system" of government in the Transkei that had produced the new Constitution; and (c) whether to work for the independence of the Transkei or to hold out for greater opportunities for all Africans throughout the Republic.

In his manifesto, Matanzima said he would appeal to the Republican government to train African civil servants for "independence" and announced himself "competent to deal with any situation on a national or international level." In practice his occasional wily toughness in dealings with Pretoria has alternated with statements revealing a narrow provincialism. Poto's manifesto failed to mention Transkeian independence. It contained a pledge to work for equal pay for equal work and an unrestricted labor market "not only in the Transkei but in the whole of South Africa." On November 7 the Minister of Bantu Administration and Development said in Pretoria that the Republican government would not allow the Transkei to take a multiracial course, whatever the outcome of the election.[6] Five days later, Poto conceded that the realization of his policy of multiracialism in the Transkei would have to await Transkeian independence, which he now belatedly appeared to favor.

Both chiefs traveled widely through the Transkei during the weeks preceding the election in order to hold public meetings and to talk with candidates and chiefs. They also dispatched emissaries to voters in the urban areas of the Republic, giving particular attention to the sizable Xhosa-speaking population in neighboring East London.

Neither Matanzima nor Poto appeared in the Qaukeni region of the Transkei, since Paramount Chief Botha Sigcau of Eastern Pondoland, under whose jurisdiction the Qaukeni region falls, declined to approve their visits. Instead, Sigcau invited both Matanzima and Poto to address the eight successful candidates and fifteen ex officio members from Qaukeni *after* the election. These decisions by Chief Sigcau suggested a desire to shield both himself and his chiefs from the pressure of an electoral mandate which could prove to be in conflict with the Republican government's preference for Matanzima as chief minister.

6. *The Natal Mercury* (Durban), November 8, 1963.

Differences between Matanzima and Poto in personality, associations, and policies appear to have given the latter the initial advantage in the campaign for the support of the candidates to be elected to membership in the Assembly—except in Matanzima's own Emigrant Tembuland. A survey of the opinions of 123 of the 180 candidates taken on nomination day by an Umtata journalist showed that of the 68 candidates who expressed a preference, 47 supported Poto for chief minister. Better electoral organization by Poto's followers increased this advantage. In fact, apart from his own region, Matanzima appears virtually to have conceded the votes of the candidates to Poto and to have turned instead to winning the support of the ex officio members of the Assembly who, being government-nominated and salaried chiefs, were presumably sensitive and responsive to the desires of Pretoria. A printed copy of Matanzima's election manifesto did not even appear until early December; only a mimeographed copy was available during the campaign.

Candidates for election to the Legislative Assembly undertook four different types of political activity. More than half of all the candidates from all of the regions—except Umzimkulu, which had only two members—joined together with others in their region to contest the election as a team, or slate. Most, though not all, had as many members as there were seats to be filled from its region. The endorsed candidates within Dalindyebo and Emigrant Tembuland previously referred to constituted such a slate within their respective regions.

Being a member of a team made for more effective campaigning. Team members gained an identity that was difficult for an individual candidate to achieve campaigning alone. In consequence, the construction of one slate tended to generate competitive groupings. It was common to find two or more slates within a single region. Indeed, several candidates prudently joined more than one team!

In a number of regions—notably Emigrant Tembuland, Dalindyebo, and Fingo—one slate of candidates endorsed Poto while another openly favored Matanzima. In these regions the electoral struggle was concerned, at least in part, with substantive political issues. Elsewhere in the Transkei, some individual candidates and also some slates openly favored Poto. Matanzima appeared to have fewer followers among the candidates. In the less committed areas, the campaigns of the various candidates were not involved so much with the contest for the job of chief minister; they focused instead upon the backward conditions in the Transkei, which all agreed should be improved.

A minority of the candidates—perhaps a quarter of the total number—prepared election manifestoes and circulated copies. But only nine candidates took advantage of an offer made by the *Daily Dispatch* of East London to reproduce in its issue the day before the election all manifestoes submitted since the first announcement of the offer several weeks earlier. In general, the standards of the manifestoes varied greatly. A very few were printed, and some of these carried a photograph of the candidate. Most, however, were mimeographed.

Eighteen of these manifestoes were collected and their content analyzed. There was little agreement on the issues of the campaign among the 25 candidates (of whom about one-third were elected) represented by the eighteen manifestoes. Education in the Transkei was the most popular topic. Two-thirds of the manifestoes spoke in favor of raising teachers' salaries, of making education of African children compulsory, or of improving education facilities in the Transkei. "Multiracialism" or "separate development" were explicitly discussed in only eight of the manifestoes. Paramount Chief Poto or Chief Matanzima was cited by name in four. The need for higher wages for Africans was stated six times. The authors of ten of the eighteen manifestoes stressed their own educational qualifications. At least one candidate in Dalindyebo conceded that he had no program or experience in public affairs. On October 21, 1963, M. D. T. Skote, forwarding his "manifesto" to the editor of the *Daily Dispatch,* wrote,

I have nothing in particular to write as to what I will stand for if elected on the polling day, but that I will patiently await ammunition from the voters whom I will represent and then I will not fire until the electorate demand [it] of me.

He was not elected.

Many candidates—but by no means all—held public meetings, though few, except in East London, took place outside the Territory. Within the Transkei itself, as we have seen, Proclamation 400 of 1960 required the permission of the local Bantu Affairs Commissioner for all meetings of ten or more Africans. Some candidates risked arrest and held meetings without first applying for permission, probably expecting it to be refused, but all requests to hold pre-election meetings appear to have obtained speedy approval. In Emigrant Tembuland, however, four candidates who were opposed to Matanzima complained that although they had obtained the permission of the Bantu Affairs Commissioner, individual chiefs and headmen refused to allow them to speak to groups in areas under their particular jurisdiction.[7]

One chief in Emigrant Tembuland is alleged to have intimidated certain individuals among his tribesmen who were suspected of being politically opposed to Matanzima and to have delivered three such persons to Matanzima's Great Place at Qamata where they were assaulted by Matanzima's bodyguard. Information regarding these alleged occurrences was released to three national daily newspapers. None of the three chose to publish this information, however, possibly because to do so might have constituted an infringement of another provision of

7. *Territorial News* (Umtata), October 24, 1963.

Proclamation 400 which makes it an offense to interfere with the authority of the state or of its officers—including chiefs and headmen—in the Transkei. Elsewhere, there were no reports of violence or acts of intimidation.

Finally, there was the election-day activity of the candidates and their agents, who distributed papers to voters at the polls listing the names on their slates. Indeed, papers bearing the names of the members of one slate or another had been circulating in the Transkei since nomination day. Many voters brought such a paper with them to the polling station where illiterates—estimated to constitute more than half of the electorate—could indicate their preferences among the candidates by handing a list of names to an official standing by to assist them. That many voters were capable, however, of marking their ballots owed much to the work of the four mobile film units belonging to the Department of Information which, by election day, had completed a month-long tour of the Transkei; in this period up to 100,000 persons had received visual instruction in the mechanics of voting.

The electoral regulations provided that a ballot was spoiled if it bore fewer than the permissible number of votes (each elector had as many votes as seats to be filled in his district) or more than the permissible number. A candidate not running as a member of a slate found it desirable, therefore, to provide the voter not only with his own name but also with as many names as there were seats to be filled in his region. It was reported that in Nyanda, where four members were elected, one candidate who was running alone had printed 85,000 papers. On each paper was listed the names of four candidates, but while his name appeared on all 85,000, he had varied the names of the other three. (This imaginative if unorthodox arrangement was not sufficient, however, to secure his election. He finished fifth.)

In general, the campaign was quiet and unspectacular. There were no posters, no mass meetings, no parades, and no soapbox oratory. Foreign and South African journalists, students, and others who came to the Transkei in considerable numbers to witness the campaign saw little of it. Political activity by the candidates was simple and essentially local. In Umtata, the new politics of the Transkei was a popular topic of conversation during the weeks preceding election day, and excitement was evident. Reports from the outlying areas of the Territory indicated, however, that considerable confusion existed there regarding both the significance of the election and what it would require of the individual voter.

In part, the quietness of the campaign was a consequence of the official suppression of political activity in the Transkei since 1960, the stringency of the provisions of Proclamation 400, and the memory of numerous arbitrary acts against those who had resisted official policy or been ranged against a headman or chief. Observers noted that many persons feared arrest if they attended political meetings or engaged in political discussion. Candidates opposed to Matanzima wondered how far they might go in their opposition to separate development. (The briefcase of one anti-Matanzima candidate from Emigrant Tembuland was searched by a South African police officer while the candidate was addressing a meeting in the African township of Langa near Cape Town. Another policeman took notes of what was said.)[8] Moreover, the cost of campaigning was undoubtedly an important, limiting factor for most candidates.

Yet perhaps of greatest significance in determining the nature of the campaign were the dynamics of public-opinion formation in the Transkei. In this society public opinion is shaped by a limited number of individuals, those to whom others have come to look for guidance. What appears to be necessary is a reputation for intelligence and character, prudence, sound judgment, and "understanding." Advanced age is usually of great importance. The opinion leaders are often chiefs and headmen, but they also include businessmen, teachers, traders, and pensioners. These were the persons the candidates had necessarily to approach. If a candidate could win their support, a large following was assured. This support was not obtained "from the stump" but in private and after much deliberation. According to one keen observer of the Territory, "Soap-box oratory gets you nowhere in the Transkei. It's hours and hours of sitting and playing with a point, and going over it again, and looking at it from this angle, and hearing this old man's views—that sort of thing." This type of campaign was obviously little open to public view.

ELECTION DAY

November 20, polling day, dawned bright, clear, and warm, after three days of intermittent rain that had caused officials to fear a low voter turnout. Officials hoped for a maximum number of votes to be cast, knowing that a low turnout, for whatever reasons, would be interpreted as a popular rejection of the self-government "experiment." On November 6, Mr. H. J. Potgieter, Umtata magistrate, formally requested all headmen in his area of jurisdiction to "impress on the . . . voters . . . in your location that it is in their own interest to go and register their votes."[9] Several days before the election he encouraged employers in Umtata to allow voters in their employ enough time away from work on November 20 to vote. All bars were closed in the Trans-

8. *Daily Dispatch* (East London), November 18, 1963.
9. Mimeographed circular.

kei on election day, even those serving patrons in the exclusively White hotels of Umtata.

By 6:00 A. M., the start of the polling day within the Transkei, 80 voters had already gathered in front of the magistrate's court in the center of Umtata, where one of the 1,030 polling stations in the Territory was located. By 8:00 A. M. the crowd had grown to more than 300. At noon, with more than 500 persons waiting to vote, a second polling station was hastily set up across the street in the Umtata town hall. Personal visits to a dozen other stations within a 25-mile radius of Umtata confirmed the impression of an early-morning rush to the polls followed by hours of good-humored waiting with one's friends under a bright sun. Reports received throughout the day from other centers in the Transkei indicated that this was the common pattern. By mid-afternoon most of the voting appeared to have been completed. At 6:00 P. M., the end of the polling day, the area between the magistrate's court and the town hall in Umtata was deserted, save for a small detachment of police.

In the country districts during the morning women commonly outnumbered the men, in some instances by as much as four to one, as they waited outside the polling stations; many were wrapped in their traditional red blankets and some had babies on their backs. Seen in the Dalindyebo region were one or two young men outside nearly every polling station who handed to each voter in line a paper listing the names of the seven "endorsed" candidates. One polling official later reported that at his station all but one of the 495 persons who voted during the day presented such a paper.

At the approximately 1,000 polling stations that had been set up outside the Transkei, the polling day commenced one hour later and lasted two hours longer. Voting commonly began briskly, slowed down during the working hours, and then picked up again in the early evening. Considerable voter enthusiasm was reported in some cities. The electoral officer in Harrismith, in the Orange Free State, reported a poll of 100 per cent. Voting on the Witwatersrand proceeded slowly, however, except at polling stations within the mine compounds. Polling stations in Johannesburg reported an average of only about three voters an hour throughout the day.

In fourteen hours, 601,204 Transkeian Africans voted, one-fifth of them at polling stations outside the Transkei. The Minister of Bantu Administration and Development later estimated to the authors that the turnout of registered voters averaged 51.7 per cent at polling stations outside the Transkei and 77.1 per cent within the Territory. We calculate the overall turnout to have been 68.2 per cent. Among the nine regions of the Transkei, the highest overall poll including both Transkeian and urban returns—75.4 per cent—was recorded in Paramount Chief Poto's region, Nyanda. Among the major urban centers, the highest level of voter turnout was in Port Elizabeth, 72.4 per cent, and the lowest level in Cape Town, 29 per cent.[10]

The Republican government was especially anxious that the first Transkei election should be seen not only as a popular event but also as a genuine expression of African political opinion within the Transkei. Extensive precautions were taken to guard the secrecy of the ballot and to assure an honest election. Fairly complex electoral administrative procedures were used. Nevertheless, allegations of improper conduct by some polling officials (most of whom were African) were heard even before the polls had closed. The number of alleged instances of election abuse was small, however, and only one defeated candidate is known to have challenged publicly (but unsuccessfully) the validity of the election. Moreover, the number of spoiled papers does not appear to have been excessive. The proportion of spoiled papers varied considerably among the regions, from about 1 per cent of all ballots (202 papers) in Umzimkulu to more than 7 per cent (6,150 papers) in Dalindyebo. (The country-wide figure in the Union election of 1953 was 7 per cent). In five instances the spoiled papers, had they been counted, might have overturned the result.

THE RESULTS

The counting of the more than three million votes which were cast on November 20—every elector cast between two and eight votes— did not end until December 2. The results, when announced, disclosed the almost universal triumph of candidates supporting Paramount Chief Poto. In Emigrant Tembuland, the four candidates favoring and favored by Matanzima were easy winners, but elsewhere—and especially in Dalindyebo and Fingo, where all eleven successful candidates were supporters of Poto—those candidates supporting Matanzima were with few exceptions beaten, and beaten decisively. Of the 45 successful candidates, no less than 35 and perhaps as many as 38 could be counted as pro-Poto.

A few of the results were of special interest. One of the two women candidates, Miss Lillian Twetwa, was elected in Emboland with the second highest total of votes in that region. Of the 29 candidates who had been members of the last TTA only 7 were elected, 3 of them from Emigrant Tembuland. Among the 22 who were defeated were the last TTA deputy-chairman and Lingham Maninjwa, the man who in 1961 first raised the question of Transkeian self-government in the TTA. (However, 58 men who had been members of the TTA secured ex officio membership in the TLA.) Only one of the 8 candidates resident

10. For registration and voting figures in sixteen cities and towns outside the Transkei, see *House of Assembly Debates* (Feb. 4 and 11, 1964), cols. 720 and 1127.

outside the Transkei was successful, the Rev. B. S. Rajuili, the Progressive party member referred to earlier.

The returns for Emigrant Tembuland, Dalindyebo, and Fingo are especially interesting, for they give evidence of considerable bloc-voting in these regions. Thirteen of the fifteen successful candidates were elected by the maximum number of votes it was possible for them to obtain. Elsewhere, only ten of the thirty successful candidates were so elected. Emigrant Tembuland provided the most striking case. In this region, which elected four members, the candidate in fourth place obtained only 3,571 fewer votes than the candidate in first place, but 28,453 more votes than the candidate in fifth place. In Dalindyebo, which had seven members, the candidate who placed seventh obtained 17,000 fewer votes than the candidate in first place, but received 32,000 votes more than the candidate in eighth place. In Fingo, with four members, the candidate in fourth place received 10,000 fewer votes than the top-placed candidate, but 11,000 more votes than the one who came in fifth. In both Emigrant Tembuland and Dalindyebo, all losing candidates forfeited their deposits, while in Fingo only one of the nineteen defeated candidates did not lose his deposit. (Eighty-two of the 180 candidates lost their deposits.)

The Emigrant Tembuland, Dalindyebo, and Fingo returns indicate that the formation of slates of candidates was an important factor influencing the results of the election. In each of the regions the victors had constituted themselves as a slate. Moreover, in Emigrant Tembuland and Dalindyebo, even those candidates who formed a slate openly opposed to that of the winners placed better than did other and mostly unallied unsuccessful candidates. On the other hand, in the other regions there appears to have been no particular relationship between the formation of slates and political success. In Nyanda, for example, two members of a team of four candidates were successful while the other two were defeated.

The returns for the other regions do not in themselves show evidence of regional bloc-voting, although unidentified bloc-voting may have occurred (and probably did) within some of these regions. The top winner in these regions often received half again as many votes as the bottom winner (and in two instances more than twice as many votes), while the latter commonly received only a few more votes than the highest-placed loser. Returns from these regions showed a rough gradient, and in most regions where there was no noticeable bloc-voting fewer candidates lost their deposits.

More significant for the outcome than organization, however, were political and tribal factors. Only in Emigrant Tembuland, Dalindyebo, and Fingo, as we have seen, was the contest between Poto and Matanzima reflected locally in a struggle between two competing teams of candidates. In contrast, the formation of slates elsewhere was not part of the struggle between Poto and Matanzima, and the local reputation and perhaps tribal affiliation of the individual candidates appear to have been of paramount importance in determining their success. In both Emigrant Tembuland and Dalindyebo one slate of candidates was endorsed by the tribe, and in each of them the endorsed slate received the strong backing of the senior chief, Kaiser Matanzima in Emigrant Tembuland (his brother, George, was one of the endorsed candidates) and Paramount Chief Sabata Dalindyebo in Dalindyebo (Tembuland proper). In both regions the leadership was strong. Not surprisingly, therefore, the endorsed slates were overwhelmingly victorious in both regions.

Nyanda (Western Pondoland) is also a region with a strong paramountcy dominating subsidiary tribes. All candidates in Nyanda favored Poto, the paramount chief of Western Pondoland. Accordingly, Poto felt no necessity to expresss public preference for the election of certain candidates in his area.

In the remaining regions local chiefs were less likely to be successful in influencing the vote. Emboland and Maluti are regions of small, unrelated chiefdoms, with strong but independent tribal solidarities. Traditional paramountcies exist in both Gcaleka and Qaukeni (Eastern Pondoland), but in both they are weak. And in Umzimkulu and Fingo, chiefs have only been recently appointed and are, therefore, also weak. Only in Emigrant Tembuland and Dalindyebo, therefore, is the support of the senior chief likely to have region-wide political importance. The bloc-voting in Fingo must have a nontribal explanation. Especially in Emboland and Maluti, however, tribal relationships may have been of considerable local importance.

The authors are indebted to the Minister of Bantu Administration and Development, M. D. C. de Wet Nel, for access to the Transkei election returns on the Witwatersrand and the gold fields of the Orange Free State and in four other urban areas: East London, Port Elizabeth, Cape Town, and Durban. These figures are significant regarding the extent to which Transkeian voters in these areas outside the Territory agreed with the voting preferences of the overall Transkeian electorate.

For some regions, the urban vote was so limited as to preclude comment. Only twelve persons who had registered for Umzimkulu voted in Cape Town, for example, while only three persons registered for Fingo voted in Durban. Indeed, there were large-scale returns for all nine electoral regions only on the gold fields of the Orange Free State and on the Witwatersrand. Had the election depended only upon the Free State results, 22 of the 45 members actually returned would have been elected. The comparable figure for the Witwatersrand is 25 of the 45.

Transkeian voters in Cape Town appear to have been most in harmony with the views of the electorate as a whole, although the degree of harmony may be exaggerated because of the insignificance of the vote in Cape Town for Umzimkulu and Qaukeni. There was an important vote, however, for the seven other electoral regions which together elected 35 members. Had the vote in Cape Town solely determined the results, 26 (or 74 per cent) of the members who were returned would have been elected. Transkeian voters in Port Elizabeth would have elected 20 (51 per cent) and East London voters 22 (56 per cent) of the 39 candidates who won in all constituencies except Umzimkulu and Maluti. A sizable vote was registered in Durban for four regions and would have returned 14 (67 per cent) of the 21 who were actually elected from those regions.

In the four urban centers for which there are complete figures, if one compares voting preferences with the preferences shown in consolidated returns, it appears that the larger the urban turnout, the more its preferences varied from those shown in the consolidated returns. On the other hand, if the urban vote is viewed from the standpoint of each of the nine electoral regions, it appears that where voter certainty was evident in the consolidated returns, it was also evident but to a lesser extent in the urban returns. Again, Emigrant Tembuland provided the most extreme case. The four victors in Emigrant Tembuland (all pro-Matanzima) topped their region's poll in Cape Town, East London, Port Elizabeth, on the Free State gold fields, and along the Witwatersrand, indeed in every center for which we have figures except Durban, where only four voters from Emigrant Tembuland cast ballots. Moreover, save in Durban, the four successful candidates from Emigrant Tembuland were returned in the same order in every instance. The magnitude of their victories was not, however, as impressive as in the consolidated returns. The bloc-voting which characterized the total returns for Dalindyebo and Fingo was similarly apparent (although less marked than in the case of Emigrant Tembuland) in the Dalindyebo and Fingo returns for Cape Town, and in the Fingo returns for East London.

On the other hand, where voter confusion or uncertainty seemed common in the consolidated returns, greater uncertainty was shown in the urban returns. Emboland presented the opposite case from that of Emigrant Tembuland. None of the five winning Emboland candidates was among the top five in the poll at Port Elizabeth, while only one of the top five in the polls at East London and on the Witwatersrand was returned.

There is some evidence that voters outside the Transkei who knew little or nothing of the candidates for their region voted for a familiar name. Chief S. W. Makaula is an important chief in Emboland and is one of the ex officio members of the TLA for that region. Candidate

C. S. Makaula ranked twelfth among all Emboland candidates in the consolidated returns, but he was placed first by Emboland voters in East London and Port Elizabeth and fourth by voters on the Witwatersrand and on the Free State gold fields. Another Emboland candidate, G. K. Makaula, finally ranked sixteenth, but he was placed second by voters in Port Elizabeth, third in East London, and fifth on the Witwatersrand. Maluti provided a striking example. Five candidates were of the same family name as chiefs from that region having ex officio membership in the TLA. Only one of these candidates was actually elected, but Maluti voters on the Witwatersrand placed four of the five as the first four. The "nonresident" returns for Nyanda persistently gave top majority to C. M. Ndamase (ranking second in the consolidated poll) who bore the family name of Paramount Chief Victor Poto.

There is also some indication that candidates with their names at the top of the ballot had an advantage and that this advantage was greater with respect to the "nonresident" vote than it was in the Transkei. Emboland had 20 candidates whose names appeared, as did those of candidates in the other regions, on the ballot in alphabetical order. Candidates among the first ten on the ballot were placed among the first five by "nonresident" Emboland voters in East London, Port Elizabeth, Cape Town, on the Free State gold fields, and on the Witwatersrand. However, in the consolidated returns, only three among the first ten on the ballot were placed among the top five. The first four names on the ballot were the top four chosen by "nonresident" Nyanda voters on the gold fields of the Free State and the Witwaterstrand. Three of the first four candidates on the Nyanda ballot were actually elected. And "nonresident" Qaukeni voters on the Witwatersrand, who had to select eight names from a list of 33, placed among the top eight the second, third, fourth, fifth, sixth, seventh, eighth, and thirteenth names, four of which were actually elected.

The Transkei elections of 1963 provided considerable local excitement but few surprises. Total voter registration, the number of candidates for the election to the TLA, and the voter turnout on November 20, however, exceeded the prior estimates of many observers. Government spokesmen have taken these figures as evidence of popular enthusiasm for Transkeian self-government. The figures demonstrate to the authors the ability of the Republican government, through use of its agents of publicity and administration, to marshal, in the mass, the Africans of the Transkei for specific purposes. Despite wide participation in the electoral process, few Africans have evidenced a willingness to accept political opportunities in the Transkei as a *quid pro quo* for their continued exclusion from the political life of the Republic. The support of separate development in its present form may well rest upon the expectation of further constitutional advances for the Transkei, leading to full independence for the Territory. Moreover, a majority of the elected members of the TLA evidently intend to employ the opportunities of self-government for an attack upon the race policies of the Republic.

The results of the election of November 20 and the conclusions that have been drawn from their analysis were, in most respects, predictable. The political authority of Chief Matanzima within Emigrant Tembuland was well known. The demonstration of this authority in the results of the November election was, however, unexpectedly impressive. Moreover, Matanzima's authority was shown to be only slightly less real among those Africans from Emigrant Tembuland who were outside the Transkei. This conclusion must constitute the foremost revelation of the returns, particularly in the light of his reputed unpopularity.

No less significant, however, is the fact that the lower "nonresident" returns for the election confirmed the belief, often disputed by advocates of official race policy, that Africans in the cities, compared to those in the reserves, have markedly less interest in and knowledge of events in the tribal areas. Only one in four of those outside the Transkei who were eligible to vote actually exercised his franchise, compared to three out of four such persons in the Territory. Moreover, the greater tendency of the "nonresident" voter to be influenced by factors as irrelevant as the place of a name on the ballot further indicates his lack of knowledge about his "homeland."

The election resulted in the victory by more than 3 to 1 of candidates sympathetic to Paramount Chief Poto and, presumably, to his policy of African political rights and parliamentary representation in an undivided, multiracial South Africa. In a majority of the nine regions, however, the importance of the candidate's reputation and his tribal affiliation made it difficult to estimate the influence of wider issues in the voting. The difficulty was compounded by the electoral system, specifically the existence of several large constituencies with many members, and by the absence of territorial party organization. Nevertheless, even a more experienced electorate could hardly have demonstrated more clearly with such a system its preference for Poto and its opposition to the government's Bantustan policy.

SELECTION OF THE FIRST TRANSKEIAN GOVERNMENT

The members of the new Legislative Assembly gathered at 10:30 A. M. on December 6, 1963, in the newly refurbished and extended Bunga building in Umtata. The night before, both the Matanzima and the Poto forces had held final caucus meetings. On the eve of the election of the chief minister, both aspirants to that post expressed confidence in the election's outcome. Poto declared that he would win "provided there is no interference." Matanzima announced: "Tomorrow I will be the first chief minister of the Transkei."[11] A motorcade bringing the two popular and allied paramount chiefs, Poto and Sabata Dalindyebo, to the opening session was warmly greeted by an enthusiastic crowd of 800 as it arrived, horns blowing, in front of the Bunga building. Matanzima's entrance went unheralded, but then Umtata lies in Tembuland, near the border of Western Pondoland— politically "enemy country" for Matanzima.

The first business of the Assembly was to elect its permanent chairman. This election was viewed with particular interest as the first test of strength between the two rival groups. The Matanzima forces produced a surprise by nominating Gordon Dana, an elected member from Qaukeni and a presumed supporter of Poto. The Poto group countered with the name of N. J. Busakwe, an elected member and headman from Gcaleka, whose nomination had been assured when he defeated Dana in the Poto caucus. Observers agreed that the strategy of the Matanzima group was to create dissension in the Poto camp and perhaps, thereby, to pick up a few additional votes at the time of the election of the chief minister in the afternoon. Busakwe was elected in a secret ballot, 56 votes to 49. One member from each of the rival groups had been nominated for the post of deputy-chairman when the Assembly adjourned for lunch.

At the beginning of the afternoon meeting, the Assembly, by secret ballot, elected the nominee of the Matanzima group, Chief Petros Jozana from Umzimkulu, as deputy-chairman. The vote was 53 to 49, with two spoiled papers. After lunch, at least four members who had voted with Poto in the election of the chairman in the morning had switched and voted with Matanzima in the election of the deputy-chairman. The press and the public were left to consider this development while they waited outside the Assembly chamber for the results of the election of the chief minister, since the galleries were closed for this decisive action.

Some critics of the Republican government and Chief Matanzima and also many neutral observers of Transkeian politics had believed from the first that Poto could not be elected chief minister. Most of the 64 chiefs in the TLA, they maintained, could be and would be pressured by the White officials to vote for Matanzima. Indeed, and perhaps inevitably, soon after Matanzima had been elected, rumors began circulating in the Transkei that both the evening before and during the luncheon adjournment such pressure was exerted upon a number of chiefs among whom several had been offered and had accepted bribes. A few days earlier—and apparently to allay suspicions of interference

11. *Eastern Province Herald* (Port Elizabeth), December 6, 1963.

by officials—a spokesman of the Department of Bantu Administration and Development in Pretoria had announced that at the time of the election of the chief minister, no White official would be present in the Bunga chamber.[12] Yet when the Assembly met on December 6, Commissioner-General Hans Abraham and three other officials all took seats in the chamber. A member from the Poto group immediately objected to their presence, and for approximately one hour their right to be there was debated. Finally the officials withdrew to the vestibule of the Bunga building and joined members of the public to await the result.

At 6:30 P. M. the considerable tension both within and outside the Assembly chamber was broken with the announcement that the election had been won by Matanzima. The results of the secret ballot were 54 votes for Matanzima, 49 for Poto, and two spoiled papers. It was subsequently ascertained that Matanzima had secured the support of 42 chiefs but only 12 elected members, while Poto received the votes of 33 elected members but only 16 chiefs. The heavy overweight of ex officio members had been decisive in the result.

The victor immediately addressed the Assembly. Saying—without justification—that the people of the Transkei had through the ballot box expressed their "uncompromising rejection" of multiracialism, Matanzima promised to apply "the policy of separation of the white race now occupying the Transkei from the aborigines of the land as quickly as I possibly can" and to "view with a broad mind the important task of liberating my people to independence." The world would watch with keen interest, the new Chief Minister declared, "the changes that will be brought about as a result of the application of the new policy." His Cabinet, he said, would give priority to the Transkei's educational system.

Shortly thereafter Matanzima left the Bunga building and passed into a crowd of about 1,000 persons, including a number of Whites, who had waited to see him despite gathering darkness and a light rain. The cheers were more than matched by jeers, but most people remained quiet and then left for their homes in small groups. Two hundred or so enthusiastic followers of the new Chief Minister accompanied him to his waiting car. The decisive moment was over.

The Poto caucus remained in almost continuous session throughout the weekend of December 7–8, evaluating its position and planning strategy for the election of the five Cabinet ministers that was to follow on Monday, December 9. During this time Poto decided to accept the challenge Matanzima had issued during the campaign, namely, that the defeated candidate for chief minister should not seek election to the Cabinet but form an opposition and serve as its leader. Accordingly,

12. *Daily Dispatch* (East London), December 4, 1963.

the reported offer of the Ministry of Education to a prominent Poto supporter was turned down.

On Monday, after the Matanzima group had placed five names in nomination, the Poto forces placed a sixth name before the Assembly so as to force the decision to a vote. Then, in the secret balloting which followed, they deliberately defaced their papers in order, it was said, to "dramatize" their opposition to the new Transkeian government. The chairman announced that four of the six candidates had received 56 votes, one had received 55 votes, and one vote had been cast for Walter Singata, the Poto candidate. Three papers had been spoiled, and 45 ballots had had "lines drawn across them."[13]

Four of the new ministers were elected members: George Matanzima, brother of the Chief Minister, became Minister of Justice; B. B. Mdledle, Minister of Education; Columbus Madikizela from Qaukeni, Minister of Agriculture and Forestry; and M. Selby Mvusi from Umzimkulu, Minister of Roads and Public Works. Only one of the new ministers was an ex officio member of the TLA, Chief Jeremiah Moshesh from Maluti, who became Minister of Interior. Matanzima and Mdledle were from Emigrant Tembuland, and of the three others, two plus the deputy-chairman of the TLA were from Umzimkulu. Thus the two smallest and most peripheral areas of the Transkei received an overwhelming proportion of the executive positions of the new Assembly, a confession of weakness rather than an assertion of strength.

At the end of the Assembly's business on Monday, Paramount Chief Poto obtained the permission of the chairman to reply to the Chief Minister's victory speech that had been given three days earlier. After chiding the chiefs for thwarting the expressed will of the people, Poto said his conscience forbade him from serving in the Cabinet under a chief minister of such a different outlook and announced that he intended to form an opposition party. Four days earlier, Matanzima had announced the imminent creation of a party of his own followers.

The formal opening of the Assembly on December 11 was attended by pageantry unprecedented in Umtata. The ranking dignitary present was the Minister of Bantu Administration and Development, Mr. de Wet Nel, who addressed the Assembly for an hour after the swearing-in of the Cabinet members. The apparently random seating arrangements of the Assembly at its earlier meetings had changed into a more parliamentary form. The Chief Minister and his Cabinet now sat along the front row of seats on the chairman's right. Across the floor facing them were the chief figures of the opposition: Paramount Chief Poto in the position of "shadow" Chief Minister, Paramount Chief Sabata, and Knowledge Guzana, an elected member from Dalindyebo and the only

13. Transkei Legislative Assembly, *Proceedings at the Meeting of Members of the Transkei Legislative Assembly, held on 6th, 9th and 11th December, 1963, for the purpose of Electing Office Bearers, Etc.* (Umtata, Territorial Printers, 1964), p. 11.

practicing attorney in the Assembly, who had already demonstrated his competence as the floor leader of the Poto group. Sitting in the V. I. P. bay reserved for non-Whites were paramount chiefs and others from some of the seven remaining "Bantu homelands" for which the government planned ultimately a similar progression to semiautonomy and self-government.

Minister de Wet Nel's speech was noteworthy for its lack of a clear statement of what could be expected as the final constitutional relationship between the Transkei and the Republic of South Africa. Members of the Assembly were advised to proceed "in the knowledge that you are a part of the Republic." Later, the Minister spoke of the Republic's policy of "creative self-withdrawal" from the Transkei and referred to the present stage as a beginning of "your process of emancipation." A considerable portion of the Minister's speech was taken up with repeated, urgent, and constitutionally incongruous warnings to members to beware of looking to "alien countries" for help. Members were told: "You will be flattered by jackals coming from many directions, not because they seek your welfare but because they wish to take from you that which is yours as well as that which is ours."[14]

On behalf of the Assembly, Matanzima responded graciously to the speech of the Minister. He thanked the Republican government for helping the Transkei through a "bloodless transition period" unlike that which had occurred in "other conquered countries."[15] The chairman announced a meeting of the Cabinet and the Assembly was adjourned.

The Transkei had been launched on its new road of semiautonomy under an all-African legislature, two-fifths of whose members had been elected by a universal franchise. It had an African chief minister and Cabinet. Nonetheless, major positions of power and influence remained in White hands, in particular those of the experienced permanent officials transferred for this purpose from the Pretoria administration. Among the latter, J. H. T. Mills, Secretary of the Chief Minister's office, played a pivotal role. Moreover, as in the past, there were the White magistrates whose influence in their own spheres was little if at all diminished by the existence of the new African government. More than ever, in fact, the Transkei resembled a colony in the stage between the establishment of a national legislature and the extension to it of power to control the implementation of policy. Would it move to that next stage?

It may be questioned whether, despite the popular support evidenced for him, Paramount Chief Poto (or the Transkei) would have been better off had he become chief minister at the start of the TLA's life.

14. *Ibid.*, pp. 14–15.
15. *Ibid.*, p. 15.

The Republican government's commitment to Chief Matanzima, the Chief's experience in the TTA, and his demonstrated toughness taken together suggest that he had a better chance than his rival to carry out policies which challenge Nationalist tenets. At the same time it is clear that the exclusivist strains in Matanzima's outlook do not confine him to Xhosa nationalism but can encompass a Black nationalism that might appeal to Africans throughout South Africa. South African Africans on the whole have been remarkably free from the intolerance and exclusiveness that characterizes so many South African Whites. It remains to be seen what effect Matanzima's bitterness and ambitions will have on his use of his position.

The selection of Matanzima as chief minister of the Transkei was not surprising, however frustrating to those who had worked for Poto. In view of the political sagacity frequently demonstrated by the Republican government, its overwhelming commitment to the selection of Chief Matanzima, and its presumed influence on the ex officio members of the TLA, what was noteworthy was not his election but the closeness of the vote. Still more important was the division in sentiment, or at least in votes, between elected members and chiefs as demonstrated in that choice. At the end of 1963, the political situation in the Transkei was still in flux. At that moment, however, a two-thirds majority of the elected members of the TLA, and by implication an equally large majority of the electorate, were opposed to the new Transkeian government. Chiefs, on the other hand, were equally strong in its support.

Four important deductions may be made. First, a majority of the Transkeian citizenry appeared to reject the principle of separate development. Thus the new Transkeian government, which endorsed separate development, threatened to be a weak government, and therefore possibly an authoritarian one. Second, the lack of popular support might undercut the political leverage of the new ministers in dealing with the Republican government, whose support had probably been decisive in bringing them to power. The opposite side of this coin, however, was Matanzima's need to adopt some popular policy or policies to rally support, while only policies that were in some degree in opposition to Nationalist ones seemed likely to win favor. Third, as long as the Transkeian government remained dependent upon the support of the chiefs in the TLA, no democratization of the membership of the Assembly could be expected. Yet the continued opposition in the TLA of most elected members to most chiefs could be expected to discomfort the latter in their traditional role of standing above political controversy and might well further undermine the institution of chieftainship in the Transkei.

In the face of these conflicting pressures, the future course both of the Assembly and of the Transkei remained open to question. Still more significant than internal objectives and rivalries, however, in determining future actions were the limits the Republican government would impose on the use by Transkeians of their new platform.

8

The Rise of Political Parties

THE ELECTION had thrown into relief the differences between the two major leaders, Matanzima and Poto, and their programs. The decision of the Poto group to reject portfolios in the new government if they were offered presaged the formal organization of political parties. Within three months of the selection of Chief Kaiser Matanzima as chief minister, the first two officially accepted African political parties in the history of South Africa confronted each other in the Transkei.

FORMATION OF PARTIES

On January 4, 1964, in Umtata, the first formal moves were taken by the Poto group. Paramount Chief Victor Poto and several of his more prominent supporters decided to appoint an action committee to draft a constitution for a political party to oppose the Matanzima government. Knowledge Guzana, MLA (Member of the Legislative Assembly), and, as already noted, the only practicing attorney in the Assembly, was appointed chairman of the action committee. Certain general principles and objectives of the party were agreed upon which were, in fact, very much a restatement of the principles set out in

Chief Poto's election manifesto. It was tentatively agreed that the party should be named the Democratic party (DP).

The action committee completed its work over the next month, and on February 7, 1964, an inaugural meeting of delegates from the nine regions of the Transkei accepted its report,[1] which outlined the structure of organization and membership rules of the new party. Paramount Chief Poto was named leader of the party. Under the leader the party hierarchy corresponds to the district, regional, and all-Transkei levels of the administration. An annual party conference is declared to be the highest authority of the party. Committees at each of the three levels are responsible for executive functions. The manner of recruitment of committee members is not wholly specified, but the Constitution provides that all paramount chiefs who are members of the party are ex officio members of the National Executive Committee. Membership in the party is said to be open to *all* who subscribe to the party's aims and principles,[2] a reflection of its multiracial or nonracial approach.

The Democratic party held its first conference in Umtata on April 6. About 100 supporters attended the conference, coming from all parts of the Transkei and including most of the MLAs who had supported Poto for chief minister. After adding a preamble and effecting a few small changes to its statement of principles, the meeting unanimously approved the party's constitution. Otherwise, the principal work of the first conference was the election of officers. As had been expected, Knowledge Guzana became chairman. Chief Sandy Majeke, MLA for Emboland, and the Rev. B. S. Rajuili, MLA for Maluti but a Johannesburg resident, were elected first and second vice-chairmen, respectively. T. H. Bubu, MLA for Qaukeni, became secretary and Dr. P. H. Bala, MLA for Fingo, was elected treasurer. The broad geographic representation on the first National Executive Committee is noteworthy.

The Matanzima group had not been far behind the Poto group in developing a formal organization. On February 14, 1964, just one week after the inaugural meeting of the Democratic party, Chief Kaiser Matanzima emerged from a well-attended Umtata meeting of his supporters and announced that a committee had been formed to establish a "Government party" for the Transkei.[3] Nearly four weeks later, on March 11, the Chief Minister declared that the name of his party would be the Transkei National Independence party (TNIP). He released a draft "Programme of Principles" for the party, which had been prepared by the committee the day before but appeared chiefly to be a restatement of Matanzima's election manifesto. The Programme pledged the TNIP to retain the automatic membership of chiefs in the TLA, to continue support for the principle of separate development in oppo-

---

1. *The Star* (Johannesburg), February 8, 1964.
2. "Draft Constitution" (mimeographed).
3. *Daily Dispatch* (East London), February 15, 1964.

sition to "integrated multiracialism," and to maintain "close and friendly relations" with the Republic after full independence for the Transkei had been achieved.[4]

Six weeks later, on April 23, more than 70 delegates, including eight from the Witwatersrand, gathered in Umtata for the TNIP's inaugural congress. Chief Kaiser Matanzima was naturally elected leader of the TNIP, and his brother, George Matanzima, became chairman. Of the four other members of the Transkeian Cabinet, only the Minister of Education, B. Mdledle, received an office, that of treasurer. On the other hand, M. S. Sinaba, MLA for Maluti, and M. Canca, MLA for Emboland, both of whom had been considered supporters of Chief Poto, were elected TNIP vice-chairman and assistant secretary. D. Makongolo, who had been defeated in Dalindyebo for the TLA, was elected party secretary.[5]

The first TNIP congress also endorsed a constitution for the party, which had been prepared under the leadership of George Matanzima, and confirmed the name of the party and its Programme. The constitution provides for a party executive consisting of the "national" officers of the party, together with all paramount chiefs who are party members, plus one representative of each of the Transkei's nine regions.[6] The Transkeian party system had come into existence.

While party activity in both the Matanzima and Poto camps was largely confined to the Transkei, it was not exclusively so. On August 24, 1964, Chief Minister Matanzima, with four of his fellow ministers, commenced a seventeen-day good-will tour of the Orange Free State and the Transvaal. L. Ncwana, chairman of an African committee formed in Johannesburg to look after the Transkeian ministers during their stay in the city, revealed a short while later that Matanzima had asked his supporters there to form a TNIP Witwatersrand branch. At a final meeting of the reception committee on September 20, the members appear to have decided to transform the organization into the nucleus of such a political body. Concurrently, committee members learned there would be a TNIP admission fee of twenty cents, of which one-quarter would be retained by the branch and the remainder sent to TNIP headquarters in the Transkei.[7] In October, leaders of the Democratic party developed plans for their own tour of urban areas of the Republic.[8] Despite all difficulties, African party politics were spreading into the urban areas—not, it was true, the kind of poli-

4. "Programme of Principles of the Transkei National Independence Party" (mimeographed).
5. *Daily Dispatch* (East London), April 24, 1964.
6. *Ibid.*
7. *Ibid.*, September 21, 1964.
8. *Ibid.*, October 15, 1964.

tics African nationalist leaders had aimed for, but party politics nonetheless.

Party Alliances

At the February 7 inauguration of the Democratic party, the delegates had resolved not to associate ("link up") their organization with any other political party in South Africa. Nevertheless, following a meeting in Umtata in March with Knowledge Guzana and Paramount Chiefs Poto and Sabata, Dr. Jan Steytler, leader of the Progressive party, announced that there would undoubtedly be a "natural liaison" between the two parties because both "are based on the same ideas." A reporter wrote that this statement of Dr. Steytler was met with "nods of approval" by the leaders of the Democratic party standing alongside.[9] It will be remembered that the Rev. B. S. Rajuili, second vice-chairman of the Democratic party, was already a member of the Transvaal executive committee of the Progressive party. While Steytler emphasized that there would be no question of a "link-up" between his party and the Democratic party, it seemed clear that the latter would welcome advice from the Progressives, especially on tactics. Without some outside aid they were, of course, seriously handicapped in comparison with Matanzima and his followers who had skilled and experienced White officials on whom to call. Nonetheless, the Republican government, anxious to prevent communication between its opposition political parties and Africans, particularly those in rural areas, ultimately attempted to use the Progressive party tie and other alleged political contacts to the disadvantage of the Democratic party.

On August 24, 1964, nearly five months after the Poto-Steytler meeting in Umtata, Security Branch policemen searched Guzana's law offices, his automobile, and later his home in Umtata.[10] Guzana subsequently disclosed that the police had asked him about an alleged meeting with Alan Paton, the novelist and national president of the Liberal party.[11] At about the same time, the Special Branch searched the Umtata home of Lewis Majija, assistant secretary of the Democratic party, MLA for Dalindyebo, and reputedly a member of the Liberal party.[12] Then, on August 28, police raided the temporary residence in Langa African township, outside Cape Town, of Chief Tutor Ndamase, MLA for Nyanda and Paramount Chief Poto's son and heir. In their search the police removed a copy of the Constitution of the Democratic party, but this was later returned to Chief Ndamase, with apologies.[13]

At the least, these searches created an atmosphere of tension; the

9. *The Star* (Johannesburg), March 3, 1964.
10. *Daily Dispatch* (East London), August 28, 1964.
11. *Ibid.*, September 2, 1964.
12. *Ibid.*, October 8, 1964.
13. *Ibid.*, September 4, 1964.

Republican government's supervision of Transkeian party affairs was not only deeply disturbing to its leaders but also to any observers who had believed the Verwoerd administration would respect the independence of party politics in the Territory. At an earlier date, the Democratic party had been seriously hampered, to the authors' personal knowledge, by magisterial dilatoriness in giving permission for a meeting of Democratic party members—this permission being suddenly provided with a timetable of only a few hours in which to organize the gathering. Now it appeared that these potentially threatening actions by the police had also another motive: to restrain Africans from seeking advice or support from Whites other than government personnel or supporters.

The Republican government had still an additional motive. The Prime Minister and several of his colleagues in the Cabinet in the second week in September, 1964, condemned White "meddling" in non-White politics and broadly hinted that legislation would be introduced to proscribe these associations.[14] Administrative restraints were in fact instituted in August, 1965, to hinder the Progressives in campaigning for support among the Coloureds.

An Early Problem

Well before the Transkei's political parties had taken formal shape, word of a scandal concerning Matanzima's Minister of Justice, his brother, had caused critical publicity, though little more. On January 12, 1964, the *Sunday Times* momentarily broke the calm that had quickly returned to Umtata after the inauguration of Transkeian self-government one month earlier. The paper disclosed that the newly elected Transkeian Minister of Justice, George Matanzima, had only seven months earlier, in June, 1963, been struck from the roll of attorneys for misappropriating trust funds, and that at the same time Mr. Justice van der Riet had declared him to have made a false statement before the Eastern Cape Division of the Supreme Court. Approached about these disclosures on the same day, the Minister of Bantu Administration and Development, De Wet Nel, suprisingly denied knowledge of the matter, or much knowledge of the Minister.[15] Chief Poto, hampered by the fact the TLA was not in session, promised to raise the question of the fitness of the Minister of Justice to hold his office when the TLA convened in May;[16] he subsequently declared that the honor of the Transkeian government required the resignation of the Minister of Justice.[17]

Save for accusing the *Sunday Times* of acting maliciously and of

14. *The Star* (Johannesburg, air edition weekly), September 19, 1964.
15. *Natal Mercury* (Durban), January 13, 1964.
16. *Evening Post* (Port Elizabeth), January 13, 1964.
17. *Sunday Times* (Johannesburg), January 19, 1964.

meddling in affairs of concern only to the Transkei, the Chief Minister and his brother remained silent on the questions that had been raised. On February 10, De Wet Nel decried what he called a "mean press campaign" against George Matanzima, whom he now knew to be a "capable man."[18] Except for a brief mention by Paramount Chief Poto at the time of the no-confidence debate in the TLA on May 8, this last statement ended public discussion of the matter. The Transkeian government's reputation had not been enhanced but its grip on power was unshaken.

THE GOVERNMENT TAKES SHAPE

Meanwhile, the Transkeian administration began to adjust to its new responsibilities and to the combination of African policy-making power and White civil servants. Apart from teachers and casual workers, the Transkeian civil service at the beginning of 1964 consisted of 2,476 posts, approximately one-quarter of which were filled by Whites.[19] These civil servants remained employees of the Republican government, which undertook to pay their salaries. Moreover, just prior to the Transkeian transition to "self-government" in 1963, approximately sixty senior White civil servants were newly posted to Umtata, where they not only pervaded the administration but also created a sudden boom in the market for real estate.

The most senior of these White civil servants were six who became the permanent secretaries of the new Transkeian departments. Two of these, R. A. Midgley, Secretary of the Department of the Interior, and I. J. M. van Rooyen, Secretary of the Department of Education, were "old hands" in the Transkei. J. H. T. Mills, Secretary of the Department of Chief Minister and Finance, had been intimately involved, as we have seen, in the process of drafting the Transkeian Constitution. Upon Mills, acting with Commissioner-General Hans Abraham, of the Xhosa National Unit, fell primary responsibility for the maintenance of harmony between Umtata and Pretoria.

The official policy of the South African government is to replace White civil servants in the Transkei as rapidly as qualified Transkeian Africans become available. This will take a long time. In 1964, Whites filled all the top posts in the Transkeian administration and, excepting the ministers, no African was closer than about three echelons from the most senior positions in the administration. On the other hand, quite a large number of Whites were in positions substantially junior to those held by the most senior Africans. In consequence, to safeguard traditional South African practices, each department was carefully

18. *Rand Daily Mail* (Johannesburg), February 11, 1964.
19. *Daily Dispatch* (East London), August 16, 1963.

organized so that no White, save for the six department secretaries, ever came under the direct authority of an African. Initially, it appeared also that the African ministers were content to confine their role to matters of policy, and then only after drawing liberally upon the advice of their top civil servants. Thus questions of administration were entirely in the hands of their White department secretaries.

At the start of the new administration both African and White civil servants in Umtata were separately instructed in tactful dealings across the color line. Early reports suggested that Whites in government service in Umtata had been punctiliously correct in their dealings with Africans and that no racial incident had been encountered. There was no question, however, of interracial fraternization; social mixing of the races was discouraged both during and after working hours.

On January 15, 1964, the Chief Minister announced the names of the three members of the Transkeian Civil Service Commission. Price Sobahle, a defeated pro-Matanzima candidate for the TLA from Qaukeni, was appointed chairman, and the two other members were C. W. Monakali from Fingo, another defeated pro-Matanzima candidate and a former deputy-chairman of the TTA, and J. D. Moshesh, also pro-Matanzima, of the Maluti region. There was no provision, as in the United States, for either nonparty or biparty representation.

In the middle of February the Commission advertised its first vacancies: 246 posts, varying from that of messenger—minimum salary R3.54 ($4.95) per week—to Inspector of Education with a maximum salary of R48.46 ($67.84) per week. When the Commission first met on March 3 to consider applications for employment, 1,700 had already been received. An early report placed the number of applicants with a minimum of high-school education at more than one-third the total number.[20] Thus the number of educated Africans interested in the new posts seemed larger than had been expected.

TLA CONVENES

Well before the TLA convened in May, the new political parties had been gauging their strength in that body. At the end of February, Chief Minister Matanzima announced that he could already count on nine members, three chiefs and six elected members, who had supported Poto in December.[21] The Democratic party maintained that only one MLA had "changed" to Matanzima.[22] The end result was between these two estimates, for soon after the State President, C. R. Swart, had

20. *The Star* (Johannesburg), February 21, 1964.
21. *Daily Dispatch* (East London), February 25, 1964.
22. *Ibid.*, February 26, 1964.

opened the Assembly, the first division of the House made it clear that at least two members had crossed the aisle to join the government.

That first vote was to remove N. Joel Busakwe from the office of chairman of the Assembly. The charge against Busakwe, levied by the Chief Minister on the second day of the session, was that he had attacked the rules of the TLA in a public meeting in East London on April 18, 1964. In evidence, Matanzima cited a newspaper report whose accuracy Busakwe promptly denied. Busakwe then moved to the attack by implying that the Chief Minister was motivated by pique at the former's refusal to accept repeated invitations to join the TNIP. Taken to a vote, the motion to remove was carried by 63 votes to 0, the Democratic party abstaining in protest.[23] Two days later the deputy-chairman, Chief Petros Jozana, was elevated unopposed to the post of chairman of the Assembly, while S. M. Sinaba, also of the TNIP, was elected deputy-chairman.

Thereafter, there could be no doubt that the Chief Minister was in complete command of the Assembly. On Paramount Chief Poto's motion of no-confidence in the government presented on May 12, the government was upheld by 61 votes to 39.[24]

Yet Matanzima's dominance of the Assembly could not be equated with an automatic acceptance of Nationalist government policies. In two areas—on border industries and on education—the Chief Minister showed himself ready to strike out along more locally acceptable lines.

Independent Approach by Matanzima's Government

The first evidence of an independent line appeared on June 3, 1964, during the second-reading debate on the Transkei Development and Reserve Fund Bill, when Chief Matanzima declared that as far as the Transkei was concerned, the Republican government's border-industries scheme was impractical as a solution to developmental needs and that it was necessary to have industrial development *within* the Territory. The Chief Minister also asserted that it would be an "idle dream" to depend solely on private African capital and initiative for the industrial development of the Transkei. "Serious consideration" should be given to allowing private White enterprise to establish industries in the Transkei, he concluded, provided that the Transkeian government retained a controlling financial interest in any such industries.[25] The Nationalist response was both quick and tart. On June 7, four days later, the newspaper *Dagbreek en Sondagnuus*, which was controlled by a board headed by Prime Minister Verwoerd, gave prominent position to

23. Republic of South Africa, Transkei Government, *Debates of the Transkei Legislative Assembly. Second Session—First Assembly, 5th May to 19th June, 1964* (Umtata: Elata Commercial Printers [Pty.] Ltd., 1964), p. 9.

24. *Ibid.*, p. 45.

25. *Ibid.*, pp. 170–71.

a report by the paper's Transkeian representative that Chief Matanzima's deviation from the policy of the Republican government had created "concern in certain circles." Nonetheless, the obvious challenge on economic policy had been made.

This challenge had still more significance against the backdrop of the grim economic realities of Transkeian self-government revealed in the TLA debate on the Transkei Appropriations Bill. At that time, the Chief Minister disclosed that the estimated total revenues derived from the Territory's own sources amounted to less than one-fifth of the estimated total expenditures of the six departments under the Transkei government: R3,126,000 ($4,376,400) out of R16,120,000 ($22,568,000). Moreover, this latter figure did not include an estimated R1,610,000 ($2,256,800) for salaries for the White civil servants in the Transkei, which were being paid directly to them by the Republican government.

The deficit of more than four-fifths of the total estimated expenditures was to be met, Matanzima disclosed, by an annual grant from the Republican government of R11 million ($15,400,000) and a special additional grant of R2 million ($2,800,000).[26] The larger of these grants was supposedly equivalent to the total expenditures by the Republican government in the last financial year prior to Transkeian self-government for the branches now handled by the Transkeian government, less the aforementioned salaries of White civil servants in the Transkei. Thus the *added* investment of the Republic in the Transkei during the first year of self-government was only R2 million. Far more serious was the obviously almost complete financial dependence of the Transkeian government on Republic subventions. The need for sources of local revenue was obvious.

Still more striking evidence of some political independence on the part of the Transkeian government was shown on June 9-10, 1964, when the TLA considered the interim report of its select committee on education. This committee had been set up on May 13 to consider the report of the Cingo Commission, which the Minister of Bantu Administration and Development had appointed in 1962 to review the teaching of the official languages and the use of instruction in the mother tongue for the primary schools of the Transkei. Ten resolutions of the opposition that dealt with educational matters had also been referred to the select committee for consideration.

The report of the select committee unanimously recommended that in place of the vernacular either English or Afrikaans be introduced as the medium of instruction in the fifth year of school. It also proposed that primary schools in the Transkei adopt, with certain alterations, what was termed the "Cape European Education Syllabus," that is,

26. *Ibid.*, p. 49.

the Cape Provincial Administration Syllabus. Both this interim report,[27] and the final report tabled on June 19, which advised that Transkei secondary schools should also adopt the "Cape European Education" syllabi,[28] were unanimously endorsed by both government and opposition members.

Thus the TLA rejected for the Transkei two cardinal principles of the Afrikaner Nationalist government's Bantu Education policy: instruction of African children through the medium of the tribal vernacular; and separate and environmental determination of the goals of African education. African opposition to both principles had been central to the controversy which had surrounded Bantu education since its introduction a decade earlier.

The Transkeian decision was made despite appeals and warnings from official sources. In April, 1964, the *Bantu Education Journal,* official organ of the Department of Bantu Education, had editorially advised the Transkeian government to retain the system of Bantu education inherited from the Department. It warned the new government not to be "influenced by superficial advisors when the education of the Xhosa nation is at stake." In this perspective it was not surprising that many opposition newspapers in the Republic interpreted the Assembly's unanimous decisions on education as a serious blow to South African government policies.

In a rather puzzling outburst, prompted by what he termed the "gloating" of "Progressive and Liberal papers," Chief Matanzima issued a public statement on June 25, 1964, declaring that their deductions were unwarranted and that the Transkei had not deviated from the aims of Bantu education. He also asserted his own belief in instruction in the mother tongue and said it was an "ideal" of his government to develop Xhosa until it constituted a suitable medium for higher education.[29] The effect of this statement both on the Republican government and on the support Matanzima had presumably gained when he stood with the Transkeian opposition on the education issue was not immediately apparent. The whole situation pointed up clearly, however, the pressures from both sides to which he is constantly subject. In the no-confidence debate of the 1966 session of the Legislative Assembly, Matanzima announced preparations to develop Xhosa as a modern language to be used as the vehicle of instruction from elementary school to the universities. It was the duty of a people, he said, to make their vernacular an international language.

On June 10, 1964, the Transkeian government and the opposition also joined in calling upon the authorities to relax "influx-control" regulations—those regulations which serve to control the movement of

27. *Ibid.,* p. 218.
28. *Ibid.,* p. 289.
29. *South Africa Digest,* July 3, 1964.

Africans into and within the urban areas of the Republic, and are thus universally unpopular.

On other issues, during the six-and-one-half week session of the TLA, Chief Matanzima exploited his control of the Assembly to override, sometimes arrogantly, the opposition and to support measures that maintained tight controls in the Transkei and were consistent with, or at least neutral in relation to, the Republican government's separate development policy. On May 27, by 52 votes to 40, the Assembly defeated a motion by the opposition to repeal the highly restrictive Proclamation 400.[30] A week later a motion that called for the admission of "political fugitives" to the Transkei without the risk of prosecution was rejected, 50 votes to 35.[31]

Extensions of local responsibilities were also made. On June 11, despite the opposition's claims that the Transkei lacked the necessary personnel, the Assembly carried a motion requesting the transfer to the Transkeian government of the functions of the Department of Health.[32] Moreover, on the last day of the session, the Assembly agreed, 54 votes to 41, to the third reading of the Transkei Trading Amendment Bill, which abolished the previous requirement that there should be at least two miles between the trading stations in the Transkei.[33] The opposition had argued, on the other side, that the Transkei could not yet support many more traders and that the Bill consequently ran against the economic interests of the Transkei.

There was one unexpected exception to Chief Matanzima's mastery of the Assembly. On June 2 Mr. O. O. Mpondo (Democratic party, Gcaleka) moved that the enforcement of land-rehabilitation schemes be suspended in the Transkei.[34] Under such plans, many locations in the Transkei have been systematically replanned by government experts so that the best lands are used for cultivation and grazing and not for residential purposes. A frequent consequence of land rehabilitation is that existing huts must be destroyed and reconstructed on different sites. The government has commonly sought the cooperation of local people before commencing land rehabilitation and has compensated the owners of huts which must be broken down. Still, it is known that land-rehabilitation measures are a source of much popular dissatisfaction in the Transkei. Tribesmen of the rural Transkei are renowned for their conservatism. And in many areas, despite consultation with the people, some officials—whether magistrates, agricultural officers, chiefs, or headmen—appeared to have forced the pace of rehabilitation.

30. TLA *Debates*, May 27, 1964, p. 145.
31. *Ibid.*, p. 289.
32. *Ibid.*, p. 233.
33. *Ibid.*, p. 290.
34. *Ibid.*, p. 165.

Opposition to land rehabilitation was one cause of the Eastern Pondo-land disturbances in 1959 and 1960.

The Transkeian government opposed Mpondo's motion and Minister of Justice George Matanzima introduced an amendment which denied that there had been any enforcement of land rehabilitation.[35] But when a division of the Assembly on this amendment was called the following day, the government suffered its first and only defeat of the session by one vote, 45 votes to 44.[36] Six chiefs voted with the opposition for the first time, including, significantly, three chiefs from Eastern Pondoland. The original motion was then put by order of the chairman but was also lost, 43 votes to 0, since the opposition, arguing that the defeat of the government's amendment meant the original motion was carried auto-matically, had left the House in protest.[37]

Zoning in the Transkei

On June 11, the Chief Minister announced "with much pleasure" that the Transkei Zoning Committee, which had recently been ap-pointed by the Minister of Bantu Administration and Development, would shortly start its investigations into the zoning of the White spots of the Territory.[38] No African had been appointed to the six-man Zoning Committee; instead, it consisted of four White civil servants, including the Secretary of the Transkeian Department of the Interior, and two private citizens. One of the private citizens was a trader from the Kentani district of the Transkei, and the other was a former mayor of Umtata and the chairman of the European Liaison Committee, an organization of Transkeian Whites created specially to represent the interests of Whites of the Territory in discussions with the Republican government.

Chief Kaiser Matanzima's desire to rid the Transkei of Whites had long been apparent. His 1963 "Election Manifesto" stated that "all the land in the Transkei should belong to the Bantu including municipal land in the 26 villages." The "Programme of Principles" of the Transkei National Independence party asserts that "the gradual withdrawal of Europeans from the Transkei is a matter of paramount concern to the Party." Despite the overtones of racial exclusiveness in this objective, its appeal is obvious so long as the Whites of the Territory insist upon enjoying, as they have done for so long, the racial privileges of Whites elsewhere in the Republic. These privileges have been jealously guarded, resulting in anomalies in Umtata itself, the capital of the Transkei. For example, members of the TLA, including the Chief Minister him-self, cannot enjoy the facilities of a tearoom which stands immediately

35. *Ibid.*, p. 167.
36. *Ibid.*, p. 178.
37. *Ibid.*, p. 179.
38. *Ibid.*, p. 225.

behind the Bunga building in Umtata, in a White area of the town. While Africans may purchase refreshments, they must withdraw to the sidewalk to enjoy them. Moreover, on March 10, 1964, the Umtata Town Council had rejected a proposal of the Bantu Investment Corporation to build a hotel for Africans in Umtata on the ground that it was contrary to the Group Areas Act.[39]

On April 10, the Chief Minister told more than 600 cheering Thembu tribesmen gathered in the Cala district that the Transkeian government would see to it that the White towns were gradually taken over by Africans.[40] Speaking to a crowd of at least 4,000 persons fifteen days later at Qaukeni, the "Great Place" of Paramount Chief Sigcau of Eastern Pondoland, Chief Matanzima revealed that his government had already asked for the appointment of a committee to investigate the zoning of White towns in the Transkei. "This country is ours," declared the Chief Minister vigorously.[41]

The coming of self-government to the Transkei has had an unsettling influence upon the more than 14,000 Whites resident within the Territory, and particularly upon property owners. Comparatively few in number and represented in Parliament by a member of the opposition United party, the Transkeian Whites have feared that the government in Cape Town might regard them as being politically expendable. Accordingly, they have shunned public protest and have chosen instead to deal with the Republican government through the aforementioned European Liaison Committee.

In 1962 the Republican government appointed the Heckroodt Commission to investigate the position of all non-Africans in the Transkei; yet by the end of May, 1964, the Commission's recommendations had not yet been made public. This delay only served to increase the Whites' anxiety. In April and May, 1964, Republican government spokesmen tried to calm White fears. Speaking to the Umtata Rotary Club on April 13, J. H. T. Mills, Secretary of the Transkeian Department of the Chief Minister and Finance, spoke of the "whole volume" of provisions in the Transkei Constitution Act that serve to safeguard the interests of Whites in the Transkei.[42] The Republican government would not leave Transkei Whites "in the lurch," stated Minister de Wet Nel in the House of Assembly on May 15.[43] Speaking before the Annual Congress of the (White) Transkeian Civic Association in Umtata on May 26, Commissioner-General Hans Abraham promised that no White would be forced to leave the Transkei. He warned, however, that the South African government would not be able to apply the Repub-

39. *Rand Daily Mail* (Johannesburg), March 12, 1964.
40. *Daily Dispatch* (East London), April 11, 1964.
41. *Ibid.,* April 27, 1964.
42. *Ibid.,* April 14, 1964.
43. *Ibid.,* May 16, 1964.

lic's laws in the Transkei indefinitely.[44] Meanwhile, in the Transkei Legislative Assembly, the Chief Minister had declared on May 15: "We want to withdraw the colonists from the Transkei and give power to the aborigines of the land."[45]

On June 8, 1964, the Republican government finally released a White Paper disclosing its reactions to the recommendations of the Heckroodt Commission. (The Commission's report itself was not made available.) The government accepted responsibility for compensating Whites and Coloureds in the Transkei for property losses suffered as a direct consequence of the change in constitutional status of the Territory. The onus of proof of loss, however, would rest with the property owner. Shortly afterward, the Transkei Zoning Committee began hearings, which were completed in October, in 23 of the 26 villages in the Transkei.

PARTIES VIE FOR POWER

As the 1964 TLA session wore on, some changes took place in party allegiance. On May 26, Chief Mazauteti Diko of Qaukeni crossed from the government benches to join the opposition Democratic party.[46] Following the Assembly debate on land rehabilitation in the Transkei, Chief Qamarana Zenzile of Gcaleka similarly changed his affiliation and joined the opposition, but he died on September 16. Then after the close of the session, Chief Sigwebo Mhlanga of Qaukeni announced his resignation from the TNIP and said he would thereafter support the Democratic party. Addressing a large crowd of Africans at Lamontville Community Center, Durban, on August 2, Chief Mhlanga said that he had originally supported Chief Matanzima because of threats from Republican government officials that he would lose his chieftaincy if he did not do so. He also alleged that a majority of the chiefs who supported Chief Matanzima had been "intimidated" by officials.[47]

The fact that each of those who crossed to the opposition benches in 1964 was a chief seemed a consequence of the Democratic party's accusation that chiefs in the TLA who supported Matanzima were opposing the popular will. Speaking during the debate on his motion of no-confidence in the government, Paramount Chief Poto had cited election figures which purported to show that the electorate favored the Democratic party by a ratio of nearly 4 to 1. "The majority stand for the Democratic Party of which I am the leader," he said.[48] Concluding the debate the following day, he asserted:

44. *Ibid.*, May 27, 1964.
45. *Ibid.*, May 17, 1964.
46. *The Star* (Johannesburg), May 27, 1964.
47. *Daily Dispatch* (East London), August 4, 1964.
48. TLA *Debates*, May 6, 1964, p. 11.

I hope the chiefs on the other side will understand that I have no wish to have them thrown outside, but if they are going to think only of their own interests, they will not be regarded as representatives of the people. . . I hope you will have no trouble and that you will realize you are lost if you stick to the policy of separate development.[49]

On August 8, 1964, Knowledge Guzana returned to this topic while addressing a Democratic party meeting at Engcobo. Chiefs who continued to support separate development "were using a spade to dig their own graves," Guzana asserted; those who did not represent the views of the people would lose the "aura of chieftainship" which surrounds them. "How often," he inquired, "is the Democratic Party going to ask you to be patient with these people who betray your aspirations?"[50]

Three months earlier, on April 30, Mlingo Salakupatwa, elected MLA for Gcaleka, had been shot through a window in his hut. His wife had been killed instantly, and seventeen days later Salakupatwa died of his wounds in a Port Elizabeth hospital where he had been taken for an emergency operation.[51] At the time of his election to the Assembly in November, 1963, Salakupatwa had been thought to be a supporter of Chief Poto; yet it is believed that he voted for Matanzima for Chief Minister. On March 20, 1964, Salakupatwa had been elevated from headman to subchief of his location in the Kentani district, near Butterworth, in an installation ceremony at which all members of the Matanzima Cabinet were present. Despite the announcement by the South African Police of an unprecedented R 1,000 reward for information leading to the arrest and conviction of Salakupatwa's killer,[52] the assailant's identity was not determined. Whether or not there was a political motive for his killing, the suspicion that it was retaliation for support of Matanzima was easy to exploit.

The By-Election

Salakupatwa's death created a vacancy among the seven elected Members of the TLA from Gcaleka, thereby necessitating a by-election. Announced for November 25, 1964, this special election immediately assumed particular significance, for not only was it the first popular vote since the general election of November, 1963, but it was to be held in a region politically split between the two Transkeian parties. Indeed, a clear-cut victory for either party in the by-election could well affect several Gcaleka votes in the TLA. The position of the TNIP, which at the beginning of the TLA session had enjoyed the support of all seven of Gcaleka's ex officio members, seemed particularly vulnerable to erosion

49. *Ibid.,* p. 45.
50. *Daily Dispatch* (East London), August 12, 1964.
51. *The Star* (Johannesburg), May 18, 1964.
52. *Daily Dispatch* (East London), May 26, 1964.

were the Democratic party to be successful. On the other hand, a government victory might prove a decisive setback for the Democratic party, whose major political argument against the Matanzima government was that it lacked popular support.

The Democrats got off to a bad start. Although nomination day was September 29, both parties had announced the names of their candidates before the end of July. The choice of the Democratic party was a newly appointed Chief, Tabakile Sigcau, half-brother of the Paramount Chief of Gcaleka. Chief Sigcau is a member of the influential "Right Hand House" of the Gcaleka royal family (See Chapter 4). Through August and September the Democratic party publicized its candidate in the Gcaleka region. Then on nomination day it was discovered that Chief Tabakile Sigcau could not be nominated because his name did not appear on the Gcaleka voters' roll. At the last minute the Democrats had to find and put forward a substitute candidate; their choice was Jongilezwe M. Dumalisile, who was also a relative of Paramount Chief Zwelidumile Sigcau. As had been expected, Mr. Paul Majavu, a retired teacher, was nominated by the TNIP. He had sought election to the TLA from Gcaleka in 1963 but had finished nineteenth out of the twenty-nine candidates running and had lost his deposit.

A second surprise of nomination day was the introduction of Mr. David Gwebityala, of whom nothing had been heard before. Gwebityala declared that his political ideas were the same as those of the Democratic party and that he would contest the election as an "Independent Democrat." Guzana called Gwebityala an "imposter," however, and maintained that "We do not know him and suspect he is standing to split our vote."[53]

No unusual or unexpected issues developed in the course of the eight-week campaign. Majavu followed the Matanzima line and took his stand on behalf of the separate development of the races, automatic membership of chiefs in the TLA, and the zoning of Transkeian villages for African ownership. The manifesto of the Democratic party candidate was equally characteristic and declared in favor of a multiracial South African parliament and universal education; for repeal of "job reservation" by race and Proclamation 400; and against enforcement of land-rehabilitation measures.

The parties were otherwise distinguished from each other by the magnitude of their efforts in Gcaleka and their campaign strategies. The TNIP's campaign was clearly better organized and better financed than that of the Democratic party. The national secretary of the TNIP, Douglas Makongolo, and Minister of Justice George Matanzima spent weeks in Gcaleka preparing for the election; local organizers were appointed throughout the region. In contrast, the principal burden of

53. *Ibid.,* October 6, 1964.

directing the Democratic party's campaign fell largely on one man, Knowledge Guzana, working from Umtata.

The Democratic party sought a mass following. Through October and November until the election, Chief Poto, Guzana, and other Democratic party leaders addressed large public rallies every weekend in all parts of Gcaleka. In contrast, the TNIP adopted the typical electioneering techniques of a "patron party." Its agents visited chiefs, headmen, and other notables in an effort to persuade them that they should vote for Majavu and should urge the people under their influence to do likewise. And on October 6 an official memorandum, originating in the "Office of the Chief Minister," was circulated among chiefs and headmen in Gcalekaland urging them to "stand by the Government" and "vote for Paul Majavu."

The Daily Dispatch on October 6 stated that "the Democratic Party is very optimistic about their *[sic]* chances in the by-election." There were several good reasons, however, for supposing that the advantage lay with the TNIP: the last-minute change in the identity of the Democratic party candidate; the presence of a third candidate who would likely split the antigovernment vote; the weaker financial and organizational position of the Democratic party; and the capability and desire of the Transkeian government to determine the political affiliations of many, if not most, of the chiefs and headmen.

The results when announced were viewed by many as a significant upset.

Jongilezwe M. Dumalisile (DP)	36,137 votes
Paul Majavu (TNIP)	28,703 votes
David Gwebityala (Ind.)	4,569 votes

Forty-eight per cent of the Gcaleka electorate had voted on November 25, 62 per cent of those eligible within the region itself and 21.5 per cent of those eligible elsewhere.[54] There could be no question but that there had been a swing toward the Democratic party.

Jubilant Democrats hailed their Gcaleka victory as "full endorsement for our multiracial policy and decisive rejection of separate development."[55] In a public statement issued the day following the announcement of the results, Chief Poto called for the immediate resignation of the Chief Minister and his government.[56] But on December 1, the Chief Minister dismissed his party's by-election defeat as "something common in parliamentary systems." He also observed that the TNIP had a majority of 23 seats in the TLA and promised that "the Government with its big majority will continue its business, acting on the mandate of the people of the Transkei."[57]

54. *Ibid.,* November 28, 1964.
55. *Ibid.*
56. *Ibid.,* November 30, 1964.
57. *Ibid.,* December 1, 1964.

THE TRANSKEI AFTER ONE YEAR
OF SELF-GOVERNMENT

The Gcaleka by-election came approximately at the end of the first year of Transkeian self-government. What can be said in general of this experience? In the first place, self-government had meant little change in the economic life of the Transkeian people. Apart from, at most, several hundred new jobs for Africans in the Transkeian civil service, and the prospect, now closer but still unrealized, of African-owned enterprise in the villages of the Transkei, the economic horizons of the Transkei remained as before. The Republican government had provided no marked financial or economic aid for its first Bantustan and "showpiece" of South African race relations.

Such changes as had resulted from the Transkei's increased local autonomy were almost exclusively political and administrative. Two political parties had been formed in the Territory. Indeed, helped by the necessity of fighting the Gcaleka by-election, the development of parties in the Transkei had proceeded rapidly; recognized leaders and a tentative electoral organization had clearly emerged in both political groups. These two parliamentary parties seemed to have mastered easily the procedural and other complexities of the new governmental system.[58]

The first year of self-government ended, as it had begun, with Chief Matanzima in firm control. Yet while the Chief Minister had consolidated his political power in the Transkei, he had evidently not extended it. The opposition, surmounting greater obstacles, had also entrenched its position. The Gcaleka by-election, in fact, suggested the Democratic party had genuine popularity. The Transkeian government, in contrast, still owed its existence to the support given to it by the chiefs. In the long run this position would be untenable. Clearly the chiefs cannot permanently flout popular views and retain their positions. The same is true of Matanzima and the TNIP; they will either have to adopt a more independent, even broadly nationalistic line or be ultimately rejected.

Three events of the first year of Transkeian self-government were of general South African interest: the Chief Minister's assertion of the need to admit private White capital to the Transkei, and concurrently his dismissal of the value of "border industries" for the Transkei; the Assembly's unanimous rejection of the philosophy of Bantu education; and the somewhat unexpected success of the Democratic party in the Gcaleka by-election. All three raised doubts about the ability of the Nationalist party government to control Transkeian development.

58. In March, before the opening of the TLA, all members had taken a two-day course in Umtata in parliamentary procedure. Probably of greater educational importance, however, was the continued consultation of leaders on both sides with White allies.

Yet these events did not seriously weaken Dr. Verwoerd's standing with the White electorate. Other events occurring elsewhere over the same period—in particular, police discovery of White and African sabotage rings—had tended to solidify White support for stronger police measures. Events concerning the Transkei had become remote to the lives of most Whites in South Africa. Nor did they appear to be having practical and positive relevance to the lives of those approximately one million Transkeian citizens and the millions of other Africans residing outside the Territory. Thus it was difficult to perceive that Transkeian "self-government" was in any significant way reducing race tensions in the Republic.

Epilogue

South Africa Fails
to Meet the Challenge

Ⅰ N ESTABLISHING the Transkei—or, at least, its rural areas—as the first semiautonomous African territory under an African Chief Minister and Cabinet and an all-African legislature, partially elected by universal Transkeian suffrage, the South African government took a step with potentially far-reaching consequences, and for calculated purposes. Confronted with world-wide opposition to its policies of racial discrimination, the Nationalist government sought to divert both internal and external criticism and pressures by starting to transform its domestic colonies, the African reserves, from mere sources of unskilled labor for the country's vigorous economy into genuine "homelands" which would form counter magnets to draw African attention and even African residents away from the so-called White areas, where they so heavily outnumber the White inhabitants.

In this perspective, the long discussions and complicated processes involved in establishing the Transkeian "Bantustan" find their justification. Insignificant in themselves both in the number of persons affected and the extent of change, the developments in the Transkei might have been crucial to the character of South African racial policy had they provided a strikingly attractive alternative to opportunities in the country's urban areas. The Transkei might then have seemed an example to be followed eagerly by other predominantly African areas, such as Zululand (although the Zulu are scattered in small reserves all over

Natal), and even the dispersed pockets of land of the Tswana and Sotho. Taken together with the imminence of independence for the former High Commission Territories—Bechuanaland, Basutoland, and Swaziland—the Africans' opportunities in their own areas in South Africa might have dulled the edge of African resentment at overt discrimination and restrictions elsewhere.

That the Transkeian development has opened the way to some constructive opportunities cannot be denied. For the first time in South African history, Africans have taken leadership in officially sanctioned party political activity. For the first time, the principle of "one man (or woman), one vote" has been officially accepted, at least for Transkeian Africans outside as well as inside the territory, and by implication for members of any African group accepting comparable semiautonomous status. It is undoubtedly true, however, that although the South African government may try to restrict the implication of this franchise to narrow territorial areas, its relevance for national political representation will not be overlooked. Indeed, this experience may well undercut whatever frail hope the Progressives might have of persuading Africans that they should consider a more restrictive although nonracial franchise in the broader, national sphere.

Beyond the experience of political activity involved in elections and the operations of political parties lies the opportunity for a small, but not unimportant, group of Africans to exercise limited legislative and administrative responsibilities. However much these opportunities remain hedged, and no matter how powerful the behind-the-scenes—and occasionally public—role of the White officials becomes, the very grappling by Africans with specific problems, the necessity of consulting African representatives, and the fact of their holding executive positions have both practical and psychological effects. All colonial experience, and particularly that of the former Belgian Congo, documents the need for practical experience by Africans in administration and political decision-making as an essential step toward constructive use of such opportunities.

But in spite of the possibilities offered for political maturity, it is equally important to note the overwhelming economic problems of the Transkei, and what must seem the almost calculated lack of financial or economic aid to meet these problems. Whatever sins of inadequate preparation or aid can be laid at the doors of British and French colonial administrations, their achievements contrast most favorably with the parsimony of the South African government in regard to the economic development of the Transkei and other African areas.

The Transkei's share of South Africa's five-year development plan, 1961–66, called for an expenditure of only £9.5 million ($26,600,000) for an area larger than that of the Netherlands.[1] Under this plan the average annual investment in the Transkei was only .5 per cent of the total expenditure of the South African government in 1961–62. Even the special additional grant of R2 million made to the Transkei by the Republican government in 1964 (R1 million of which will indirectly capitalize the new Transkei Development and Reserve Fund) is not sufficient to suggest that existing plans constitute a serious effort to develop the reserves in general or the Transkei in particular.

It is clear that the basic problem in the African reserves is the lack of nonagricultural wage-employment opportunities,[2] a situation in which the Transkei is no better off than other African areas within South Africa. As late as 1962, only 20,592 of the 1,400,000 Africans in the Transkei had paid jobs within the Territory. Of this total more than 8,000 were in domestic service.[3] In 1962 alone, at least 115,000 Africans from the Transkei sought work in the mines of the Republic, while about 30,000 more were recruited for agriculture and industry.[4] Moreover, as we have seen, in order to carry out the plans for the agricultural development of the reserves it will be essential to remove from the land at least one-half, and perhaps two-thirds, of the persons now on it. This conclusion is supported by the South African government's experience in the Ciskei, to say nothing of the annual increase in population, which would have to be taken care of by secondary and tertiary activities. In the Transkei this could mean as many as 500,000 people seeking new jobs, for whom such opportunities clearly are not now available within the Territory. Indeed, Professor Hobart Houghton, a leading South African economist, wrote in 1962 that his slogan for the economic development of the African areas was "Wanted: 300,000 non-agricultural jobs at R20 [$28] per month!"[5]

Despite the concessions so far offered by the government for its border-industries scheme, industrialists have formidable practical objections to moving industry to border areas. As early as 1958, the Viljoen Commission of Enquiry into Policy Relating to the Protection of Industries reported that from a purely economic standpoint the scales were "heavily weighted" against industrial decentralization.[6] In any case, the areas which have been selected for border industries are those already impinging on existing urban centers, particularly Pretoria, Durban, East London, and Pietermaritzburg. While the success of

1. Department of Information, *The Progress of the Bantu Peoples Towards Nationhood* (occasional pamphlet), p. 20.
2. Hobart Houghton, "Economic Development in the Reserves," *Race Relations Journal,* XXIX, No. 1 (January–March 1962), 15.
3. *House of Assembly Debates* (May 28, 1963), col. 6772.
4. *Ibid.* (March 18, 1963), col. 2962.
5. Houghton, *op. cit.,* p. 19.
6. *Report of the Commission of Enquiry into Policy Relating to the Protection of Industries,* 1958 (U. G. 36/1958), paras. 45–48.

industries established in such border localities seems assured, the degree of wider dispersal, as Professors Fair and Green had suggested earlier, is "very limited."[7] By 1962, the border industries had created only about 1,850 new jobs in the reserves.

Moreover, it is apparent that the larger the reserve area, the less border industries can do to cut down migratory labor. Very small reserve areas can become virtual "company towns," as has happened at Rosslyn, just outside of Pretoria. In large areas like the Transkei, however, the effect of border-industry development can be little more, in most cases, than a reduction in the distance the migratory worker is away from his family. This fact, plus uncertainty about the future boundaries of the Bantustans, have been factors inhibiting interest in the border program for industry in the East London-Port Elizabeth-Queenstown circumference of the Transkeian and Ciskeian Territories.

The Bantu Investment Corporation, the government's instrument for promoting industrial and commercial development *within* the homelands, has been no more promising to date in creating employment opportunities for Africans in the reserves. Established in 1959, the Corporation was initially capitalized by the government at £500,000. In early 1962 its capital was doubled, and in 1964 the Transkeian government invested an additional R500,000 in the Corporation. The purpose of the Corporation is to assist Africans with loans to set up businesses for themselves in the homelands. Concurrently, in order to exert pressure on Africans to invest in the reserves, the government limited each individual African businessman to only one trading license in the African urban townships located in the so-called White areas.

From mid-1959 through mid-1966, the Bantu Investment Corporation contracted for more than 800 loans. The number of new jobs which had been or would be thereby created is unknown, but it is certainly not more than several thousand, far short of the 50,000 new jobs which the Tomlinson Commission said should be newly created each year for 25 years.

The amount of capital available to the Bantu Investment Corporation is not, however, the major difficulty for African investment in the Transkei, or in any of the reserve areas. The chief limiting factor is the scarcity of Africans who both wish to live in the reserves and have the entrepreneurial skill and experience required before a loan can be granted.[8]

An additional problem is the lack of exploitable resources. On May 18, 1964, Chief Minister Matanzima optimistically told the members of the Transkei Legislative Assembly that although the mineral re-

7. T. J. D. Fair and L. P. Green, "Development of the Bantu Homelands," *Optima,* XII, No. 1 (March, 1962), 15.

8. See Professor Hobart Houghton's address to the seventh regional congress of the Midlands Chambers of Commerce at Grahamstown (*Daily Dispatch* [East London], June 12, 1964.)

sources of the Territory had not yet been "thoroughly investigated, sizeable deposits" existed.[9] Two days later, however, while addressing the annual conference of the Trankei Civic Association, Mr. N. G. Venter, Manager of the Umtata branch of the Bantu Investment Corporation, declared that the "extreme poverty" of the Transkei in natural resources stood out like a "sore thumb." This condition, he said, was the foremost reason why there were virtually no important industries in the Transkei. He concluded that the Transkei could not be made free of the need for outside assistance.[10] But, as we have seen, the degree of this assistance by the South African government is hardly more than enough to maintain the Transkei (and other African areas) at their existing level.

Even in the political sphere, events have not proved encouraging. In 1966, five members of the opposition Democratic party—Majija, Raziya, Nkosiyane, Nogcantsi, and Cromwell Diko—were arrested on a charge of conspiring to murder Kaiser Matanzima. About the same time, Paramount Chief Victor Poto resigned as leader of the Democratic party because of advanced age and ill health. Knowledge Guzana took his place. Refused a passport to visit the United States on the State Department's Leader Exchange Program (as was Chief Butileze of Zululand), Guzana has concentrated on his work as leader of the opposition without the benefit of outside experience. Reportedly he has made an excellent impression, but he is operating in a situation in which the cards are stacked against him.

Relations between the Republican government and Chief Minister Matanzima have not been free from strain. In two respects, however, Matanzima has won his own way. His desire for the status of Paramount Chief has been granted. More striking, his protest over the banning of Curnick Ndamase, a former lecturer at Fort Hare, resulted in the unprecedented, though partial, lifting of that ban. The case is a particularly interesting one since Ndamase, who had been dismissed for criticizing the administration in a private talk, was subsequently appointed by Matanzima—on the advice of the Civil Service Commission but over the opposition of Commissioner-General Hans Abraham —to the top African educational post in the Transkei. The government's banning of Ndamase was intended, it appeared, to prevent him from assuming that position. Matanzima and other ministers took the unusual step of flying to Cape Town to protest the ban. Apparently a compromise was reached, with Ndamase taking, at least for the present, a minor post away from Umtata, probably as a school principal.

Despite extremely limited local funds, the Transkeian government successfully negotiated the transfer of three more ministries—Post and Telegraphs, Transport, and Information—to African control in 1966.

9. TLA, *Proceedings*, p. 77.
10. *The Star* (Johannesburg), May 21, 1964.

More significant has been the pressure inside the TNIP, particularly from the Maluti region, for independence by May, 1967. So persistent was this party pressure that Matanzima found himself forced to state repeatedly that the Transkei was not yet ready for independence and even to suggest that ANC infiltrators of the TNIP were responsible for the independence demand.

The moving spirit in the appeal for independence was Shadrack Sinaba, who had switched his allegiance from the Democratic party to become Matanzima's Chief Whip. Sinaba left the Transkei National Independence party in December, 1965, and sat during the 1966 Assembly as an Independent. His proposed new party, the Transkei People's Freedom party, was founded later in the year. Once the TLA session began in mid-April, 1966, he tempered his earlier appeal for independence and requested to know "when independence is going to be achieved." He appeared, however, to have gained considerable support within the ranks of Matanzima's party. Whether such pressures were in practice unpopular with Matanzima was not clear, for he reportedly asked for a speedier process toward independence when he was protesting Ndamase's ban during his Cape Town trip.

Even the Democratic party, despite its earlier emphasis on multi-racialism, was moving more openly toward support of independence—largely, as suggested before, because it realized that the Republican government would not otherwise permit the policies that the party stood for. The most prominent supporter of independence appeared to be the Rev. B. S. Rajuili, himself from the Maluti area though resident in Johannesburg. It was becoming increasingly apparent, therefore, that at the next Transkeian general election in 1968, independence, and its date, would be the dominant issue.

But what would independence for the Transkei mean, even if it were conceded? Would such an economically impoverished area be able to make more than technical use of such a status? Or could it be something of a Trojan horse, as the United party has warned, by attracting outside capital and, more important, becoming subject to outside political influence?

In the light of the external as well as the internal pressures that formed the setting within which the South African government embarked on the Transkeian experiment, would independence for the territory do anything to assuage foreign criticism and African resentment? By itself, and with its extremely limited resources, such a development would seem almost meaningless except, perhaps, to its small group of leaders and local inhabitants. The almost total dependence on the South African economy for even the livelihood of those in the territory, the lack of attractiveness of rural life to Africans brought up in urban areas, and the relatively small numbers affected in relation to the total African population of South Africa would all seem to make independence for the Transkei relatively unimportant in the total context. Even if the South African government should decide to pour massive funds into the Transkei and other African areas for which it plans comparable developments, it can hardly be expected that either the Africans themselves or the outside world would feel that what was virtually a unilateral settlement by Whites for a small, impoverished area could compare with the progressive extension of political, social, and economic rights for Africans within the present boundaries of South Africa.

Could any plan for separation offer possibilities for racial harmony in South Africa? Looking from outside, the authors see separate territorial development as worthy of consideration only if it meets three distinct requirements and shows great promise of leading to a corollary that goes to the heart of the South African situation. In the first place, White and African areas would have to be separated in a manner that provided both groups with urban and economic resources and with port facilities and communications related to their population needs and geographical spread. Secondly, and intimately related, is that non-White areas would not be shut off from the world outside and from each other by White-controlled strips of territory and pockets such as Port St. Johns. In the third place, the settlement would have to be the product of genuine and extensive discussion, and of agreement by representative national as well as local leaders of the groups concerned.[11] And beyond these three requirements would lie the basic

11. Many proposals have been made since the end of World War II for calling a new national convention that would be representative of all racial groups. The unreality of such hopes today is indicated by the conditions that necessarily should precede the calling of such a convention and the status of many of the non-White leaders who should be present. According to the Progressive party's Molteno Commission in 1962, before such a convention met, in accordance with an act of Parliament, "legislation restricting in any way freedom of political organization of any non-White community . . . should . . . be repealed and freedom of organization restored to all." (*Final Report of the Commission set up by the Progressive Party to make recommendations on a Revised Constitution for South Africa extending Franchise Rights to all civilized subjects of the Republic,* Molteno Report, II [August, 1962], 73.)

The African delegates emerging from the process of selection discussed by the Molteno Commission might include a number of leaders who were not members of the ANC and the PAC before those organizations were outlawed—for example, Matanzima and Poto. But the delegation could hardly exclude other Africans who have been leaders in the sense that Albert Luthuli, President-General of the ANC, had in mind when he expressed disappointment in January, 1961, that Dag Hammarskjold was meeting "tribal chiefs and others who are not representative of the African people." "I have the highest respect for the chiefs," Luthuli said, "but they are not necessarily leaders of the people. . . . They are not leaders in the sense of voicing the aspirations of the people." Agreeing with Luthuli, in effect, Dr. A. B. Xuma, President-General of the ANC from 1940 through 1949, told Hammarskjold that it was worthwhile for him (Xuma) to continue discussions only if elected leaders like Luthuli and Robert Sobukwe, leader of the PAC, were present. (*The Star* [Johannesburg], January 13 and 18, 1961.)

Luthuli is under ban in his rural area. Sobukwe is being detained indefinitely on Robben Island near Cape Town, although his three-year prison term expired in mid-1963. Mandela is also on Robben Island serving a life sentence for attempted sabotage. And other ANC and PAC leaders are also in jail, under ban, or in exile.

objective: that such a partition would lead to the establishment of nonracial policies in both White and African areas. Only a realistic hope of this latter development would make separate development worthy of serious consideration as an alternative to liberal change within a united South Africa.

Such hope that racial discrimination could be eliminated by a far-reaching territorial division of South Africa rests on the assumption that discrimination arises from fear. If so, the psychological effect upon Whites of becoming either the majority or near-majority in a newly demarcated area or areas might create new attitudes toward color and race. The extensive consultation and compromise between Whites and Africans essential for a mutually agreeable division of territory would in itself help to provide an atmosphere in which nonracial societies could be organized. This process, admittedly, would require a fundamental change in attitude on the part of the White government and electors of South Africa, but they could expect at least two positive results: freedom from their underlying but pervasive fear of violence and acceptance in full measure by the Western world. Furthermore, the risk that violence might erupt during the movement toward non-racialism would need to be weighed against the near certainty of eventual racial violence if South Africa persists in its present course.

Over and over again representatives of states all over the world have assailed South Africa for its racial policies. American representatives have generally tried to indicate their awareness of the complexity of the South African racial scene and their recognition that the United States has been and is still notably inadequate in fulfilling its own objectives of racial equality. American representatives have not endorsed the Bantustan concept. Instead, they have emphasized that the first step toward a solution of South Africa's problem is recognition of the multiracial character of its society. However, official spokesmen also have emphasized that the solution would best be one devised by the South Africans themselves. This would not exclude a partition arrived at by South African representatives of all groups. In the course of the sharpest criticism of South Africa ever made by an American delegate, Francis Plimpton, U.S. representative in the United Nations, declared on October 24, 1961, that "carried to its logical conclusion, the result of apartheid would be real partition, with the Negro and other non-White inhabitants in possession of their own territory and independent government and with the White South Africans gathered in their own independent enclave."[12] But this is a possibility not in sight.

What in practice might be "a real partition"? It might begin by join-

12. U.S. Delegation to the General Assembly, *Press Release No. 3811,* October 24, 1961.

ing the Transkei and Ciskei, and continue by linking the major African areas of South Africa to the former High Commission Territories, that have achieved, or will soon achieve independence. The Transkei adjoins Lesotho (formerly Basutoland); Zululand is close to Swaziland; Tswana-land is near Botswana (formerly Bechuanaland). But, although these territories occupy some 45 per cent of all the land within the boundaries of South Africa and the three adjacent Territories, their proportion of its resources is very small. With the addition of Southwest Africa, wholly freed from South African control, both area and resources would be considerably increased.

Much more than this would be necessary, however, in order to establish an equitable and stable partition. Some part at least of the most industrial sections of Natal, as well as developed ports, whether now existing or newly constructed, would have to be incorporated in the ring of African-controlled territory that must be expected to cut off Durban and its vicinity from the rest of the Republic. Port Elizabeth and East London might well become part of the African lands stretching at least to the northern boundary of Lesotho. The wealth of the all-important Witwatersrand area would have in some way to be shared.

Moreover, the process of arriving at division is as important and even more complicated than the division itself. Today it is a White government that is defining boundaries and putting conditions on what goes on within them. But in some unforeseeable future the process might be managed by others. Only as one puts oneself in the position of those who are now the objects of policy can one appreciate the vital character of the way in which far-reaching decisions are made. Even the program suggested above, which might seem on paper to be a far more equitable plan for separate territorial development than any yet advanced, would fail utterly to establish what Dr. Hoernlé called "areas of liberty" if it were not the result of full, free, and widespread consultation between Africans and Whites of all groups, national and local, such as has not yet been seen in South Africa.

Of itself, the Transkei is of minor importance. What made it significant was that it was chosen for the most dramatic illustration of the official South African race policy of separate territorial development. What has happened to and in the Transkei has made it clear, however, that far more has been claimed for separate development than either the process or the accomplishments warrant. And yet of all African territories controlled by South Africa the Transkei is the one best suited for political responsibility and economic development. To consider the parody of separate development which the Odendaal Commission proposes for small isolated groups in Southwest Africa is to recognize the devastating extent to which the policy might be pushed.

What is chiefly important is that Transkeian developments have taken territorial separation out of the realm of theory into that of practice and disclosed the hollowness of its pretensions. More constructively, the experience underlines for us the basic changes both in policy and procedure that are needed if South Africa is to move toward a realistic accommodation between Africans and Whites.

What is essential to remove the bitterness and tension between Africans and Whites—and what the development of the Transkei has not provided—is full and open consultation, as well as mutually acceptable plans. If the Transkei had been moved rapidly to independence, as Lesotho was, this process might have stirred the imagination of local Africans and of world opinion. But what has taken place in the Transkei has done more to remind Africans of imposed limits than of widening opportunities. Moreover, few if any Africans inside or outside South Africa consider that even a relatively equitable partition of that country would be a satisfactory alternative to the extension of political rights to non-Whites within an undivided country.

Africans, no less than Whites, view themselves as South African citizens who should receive all the rights and privileges of citizenship in an undivided country. In this perspective, the whole complicated procedure resulting from the Republican government's conception of separate development—what we have called domestic colonialism— becomes largely meaningless. Only when Whites accept for the whole of South Africa the implicit challenge of separate development—that Africans must have the same rights and opportunities as they themselves enjoy—can that country hope to attain the internal consensus that would enable South Africa to assume the role in Africa and the world that its resources and development would justify.

Appendix

THE EXTRACTS that follow are from the Transkei Constitution Act and are the sections most relevant to its purposes. The Act is known officially as the "Act to confer self-government in the Transkei on the Bantu resident in the Transkei and on certain Bantu related to the Bantu of the Transkei and to provide for matters incidental thereto" (The Republic of South Africa, Act. No. 48, 1963).

LEGISLATIVE POWERS OF THE LEGISLATIVE ASSEMBLY

37. (1) Subject to the provisions of this Act the Legislative Assembly shall have the power—
   (a) to make laws not inconsistent with this Act in relation to all matters appearing in part B of the First Schedule of this Act; and
   (b) to provide in any such law for the amendment or repeal of any law, including any Act of Parliament, in so far as it relates to any such matter and applies in the Transkei or to any citizen of the Transkei whether such citizen is or is resident within or outside the Transkei.

(2) Where in terms of the said Schedule the Legislative Assembly is empowered to make laws applicable in any area outside the Transkei

or in relation to citizens of the Transkei who are or are resident elsewhere than in the Transkei but within the Republic, any such law shall have effect and may contain provision for the due enforcement thereof in any such area or, as the case may be, in relation to any such citizen in any place within the Republic wherever such citizen may be or may be resident.

(3) No law made after the commencement of this Act (including any Act of Parliament or Ordinance of a Provincial Council, but excluding a law made by the Legislative Assembly or any such Act or Ordinance as is referred to in sub-paragraph (ii) or (iii) of paragraph (a) of sub-section (1) of section *fifty-two*) which relates to any matter referred to in sub-section (1) shall apply to the Transkei or in relation to any citizen of the Transkei in respect of which the Legislative Assembly is empowered to make laws in so far as that matter is concerned.

First Schedule.

PART B.

MATTERS FALLING WITHIN THE CLASSES OF SUBJECTS IN RESPECT OF
WHICH THE TRANSKEIAN LEGISLATIVE ASSEMBLY SHALL HAVE POWER
TO MAKE LAWS AND REFERRED TO IN SECTION *thirty-seven* OF THIS ACT.

1. Direct taxation on citizens of the Transkei, whether resident within or outside the Transkei, and on property situated within the Transkei.

2. Bantu education in the districts mentioned in section *two* of this Act, whether within or outside Bantu areas in any such district, but not within any area in the district of Matatiele or Port St. John's which is not a Bantu area.

3. Agriculture including soil and veld conservation, stock improvement, development, maintenance and conservation of water supplies, irrigation, forestry and veterinary services in the Transkei, but excluding control over the importation into and the exportation from the Republic of stock, exotic animals, poultry, birds, insects, agricultural or other products, plants, farm feeds, seeds, fertilizers, stock remedies, vaccines, biologicals or anything liable to spread disease or infection.

4. Subject to the provisions of sections *forty-eight* and *forty-nine* of this Act, the establishment, administration and control of inferior courts in any district mentioned in section *two* of this Act.

5. The appointment, powers, duties and functions of justices of the peace and commissioners of oaths in the Transkei.

6. The protection of life, persons and property and the prevention of cruelty to animals in the Transkei.

7. The control, organization and administration of such personnel or such part of the Police Force stationed in the Transkei as may have

been transferred to the government of the Transkei by the Minister of Justice of the Republic, and charged with the maintenance of law and order, the investigation of any offence or alleged offence, the enforcement of any law and the prevention of crime in the Transkei to the extent and subject to such conditions as may be determined by the said Minister.

8. The administration of deceased estates, the execution of wills and matters relating to succession in respect of citizens of the Transkei resident in any of the districts mentioned in section *two* of this Act.

9. Land settlement, registration of deeds and surveys in the Transkei but excluding trigonometrical surveys.

10. Public works and undertakings, roads, outspans, ponts and bridges in the Transkei, excluding bridges between the Transkei and any other part of the Republic and roads which have been declared to be national roads.

11. (a) Municipal institutions, Bantu authorities referred to in section *forty-six* of this Act and other local institutions of a similar nature in the Transkei.

    (b) Institutions or bodies in the Transkei other than such institutions as are referred to in paragraph (a) which have in respect of one or more areas (whether contiguous or not) outside the area of jurisdiction of any institution contemplated by that paragraph authority and functions similar to the authority and functions of any such last-mentioned institution or in respect of the preservation of public health in such area or areas, including any such body as is referred to in section *seven* of the Public Health Act, 1919 (Act No. 36 of 1919).

12. The regulation and control of road traffic, including the licensing and control of vehicles and the drivers of vehicles in the Transkei, but excluding all matters dealt with in the Motor Carrier Transportation Act, 1930 (Act No. 39 of 1930), or the Motor Vehicle Insurance Act, 1942 (Act No. 29 of 1942).

13. Labour matters in the Transkei but excluding all matters dealt with in the Workmen's Compensation Act, 1941 (Act No. 30 of 1941), or the Unemployment Insurance Act, 1946 (Act No. 53 of 1946).

14. Welfare services including child welfare and the administration of social benefit schemes for the aged, infirm and blind, as well as disability grants and pauper relief for citizens of the Transkei in the districts referred to in section *two* of this Act, but not within any area in the district of Matatiele or Port St. John's which is not a Bantu area.

15. Births, deaths and marriages in respect of citizens of the Transkei in the districts mentioned in section *two* of this Act.

16. Registration of voters and the conduct of elections for the purposes of this Act and matters incidental thereto, including such regis-

tration and the conduct of such elections at any place in the Republic outside the Transkei.

17. The appointment, conditions of office, discipline, retirement, discharge and pensioning of public officers or employees of the Government of the Transkei and generally the administration and control of departments and matters assigned to that Government.

18. Intoxicating liquor in the Transkei.

19. Markets and pounds in the Transkei.

20. Fish and game preservation in the Transkei subject to the provisions of section *fourteen* of the Sea Fisheries Act, 1940 (Act No. 10 of 1940).

21. The control and licensing of trading and business in the Transkei but excluding the licensing of dealings in arms and ammunition and explosives.

22. The collection of and the control over all revenue and income payable to the Government of the Transkei in terms of any law, or deriving from any other source, or specially assigned to the Government of the Transkei by the State President by Proclamation in the *Gazette.*

23. The imposition of punishment for enforcing any law of the Legislative Assembly made in relation to any matter coming within any of the classes or subjects enumerated in this schedule.

24. Generally all matters which in the opinion of the State President and according to his written directions are of a merely local or private nature in the Transkei.

Selected Bibliography

GENERAL WORKS ON SOUTH AFRICA

South Africa is easily the most thoroughly documented African country south of the Sahara; there exists a vast literature. The following listing of general works for the serious but unfamiliar student is therefore merely suggestive. Works dealing with race relations in South Africa are included in keeping with the larger context of the subject of this book.

BENSON, MARY. *The African Patriots: The Story of the African National Congress of South Africa.* London: Faber and Faber Ltd., 1963. Revised as *South Africa: The Struggle for a Birthright.* Harmondsworth, Middlesex, England: Penguin Books, 1966.

BROOKES, EDGAR HARRY. *The Colour Problem of South Africa; being the Phelps-Stokes Lectures delivered at the University of Cape Town.* London: K. Paul, Trench, Trubner, 1934.

———. *The History of Native Policy in South Africa from 1830 to the Present Day.* 2d rev. ed. Pretoria: J. L. van Schaik, 1927.

CARTER, GWENDOLEN M. *The Politics of Inequality: South Africa Since 1948.* Rev. ed. New York: Frederick A. Praeger, 1959.

COLE, MONICA M. *South Africa.* New York: E. P. Dutton & Co., 1961.

DE BLIJ, HARM J. *Africa South.* Evanston: Northwestern University Press, 1962.

GREEN, L. P., and T. J. D. FAIR. *Development in Africa: A Study in Regional Analysis with Special Reference to Southern Africa.* Johannesburg: Witwatersrand University Press, 1962.

SELECTED BIBLIOGRAPHY

HELLMAN, ELLEN (ed.). *Handbook on Race Relations in South Africa*. London: Oxford University Press, 1949.

HOERNLÉ, R. F. ALFRED. *Race and Reason*. Johannesburg: Witwatersrand University Press, 1945.

_____. *South African Native Policy and the Liberal Spirit*. Johannesburg: Witwatersrand University Press, 1945.

HOUGHTON, D. HOBART. *The South African Economy*. Cape Town: Oxford University Press, 1964.

KARIS, THOMAS. "South Africa," in Gwendolen M. Carter (ed.), *Five African States: Responses to Diversity*. Ithaca: Cornell University Press, 1963, pp. 471–616.

KUPER, LEO. *An African Bourgeoisie: Race, Class, and Politics in South Africa*. New Haven: Yale University Press, 1965.

LEWIN, JULIUS. *Politics and Law in South Africa: Essays on Race Relations*. London: Merlin Press, 1963.

LUTHULI, ALBERT. *Let My People Go*. New York: McGraw-Hill Book Co., 1962.

MACMILLAN, R. G., P. D. HEY, and J. W. MACQUARRIE. (eds.). *Education and Our Expanding Horizons: Proceedings of the National Conference on Education, University of Natal, 1960*. Pietermaritzburg: University of Natal Press, 1962.

MARQUARD, LEO. *The Peoples and Policies of South Africa*. 3d ed. London: Oxford University Press, 1962.

MOHAPELOA, J. *Africans and Their Chiefs*. Cape Town: The African Bookman, 1945.

PAUW, B. S. *The Second Generation: A Study of the Family Among Urbanized Bantu in East London*. Cape Town: Oxford University Press, 1963.

PIENAAR, S., and ANTHONY SAMPSON. *South Africa: Two Views of Separate Development*. London: Oxford University Press, 1960.

RHOODIE, N. J., and H. J. VENTER. *Apartheid: A Socio-historical Exposition of the Origin and Development of the Apartheid Idea*. Cape Town: H.A.U.M., 1959.

ROUX, EDWARD. *S. P. Bunting: A Political Biography*. Cape Town: The African Bookman, 1944.

_____. *Time Longer than Rope: A History of the Black Man's Struggle for Freedom in South Africa*. 2d ed. Madison: University of Wisconsin Press, 1964.

SOGA, J. H. *The Ama-Xhosa*. Lovedale, Cape Province, 1932.

TABATA, I. B. *The All African Convention: The Awakening of a People*. Johannesburg: People's Press, 1950.

TATZ, C. M. *Shadow and Substance in South Africa: A Study in Land and Franchise Policies Affecting Africans, 1910–1960*. Pietermaritzburg: University of Natal Press, 1962.

THOMPSON, LEONARD M. *Politics in the Republic of South Africa*. Boston: Little, Brown and Co., 1965.

VAN DEN BERGHE, PIERRE L. *South Africa, A Study in Conflict*. Middletown, Conn.: Wesleyan University Press, 1965.

WELLINGTON, JOHN H. *Southern Africa: A Geographical Study*. 2 vols. Cambridge: Cambridge University Press, 1955.

MATERIALS RELATING TO THE TRANSKEI

There are few books which deal in their whole or in substantial part with the Transkei, one indication of the slight importance which has been ascribed to this region in the past. The list below includes not only books but pamphlets, articles, and other material relating to the Transkei.

BELLWOOD, W. A. *Whither the Transkei?* Cape Town: Howard Timmins, 1964.

BOARD, CHRISTOPHER. "The Rehabilitation Program in the Bantu Areas and Its Effect on the Agricultural Practices and Rural Life of the Bantu in the Eastern Cape," *South African Journal of Economics,* XXXII, No. 1 (March, 1964), 36–52.

BRIDGMAN, FREDERICK B. "The Native Franchise in the Union of South Africa." Unpublished Ph.D. dissertation, Yale University, 1939.

BROWNLEE, FRANK. *The Transkeian Native Territories.* Historical Records. Lovedale, Cape Province, 1923.

BUCKLEY, WILLIAM F., JR. "South African Fortnight," *National Review,* XIV, No. 2 (January 15, 1963), 17–23.

BUNTING, BRIAN. "Verwoerd's Bantustan Bluff," *Revolution: Africa, Latin America, Asia,* I, No. 7 (November, 1963), 68–74.

CLARKE, FRED. *Quebec and South Africa: A Study in Cultural Adjustment.* London: Oxford University Press, 1934.

"Constitutional Developments in the Transkei," *International Bulletin of the Africa Institute,* II, No. 2 (February, 1964), 54–64.

EISELEN, W. W. M. "Harmonious Multi-Community Development," *Optima,* IX, No. 1 (March, 1959), 1–15.

EVANS, GILL. "Partition and South Africa's Future," *Journal of International Affairs,* XVIII, No. 1 (Spring, 1964), 241–52.

FAIR, T. J. D., and L. P. GREEN. "Development of the 'Bantu Homelands,'" *Optima,* XII, No. 1 (March, 1962), 7–19.

FLEMING, IAN G. "The Secondary and Tertiary Economic Development of the Transkei," *Journal of Racial Affairs,* XIV, No. 1 (January, 1963), 43–56.

GALBRAITH, JOHN S. "Apartheid as Seen by an American," *New Commonwealth,* XXXII, No. 9 (October, 1956), 417–18.

GEYER, A. L. "The First Bantu Parliament," *Optima,* XIV, No. 2 (June, 1964), 101–7.

GINIEWSKI, PAUL. *The Two Faces of Apartheid.* Chicago: Henry Regnery, 1965. Issued originally as *Bantustans: A Trek towards the Future.* Cape Town: Human & Rousseau, 1961.

HAINES, E. S. "The Transkei Trader," *South African Journal of Economics,* I, No. 2 (June, 1933), 201–17.

HAMMOND-TOOKE, W. D. *Bhaca Society.* Cape Town: Oxford University Press, 1962.

———. "Chieftainship in the Transkeian Political Development," *Journal of Modern African Studies,* II, No. 4 (December, 1964), 513–29.

———. "Segmentation and Fission in Cape Nguni Political Units," *Africa,* XXXV, No. 2 (April, 1965), 143–46.

SELECTED BIBLIOGRAPHY

HAMPTON, J. D. "The Role of the Coloured and the Bantu in the Economic Pattern of the Cape Province," *South African Journal of Economics*, XXX, No. 4 (December, 1962), 253–68.

HILL, CHRISTOPHER R. *Bantustans: The Fragmentation of South Africa*. London: Oxford University Press, 1964.

———. "Elections in the Transkei," *World Today*, XX, No. 4 (February, 1964), 47–49.

HORRELL, MURIEL *The Economic Development of the "Reserves": The Extent to Which the Tomlinson Commission's Recommendations Are Being Implemented*. Johannesburg: South African Institute of Race Relations, Fact Paper No. 3, Mimeographed, 1959.

———. *Second Interim Report on the Establishment of Bantu Authorities*. Johannesburg: South African Institute of Race Relations, Mimeographed, 1959.

———. (comp.). *A Survey of Race Relations in South Africa*. Johannesburg: South African Institute of Race Relations. Annual since 1951.

HOUGHTON, D. HOBART. "Land Reform in the Bantu Areas and Its Effect upon the Urban Labour Market," *South African Journal of Economics*, XXIX, No. 3 (September, 1961), 165–75.

———. "Men of Two Worlds: Some Aspects of Migratory Labour," *ibid.*, XXVIII, No. 3 (September, 1960), 177–90.

———. *Some Implications of Bantu Homeland Development*. Johannesburg: South African Institute of Race Relations, Mimeographed, 1964.

———. "The Significance of the Tomlinson Report," *Africa South*, I, No. 2 (January–March, 1957), 13–22.

HUNTER, MONICA. *Reaction to Conquest: Effects of Contact with Europeans on the Pondo of South Africa*. 2d ed. London: Oxford University Press, 1961.

International Commission of Jurists. *South African Incident: The Ganyile Case*. Geneva: International Commission of Jurists, 1962.

KENYON, J. T. *An Address on the General Council Administrative System of the Transkeian Territories*. Rev. ed. Umtata, Cape Province: Transkeian Territorial News, 1939.

KILEY, DENIS. "The Pondoland Massacre," *Africa South in Exile*, V, No. 1 (October–December, 1960), 7–12.

KLAASTE, AGGREY. "Black—or Black and White? Progress Report on the Transkei," *Drum* (July, 1964), pp. 32–34.

KOTANE, MOSES. "Looking at Bantustans: One Nation—Not Several," *Fighting Talk*, XVI, No. 3 (April, 1962), 3–4.

KRUGER, J. D. L. *Bantustans: A Study in Practical Apartheid*. Queenstown: The Author, 1951. (Printed by *The Daily Representative*.)

KUPER, LEO. "Racialism and Integration in South African Society," *Race*, IV, No. 2 (May, 1963), 26–31.

LEWIN, JULIUS. "Tribalism Coming to Town," *Africa South*, III, No. 3 (April–June, 1959), 42–49.

MANDELA, NELSON R. "Bantu Self-Government," *Liberation*, No. 36 (May, 1959), 7–17.

———. "Bluffing the Bunga into Apartheid," *Fighting Talk*, XI, No. 5 (July, 1955), 6–7.

192

MAYER, PHILIP. "Migrancy and the Study of Africans in Towns," *American Anthropologist,* LXIV, No. 3 (June, 1962), 576–92.

————. *Townsmen or Tribesmen.* Cape Town: Oxford University Press, 1961.

MBEKI, GOVAN. "Jackboot over Pondoland," *Fighting Talk,* XV, No. 1 (February, 1961), 3–4.

————. *South Africa: The Peasants' Revolt.* London: Penguin Books, 1964.

————. *The Transkei in the Making.* 1939 (no copy located).

————. "The Transkei Tragedy (A Study in the Bantu Authorities Act)," *Liberation,* No. 21 (September, 1956), pp. 7–11.

————. "The Transkei Tragedy. Continuing a Detailed Study of the Effect of the Bantu Authorities Act in the Union's Biggest Reserve," *ibid.,* No. 22 (November, 1956), pp. 14–19.

————. "The Transkei Tragedy. A Study in the Bantu Authorities Act. III: National Grave-Diggers," *ibid.,* No. 24 (February, 1957), pp. 16–20.

————. "The Transkei Tragedy. A Study in the Bantu Authorities Act. IV: The Last Word," *ibid.,* No. 24 (April, 1957), pp. 11–14.

MOLNAR, THOMAS. *Africa: A Political Travelogue.* New York: Fleet Publishing Corp., 1965, pp. 174–92.

————. "The Transkei: International Decolonization," *Worldview* (June, 1964), pp. 7–11.

MOLTENO, DONALD. "Transkei Travesties," *Forum* (April, 1962), pp. 17–18.

MULLER, H. E. "Separate Development in South Africa," *African Affairs,* LXII, No. 246 (January, 1963), 53–65.

MUNGER, EDWIN S. *Problems of the Transkei: A South African Tribal Reserve in Transition.* American Universities Field Service Reports: Central & Southern Africa Series, Vol. X, No. 3 (September, 1962).

NIEUWENHUYSEN, JOHN. "Bantustan Fantasia," *Africa South,* IV, No. 2 (January–March, 1960), 36–41.

————. "The Development of the African reserves in South Africa with special reference to the period since 1948." Unpublished Ph.D. dissertation, University of London, 1963.

————. "Economic Policy in the Reserves since the Tomlinson Report," *South African Journal of Economics,* XXXII, No. 1 (March, 1964), 3–25.

————. "Prospects and Issues in the Development of the Reserves," *ibid.,* XXXII, No. 2 (June, 1964), 128–47.

NOKWE, DUMA. "The Voice of Matanzima: The Transkei," *Fighting Talk,* XVI, No. 3 (April, 1962), 2–3.

PATTEN, J. W. "Separate Development: A Look at the Facts," *Optima,* XIII, No. 1 (March, 1963), 17–26.

PIERCY, M. V. "The Promise of 'Separate Development,'" *South African Journal of Economics,* XXIX, No. 4 (December, 1961), 294–98.

PIM, HOWARD. *A Transkei Enquiry,* 1933. Lovedale, Cape Province: Lovedale Press, 1934.

"Program of Principles of the Transkei National Independence Party." Mimeographed, n.p., n.d.

READER, D. H. *The Black Man's Portion.* Cape Town: Oxford University Press, 1961.

SELECTED BIBLIOGRAPHY

Roux, Edward. "Decline of the Reserves: Agriculture Cannot Prosper under Tribalism," *Forum* (June, 1959), pp. 7–8.

Sadie, J. L. "The Industrialization of the Bantu Areas," *Journal of Racial Affairs,* XI, No. 2 (January, 1960), 57–81.

Schutte, H. G. *Weisse Ismen, schwarze Fakten: Von Sinn und Notwendigkeit des gegliederten Volkerorganismus insbesondere in Sud-Afrika.* Vaterstetten: Arndt, 1963.

Sisulu, Walter. "Those 'Bantu Homelands,'" *Fighting Talk,* XV, No. 8 (September, 1961), 6–7.

Spence, J. E. "The Political Implications of the South African Bantustan Policy," *Race,* III, No. 2 (May, 1962), 20–30.

Stanford, W. E. "Self-Rule in the Transkei: Government Offloads the Task It Cannot Face," *Forum,* VIII, No. 11 (February, 1960), 21–22.

Sterling, Thomas. "The Black Pawns of Bantustan," *Reporter,* XXIX, No. 6 (October 10, 1963), 42–44.

Stultz, Newell M. "'Creative Self-Withdrawal' in the Transkei," *Africa Report,* IX, No. 4 (April, 1964), 18–23.

Tatz, C. M. "Dr. Verwoerd's 'Bantustan' Policy," *Australian Journal of Politics and History,* III, No. 1 (May, 1962), 7–26.

Toerien, P. S. "Primary Economic Development of the Transkeian Territories," *Journal of Racial Affairs,* XIV, No. 2 (March, 1963), 103–14.

"Trouble in Pondoland," *New Statesman,* LX, No. 1552 (December 10, 1960), 910.

Tsvetayev, Oleg. "Verwoerd's Colonial Empire," *New Times,* No. 50 (December 12, 1962), pp. 7–8.

Turok, Ben. *The Pondo Revolt,* n.p., n.d.

Vandenbosch, Amry. "Reappraisal in South Africa," *Yale Review,* LIII, No. 1 (October, 1963), 11–25.

Van Heerden, W. "The Road to Separate Development in South Africa," *Optima,* X, No. 4 (December, 1960), 184–93.

———. "Why Bantu States?" *ibid.,* XII, No. 2 (June, 1962), 59–65.

Van Lille, Abraham J. *The Native Council System, with Special Reference to the Transvaal Local Councils.* Pretoria: De Bussy, 1938.

"Verwoerd's Crown Colony: The Transkeian Scheme and the Future of the Chiefs," *Fighting Talk,* XVI, No. 2 (March, 1962), 3–4.

Vicker, Ray. "South Africa's Experiment: Africans Seem Willing To Set Up Separate State," *Wall Street Journal,* CLXII, No. 90 (November 5, 1963), 14.

Vigne, Randolph. "Birth of Bantustan," *Forum* (March, 1962), pp. 10–12.

Walshe, A. Peter. "The Changing Content of Apartheid," *Review of Politics,* XXV, No. 3 (July, 1963), 343–61.

Wilson, Monica. "The Early History of the Transkei and Ciskei," *African Studies,* XVIII, No. 4 (1959), 167–79.

Z. S. N. "Down at Mqanduli: A Transkei Report," *New African,* I, No. 7 (July, 1962), 4–5.

OFFICIAL PUBLICATIONS

[Republic of South Africa], Department of Bantu Education. *Report of the Commission of Inquiry Into the Teaching of the Official Languages and the Use of the Mother Tongue as Medium of Instruction in Transkeian Primary Schools, October, 1962.* Pretoria: The Government Printer, R.P. 22/1963.

_____, Department of Information. *Progress through Separate Development: South Africa in Peaceful Transition.* n.d.

_____, Department of Information. *The Progress of the Bantu Peoples Towards Nationhood.* n.d.

_____, Department of Information. *The Transkei: Emancipation Without Chaos.* n.d.

_____, Department of Information. *The Transkei: Major Steps on the Road to Self-Determination.* Fact Paper No. 102 (June, 1962).

_____, Department of Information. *To Each His Own.* Fact Paper No. 106. n.d.

_____. *House of Assembly Debates.* Since June 5, 1961.

_____. *Instructions and Legal Provisions in Regard to the General Registration of Transkeian Voters 1963 For Use by Registration Officers.* Pretoria: The Government Printer, 1963.

_____, Transkei Government. *Debates of the Transkeian Legislative Assembly. Second Session—First Assembly, 5th May to 19th June, 1964.* Umtata: Elata Commercial Printers (Pty.) Ltd., 1964.

Transkei Legislative Assembly. *Proceedings at the Meeting of Members of the Transkei Legislative Assembly, held on 6th, 9th and 11th December, 1963, for the purpose of Electing Office Bearers, Etc.* Umtata, 1964.

Transkei Territorial Authority. *Proceedings and Reports of Select Committees.* Annual from 1956 to 1963. [Umtata]: Territorial Printers, 1963.

_____. *Proceedings, Special Session called to consider Draft Bill for the Granting of Self-Government to the Transkei.* [Umtata]: Territorial Printers, 1963.

Transkeian Territories General Council. *Proceedings and Reports of Select Committees.* Annual from 1908 to 1930. King William's Town: The King Printing Co., Ltd.

Union of South Africa, Department of Native Affairs. *Report of the Native Laws Commission, 1946–48.* Union Government No. 28. Pretoria: The Government Printer, 1948.

_____. *House of Assembly Debates.* Through May 26, 1961.

_____. *Memorandum Explaining the Background and Objects of the Promotion of Bantu Self-government Bill, 1959.* White Paper 3, 1959.

_____. *Memorandum: Government Decisions on the Recommendations of the Commission for the Socio-Economic Development of the Bantu Areas within the Union of South Africa, 1956.* White Paper F-1956.

_____. *Report of the Commission of Enquiry into Policy Relating to the Protection of Industries.* Union Government No. 36. Pretoria: The Government Printer, 1958.

Selected Bibliography

————, Social and Economic Planning Council. *The Native Reserves and Their Place in the Economy of the Union of South Africa.* Report No. 9. Union Government No. 32. Pretoria: The Government Printer, 1946.

————. *Summary of the Report of the Commission for the Socio-Economic Development of the Bantu Areas within the Union of South Africa.* Union Government No. 61. Pretoria: The Government Printer, 1955.

United Transkeian Territories General Council. *Proceedings and Reports of Select Committees.* Annual from 1931 to 1955. Umtata: The Territorial News Limited.

Verwoerd, Dr. H. F. *Separate Development (The positive side).* Speech by Dr. H. F. Verwoerd, Minister of Native Affairs, on the occasion of the opening of the Transkeian Territorial Authority, Umtata, May 7, 1957. Pretoria: Department of Native Affairs.

NEWSPAPERS

Cape Times. Cape Town. Daily except Sunday.

Contact. Cape Town. Liberal fortnightly from 1958; issued irregularly in recent years.

The Daily Dispatch. East London. Daily except Sunday.

Die Burger. Cape Town. Daily except Sunday.

New Age. Johannesburg and Cape Town. Left-wing weekly from 1954 until banned in November 1962.

Rand Daily Mail. Johannesburg. Daily except Sunday.

The Star. Johannesburg. Daily except Sunday.

The Territorial News. Umtata. Weekly.

Index

INDEX